LEADERSHIP AND SUCCESSION IN THE SOVIET UNION, EASTERN EUROPE AND CHINA

LEADERSHIP AND SUCCESSION IN THE SOVIET UNION, EASTERN EUROPE AND CHINA

Edited by
MARTIN McCAULEY
and
STEPHEN CARTER

M.E. Sharpe, Inc.
Armonk, New York

© School of Slavonic and East European Studies 1986

All rights reserved. No part of this publication
may be reproduced or transmitted, in any form
or by any means, without permission

First published 1986 by
M.E. SHARPE, INC.
80 Business Park Drive
Armonk, New York 10504

Printed in Hong Kong

Library of Congress Cataloging in Publication Data

McCauley, Martin.
  Leadership and succession in the Soviet Union,
Eastern Europe, and China.

  Bibliography: p.
  Includes index.
  1. Heads of state—Communist countries—Succession—
Addresses, essays, lectures.   2. Communist countries—
Politics and government—Addresses, essays, lectures.
I. Carter, Stephen.   II. Title.
JC474.M43   1985   351.003′1′091717   85–2370
ISBN 0–87332–346–7
ISBN 0–87332–347–5 (pbk.)

Contents

8/20/87 sc

List of Tables

Notes on the Contributors

Patrick Artisien is Lecturer in the Department of Business and Economics at the University of Wales Institute of Science and Technology Cardiff. Among his recent publications are *Joint Ventures in Yugoslav Industry* and articles on Yugoslav–Albanian relations and on foreign investment in Yugoslavia.

J. F. Brown was Director of Radio Free Europe, Munich, from 1978 to 1983. Among his many publications on East European politics are *The New Eastern Europe* and *Bulgaria under Communist Rule*. He is currently engaged on a history of Eastern Europe since 1968.

Stephen Carter is Senior Lecturer in Russian Government at the City of London Polytechnic. He is the author of *The Politics of Solzhenitsyn* and has a special interest in politics and literature and comparative communism.

Peter Ferdinand is Lecturer in Politics at the University of Warwick and has published articles on the Chinese and Yugoslav Communist Parties.

Peter Frank is Senior Lecturer in the Department of Government at the University of Essex. He is the joint author of *The Soviet Communist Party* and has published many articles on communist politics.

Martin McCauley is Lecturer in Russian and Soviet Institutions at the School of Slavonic and East European Studies, University of London. Among his publications are *Marxism–Leninism in the German Democratic Republic: The Socialist Unity Party (SED)* and *The German Democratic Republic since 1945*.

Dennison Rusinow is a member of the Universities Field Staff International, Vienna. Among his numerous publications are *Italy's Austrian Heritage* and *The Yugoslav Experiment*.

George Sanford is Lecturer in East European Studies, University of Bristol. He is the author of *Polish Communism in Crisis* and of numerous articles on Polish history and postwar politics.

George Schöpflin is Joint Lecturer in East European Political Institutions at the School of Slavonic and East European Studies and the London School of Economics, University of London. He is the co-author of *Communist Political Systems* and of numerous articles on East European politics.

Michael Shafir is Lecturer in Politics at the University of Tel Aviv. He is the author of *Romania: Politics, Economics and Society* and of many articles on Romanian politics.

Stephen White is Reader in Politics, University of Glasgow. He is the author of *Political Culture and Soviet Politics* and co-author of *Communist Political Systems* and various other works.

Gordon Wightman is a Lecturer in the Department of Political Theory and Institutions, University of Liverpool. He is the author of many articles on Czechoslovak politics.

Preface

The papers in this volume were originally delivered at a series of seminars held at the School of Slavonic and East European Studies, University of London, between January and May 1984. The inspiration for the scheme was the Soviet succession struggle of 1982 but further reflection indicated that the problem of elderly leaderships, and the apparent absence of legitimate succession mechanisms, applied to nearly all communist systems.

After a very stimulating seminar series the contributors assembled for a review conference held on 1–2 June 1984 at the School, to discuss each system – in turn and then on a comparative basis; the legitimacy of communist systems; the role of the military; the phenomenon of the cult of the personality; élite–mass relations; and church–state relations. Our thanks are due to all the contributors and indeed all who attended the conference for the enthusiasm, erudition and tolerance which rendered the series such a stimulating and fruitful exercise. Our warmest thanks are also due to Dr M. A. Branch, Director of the School, and his administrative staff, especially Philip Robinson and Katie McGill, for their encouragement, support and efficiency in providing a welcoming and central venue for the seminars and the conference. Students of the School, especially Ann Archer and Paul Feldman, also helped us most effectively over the period of the conference.

We are deeply indebted to the Nuffield Foundation and Mrs Jan Hargreaves for their financial support. A special word of thanks is due to Lady Jane Stevens for providing us with a wonderful venue for the completion of the editorial work.

MARTIN MCCAULEY
STEPHEN CARTER

Map

The Soviet Union and Eastern Europe

Map   xiii

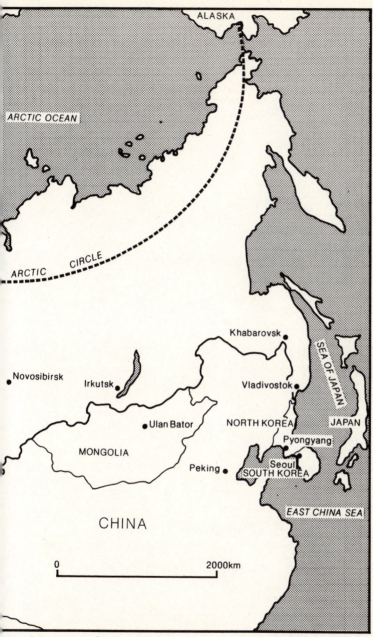

ɹRCE: W. E. Griffith (ed.), *The Soviet Empire: Expansion and Détente* (Lexington: D.C. Heath & Co., 1976). The author and publishers are grateful to Third Century Corporation for permission to reproduce this map.

Introduction

MARTIN McCAULEY and STEPHEN CARTER

Biology is the midwife of change in communist systems. It is now acknowledged that when a communist leader dies the most important office to be filled is that of head of the Communist Party. However, in order to establish himself the new leader of the Communist Party must strive to become national leader. With some exceptions, this involves occupying one of the great offices of state, that of Prime Minister or President. Once in the saddle it is very difficult to dislodge him. The leader may possess real, in contrast to cosmetic, charisma and it would appear that the cult of the personality is now endemic to communist political systems.

A tension exists in communist systems between the collectivist nature of society and its institutions and the role of the national leader. According to the official claims of the ideology, all objectives are collective and the decisions taken to achieve them are taken collectively. Yet charisma and the attendant cult of the personality have played a major part in the evolution of communist systems. Giants such as Lenin, Stalin, Mao Zedong and Tito have left an indelible imprint on their societies. During the heroic phase of the revolution a dominant figure appears to be necessary. However, when the revolution has been consolidated a different type of leader is called for. Stalin could usurp the power of the institutions of Party and state but the arbitrary nature of his rule created special problems for his successors. He did not attempt to ease the transition to a new leader, unlike Lenin and Tito, for example. Stalin, on the contrary, openly denigrated the abilities of his colleagues and perhaps it was not surprising that the Party should call on the populace not to panic when the 'great man' died.

The very nature of personalised power, which cannot physically cope with the information flows of modern government, tends to

1

create functional élites and institutions, with peculiar expertise and a stake in preserving their own bureaucratic empire. After the death of Stalin, Khrushchev and these élites seemed to place the elucidation of the 'norms of party life', the regularisation of institutional procedures, the control of the KGB and the elimination of the arbitrary power of the Stalin era, very high on their agenda. The death of Mao Zedong in 1976, of Marshal Tito in 1980, and then of Brezhnev, Andropov and Chernenko, provides scope for a comparative study of succession and change in communist systems. How, if not by death itself could a communist leader be removed and replaced? What do these obscure mechanisms tell us about the nature of communist systems and their legitimacy? Incipient institutionalisation is evident but will it develop? In which direction are communist systems developing over time?

In any State the transition from one leader to another, namely succession, tends to signify change, an opportunity for innovation in policy (Bunce 1981), and significant movement and transition in the lives of citizens. They become aware of the process of history. A nation may then change direction or ensure continuity but in one sense a new beginning is made. As Seweryn Bialer has said: 'Succession describes the order in which, or conditions under which, a person or group succeeds to political office, and the effects of this process on the structures and policies of the political system of the nation-state' (Bialer, 1980, p. 65).

What is a communist political system? A communist system has a number of characteristics which distinguishes it from any pluralistic democracy. First, the Communist Party or its equivalent will have, or effectively exercises, a monopoly of political power despite the possible existence of other political parties as, for example, in the GDR and Poland. It will usually be a party of a Leninist type, that is, a party which has a leading or guiding role in government and over society as a whole. It will be a party which operates under the principle of democratic centralism. This implies a hierarchical structure in which the decisions of higher bodies are binding upon lower ones. This places major decision-making powers in the topmost organs of the Party, namely the Politburo and the Central Committee Secretariat, or their equivalents. Secondly, the ruling Party's interpretation of Marxism – Leninism (or variation thereon) will be enforced in all realms of endeavour, and other views, such as the religious, will be more or less actively discouraged. Thirdly, the economy of such a state tends to be largely or wholly in public ownership, with emphasis on collectivism rather than on capitalist or individual private enterprise. And lastly, the media, and all intermediary institutions such as trade unions and other 'pressure groups' will tend to be controlled by, or at least strongly circumscribed by, the state (White, Gardner and Schöpflin, 1982, pp. 3–4). Using the language of sociology, there is little 'sub-group autonomy' in communist states and intermediate group cohesiveness is low. The lines of communication and power are vertical in communist states and society tends to be atomised with weak horizontal links.

It is not therefore surprising that succession processes in communist states will tend to be different from those in pluralist societies. In the West succession is usually carried out according to well-known rules, according to election procedures and party-leadership selection processes, which are clear to all. Such mechanisms as the British General Election or the US Presidential Election are openly conducted and reported upon; they are widely understood by the public; the results are generally 'system reinforcing'; and the processes themselves, to use Peter Frank's term, have a high 'technical content'. In contrast, succession in communist systems is often accompanied by some kind of crisis. Cross-cultural comparisons should really bring out differences rather than similarities. For example, Valerie Bunce (1981, p. 148) has claimed that policy innovation tends to follow from leadership successions in all polities, East and West. However this collection of studies seems to indicate that policy and personnel innovation in the 'honeymoon' period is slower and less predictable in communist systems than in pluralistic democracies. There are many reasons for this.

First, the new communist leader is chosen from among existing leaders, normally concentrated in the Politburo and the Secretariat. In this sense, there is perhaps an analogy with the principle of Papal selection, where the Pope is chosen by a secret conclave of cardinals. In one sense, then, at least in the initial stages, the new communist leader is a delegate of his peers, not their controller or selector. And he inherits a Politburo rather than choosing it. Hence when a new leader is elected he begins by being a member of a collective leadership. Then he begins to build up his authority and power and this may take years. Therefore the power of a British Prime Minister or US President to make changes in personnel and policy is greater initially than that of a new Communist Party leader.

Secondly, because of the ban on factionalism within Leninist-type Parties, the process of selection of one candidate rather than another is not known, and his probable policy orientation tends to be obscure. An aspiring leader seeks to establish good relations with all possible factions within the Politburo and will attempt to project himself as a moderate. Hence his effective policy line will only gradually emerge as he extends his political power by the steady build-up of an effective following among bureaucratic and functional élites (Breslauer, 1982, ch. 1).

Thirdly, this process – passing from Party to national leader – involves primarily a manipulation of the Party *nomenklatura*, and takes time. In contrast to Khrushchev and Brezhnev, who needed about five years (Martin McCauley, 1983b, p. 13) Andropov was able to proceed more rapidly, and achieved much during his fifteen months in office. Chernenko, on the other hand, achieved very little. The post-Mao succession also took several years to begin to clarify policy; whereas the Polish successions, Gierek–Kania–Jaruzelski, were accompanied by acute societal crisis, and provoked much more rapid policy innovation. However, we can generalise by saying that the transition from Party to strong national leader may take from one to five years. He is then in a position to put his stamp upon policy. But a Party leader may become national leader without accumulating much power. A clear example of this phenomenon was Konstantin Chernenko. Party leader, chairman of the Defence Council (which makes him Commander-in-Chief of the Soviet Armed Forces) and State President he had considerable authority but little real power. The progress of a new Party leader to that of strong national leader appears to be as follows: he secures a great state office; he builds up a secure 'tail' (*khvost* in Russian, *Seilschaft* in German) in the Party apparatus; then he engages in ideological development or innovation; a cult of the personality surfaces; he claims economic, social and foreign policy successes for the country under his guidance. Only then can he be regarded as a strong national leader.

In dealing with such a heterogeneous collection of states, distinguished by national and cultural distinctiveness rather than commonality, it is necessary to adopt some working 'model' of communist systems as they exist in the 1980s. It was felt that that the 'totalitarian model', which applied to the Stalinist and other dictatorships, did not apply to the present age. According to this model, five factors are common to all totalitarian societies: an official ideology, to which everyone is supposed to adhere, focused on a 'perfect final state of mankind'; a single mass Party usually led by one man, organised hierarchically and either superior to or intertwined with the state bureaucracy; a technically conditioned near-complete monopoly similarly exercised over all means of effective mass communication; and a system of physical or psychological terroristic police control; central control and direction of the entire economy (Schapiro, 1972, p. 18). There are three main objections to this model: it exaggerates the effect of political socialisation and assumes the Communist Party is more monolithically united than it is in reality; it neglects the policy process, assuming that all policy emanates from the leader; and it is unhelpful in understanding political change (Brown, in Solomon, 1983, p. 66).

The 'bureaucratic politics' model appears more appropriate. While accepting the claims of the totalitarian model in respect of the leading role of the Party, and its symbiotic relationship with the bureaucracy, this model plays down the influence of coercion and terror. It suggests that politics and conflict take place within the Party and state bureaucracies. Politics, it is argued, takes the form essentially of a struggle for resources among the various parts of a vast corporation. It is suggested that a kind of 'regularisation' is beginning to occur in communist systems, but at the same time, as in all bureaucracies, informal relationships are important within the context of institutional structures; there may be an accent on performance rather than principle; and rewards will accrue to the ruthless 'empire builder'. The analogy with any large corporation may be a limited one, since in communist systems, the Party has the power to appoint personnel throughout the system, and it is by no means clear that all bureaucracies in communist systems are internally united. For example, the military are usually Party members, and there is often a generational, or inter-service, rivalry, within the armed forces. However as White, Gardner and Schöpflin have pointed out:

> these shortcomings notwithstanding, the bureaucratic politics model is among the most promising of those that have been utilised in recent years, and in any case it should be regarded as complementary to, and not necessarily exclusive of, other approaches and interpretations (White, Gardner and Schöpflin, 1982, p. 23).

The states under consideration seem to fall into three categories:

(1) *Independent, indigenously communist states*: the Soviet Union, China and Yugoslavia

(2) *Communist states clearly under Soviet influence*: Poland, the GDR, Czechoslovakia, Hungary and Bulgaria

(3)   *Soviet-type states manifesting some independence* (states which place their own national interests ahead of those of the 'internationalist' interests of the Soviet-led states): Romania and Albania

It is clear that countries in category (2) will have less freedom for self-directed systemic and leadership change than those in categories (1) and (3). Societal pressures or Soviet policy are likely to influence leadership changes in category (2) states more strongly than in others. However, it can be expected that there will be more points of similarity between the USSR and the 'Soviet-type' systems of category (3), than between the independent states of category (1). In this sense Hoxha's Albania may have had something in common with the Stalinist phase of Soviet development, whereas Ceauşescu's Romania may be compared with the Khrushchev period. However it is more difficult to be certain that the thoroughgoing institutionalisation of the Yugoslav Presidency since 1980, or the decline in the leading role of the Party at the Federal level, will be repeated elsewhere in communist systems.

Category (2) states present special problems of interpretation because of the presence of the 'Moscow connection', whose precise nature and strength are always difficult to establish. In Hungary innovation and reform have been tolerated and even admired by the USSR in exchange for the unswerving loyalty of the Kádár regime. But in Poland, leadership change has sometimes been instigated by the Soviet Union, for example the replacement of Kania by Jaruzelski. The removal of Dubček and his replacement by Husák was again Soviet-inspired. We do not know the precise nature of Soviet influence over Czechoslovak internal policy today nor, for instance, do we know much about the role of the Soviet and GDR security services and their impact on the GDR leadership. One can state, however, that the post of Communist Party leader in category (2) states is on the *nomenklatura* of the Soviet Politburo. The Soviets require the hegemony of the respective Communist Parties, the recognition of the CPSU as the leading Communist Party, and the adoption of Moscow's foreign policy objectives. If these three conditions are met the communist leadership in these states may have considerable room for manoeuvre when it comes to choosing a new Party leader.

The military appear to be playing a more important role in the support of the Communist Parties, and as a consequence in the factional struggle for leadership, in all the countries considered, with the possible exception of Czechoslovakia and Hungary. It is possible to speak of the creeping militarisation of Soviet and GDR society and in China, Albania and Yugoslavia the military have always played a leading role. Three categories of states can be perceived here:

(1) *The Soviet Union* in which the military defended the revolution against its armed enemies. Afterwards the military power of the United States resulted in the Soviet armed forces being accorded the highest priority in order to catch up with and then surpass the Americans.

(2) *Countries in which the indigenous military played a key role in the success of the revolution*: China, Albania and Yugoslavia

(3) *Countries in which the indigenous military played little or no role in the conquest of power*: Poland, the GDR, Czechoslovakia, Hungary, Romania and Bulgaria. This group could be subdivided into those states which actively participated in the war against the Soviet Union: the GDR, Slovakia, Hungary and Romania

It is not an accident that the Soviet Union and the GDR are experiencing creeping militarisation. They are the two most important states of the Warsaw Pact. The military in the Soviet Union will wax as a result of mounting American military might and the GDR is a front line state. It is the country from which a Warsaw Pact invasion of the West, if it ever occurred, would be launched. The upheavals in Poland since 1980 reinforced doubts about the reliability of the Polish military machine. The same can be said about Czechoslovakia. Hence the closer military relationship between the USSR and the GDR which is now under way. In Hungary the reason why the military appear of little consequence may be connected with the fact that in the event of war, the Soviet military view Hungary merely as an access route to Yugoslavia.

The military may increase their power in category (3) states for two main reasons: the modernisation of the Warsaw Pact will raise the level of sophistication of the various armed forces and the increasing economic problems facing these countries may cause the Communist Parties to rely more heavily on the security forces and the military to keep order. The example of Poland reveals that the military, in collaboration with the security forces, are capable of suppressing opposition, at least for a time.

Military power should be distinguished from military influence. The goal of all Communist Parties is to have pliant, efficient armed forces which will act immediately on Party orders. Conflict-ridden civilian government can lead to the expansion of military influence if one faction seeks and gets military support in its struggle against other factions. The military would only benefit if that faction was victorious. Weak, crisis-ridden civilian government might also force the military to act in defence of the nation.

In which countries could the military play an important role in the selection of a new Communist Party leader? The Soviet Union, China, Albania and Yugoslavia appear to be the states in question. The Soviet Union is in a category by itself and the dismissal of Marshal Nikolai Ogarkov, the Chief of Staff, in September 1984, may indicate Party concern about the aspirations of top military figures. In Poland the generals will have a say in Jaruzelski's successor but the final decision will be taken in Moscow. In China, Albania and Yugoslavia the Party and military are so closely intertwined that one can speak of a symbiotic relationship. However, the military acknowledge the leading role of the Party.

The greater significance of the military in the GDR – defence spending over the period 1979–84 increased by almost 40 per cent, well above that of national income – is not due to the weakness of the Communist Party (SED) and its leader, Erich Honecker. Rather it is a consequence of the events in Poland and the natural military skills of the East German soldier. There has been, so far, no perceptible increase in the influence of the military over Honecker, although this could occur under his successor.

Consideration of leadership succession suggests a development of communist systems. The indigenously communist states initially went through a revolutionary 'heroic' phase, often associated with civil war. These states include, for example, the Soviet Union, China, Vietnam, Cuba, Albania and Yugoslavia. Phase two was a period of socialist construction, which may be termed a utopian phase, for its ideology is one of transformation in the name of a utopian goal, namely the achievement of communism. Those states which fell under Soviet influence after 1945 experienced phase two without any revolutionary phase of their own. Marxist ideology in the revolutionary and utopian phases is the ideology of transformation, which involves repression in the name of gigantic industrial and agricultural achievements and reorganisation and discussion about the 'new communist man and woman', or the transformation of human nature itself, under the impact of social change. However, phases one and two eventually give way to a realisation that modern economies and societies are complex, that regularisation of procedures and institutions is necessary. Eventually the accent is placed on modernisation, as exemplified by the 'four modernisations' of the People's Republic of China. At this stage, the political culture takes on salient characteristics. The ideology becomes conservative and loses much of its motivational power. Its main function becomes the legitimation and sanctification of the existing order. In the sphere of the economy, the accent shifts to efficiency, innovation and internal and external competition. In the cultural-educational sphere, a tension tends to emerge between the conservative, controlling ideology on the one hand and the need to innovate and reform on the other. In other words, the official ideology comes into conflict with the industrialist ideology. Richard Löwenthal (1970) has pointed out the dichotomy between the utopian and the modernising mentality in communist systems, and the transition from one to the other is reflected in the choice of leaders and the offices and powers accorded them.

Thus, the office of President is now accorded a Soviet Party leader in order to raise his international status and to invest him with added legitimacy. However, his powers over the state apparatus are limited by the regulation of 1964 which prevents him from acquiring the post of Chairman of the Council of Ministers. In China, it appears that Hua Guo Feng was unable to consolidate his power precisely because he aspired to the same posts and powers as those exercised by Mao. The heroic and early socialist construction phases allow the emergence of a 'great man' – itself something of an irony from the point of view of Marxism – but later, during the phase of institutionalisation and modernisation, a different type of leader is called for. Lenin and Stalin, Mao, Tito, Hoxha, Ho Chi Minh or Fidel Castro, are clearly a difficult act to follow! However the new leaders will, of course, claim the mantle of their illustrious predecessors, or in the case of Ceauşescu, claim the mantle of legitimate succession, which had been allegedly perverted by his predecessor Georghiu Dej.

Speculation about the causation of transition from the era of the heroic leader towards that of modernisation, the process referred to here as incipient institutionalisation, gives rise to the following hypothesis. Dictators are inherently unable to rule without instrumental bureaucracies, which tend to develop expertise and power. Dictators also tend to strengthen state bureaucracies, even if they weaken the Communist Party by periodic purges, because the state agencies are needed to control societies whose horizontal links are weakened under socialism. Stronger bureaucracies become more necessary as their functions expand, and when the 'great man' dies, the institutions are already in place. Initially the state bureaucracy is stronger, for instance in the Soviet Union in 1953, but the Party bureaucracy is revivified by those whose power base it becomes in the struggle for ascendancy.

Institutionalisation, however, brings with it the problem of the precise definition and delimitation of the role of the Communist Party as the leading, guiding force in communist societies. Leninism created a dual Party – state structure which has always been ambiguous. This has led some scholars to see the Party – state apparatus as a continuum (Mary McAuley, 1977, p. 186), or even to see Eastern European systems as a 'polymorphic party' (Lowit, 1979). Solutions vary, from an apparently total Party monopoly of power in Albania to a virtual abandonment of Leninism at the Federal level in Yugoslavia.

Modernisation, and its associated attempt to maintain and improve living standards, raises the crucial question of élite-mass relations in communist states. White, Gardner and Schöpflin (1982, p. 56) have claimed that communist systems have attempted to 'trade in' social and economic security for the effective depoliticisation of the masses. It was thus the failure of the élite in Poland to deliver their side of the bargain – by raising food prices and failing to rectify shortages – that triggered off the popular uprisings of 1970, 1976 and finally the formation of Solidarity in 1980.

It would appear that communist societies experience a declining acceptance of Utopian ideology during the phases of modernisation and institutionalisation. Competing ideologies, such as the influence of religion – despite official persecution – seem to become potentially important at this stage. A kind of continuum can be set up, with Poland as the most prominent example of the continuing influence of religion on society and politics, at one end, and Albania, as an officially atheist state, on the other.

An inherent problem for communist polities is that ideology is clearly a crucial ingredient of legitimation. The continuing dominance of the single Party and its leadership is based upon the claim to be the sole interpreter of the laws of dialectical and historical materialism and the sole legitimate guide of society towards the goals indicated by these doctrines. Great efforts are undertaken to convince the population that Party policy is beneficial to society. The myth of a unified Party must be maintained at all costs and the transition from one leader to another can be potentially embarrassing. No Communist Party has yet evolved a mechanism for the removal of an incumbent leader who is physically and mentally unable to fulfil his duties. Death, either natural or violent, is the usual motor of change. The only other mechanism is the staging of a *coup d'état* against the incumbent leader. If it is swift and successful, this can minimise the loss of face the Party could lose domestically and internationally. If it fails the potential damage is great. Hence the greatest single weakness of leadership in the states studied here is the absence of a mechanism for the removal of an incompetent leader. The new Party leader, in effect, becomes leader for life. When the leader is dead there are mechanisms for choosing his successor. The Politburo and Secretaries of the Secretariat together with the Central Committee in plenary session form the electoral college in the Soviet Union, for example. However, it is still too soon to speak of the institutionalisation of leadership selection. Another observable weakness applied to the country in which the revolution first took place, the Soviet Union. The USSR is 67 years old but some of the key political figures are even older. The adage, the older the revolution, the older the leadership applied to the Soviet Union until 1985. The accession of Gorbachev is a watershed. The only main exception to the above rule is Poland where the 'electoral system' is effective. Public pressure leads to periodic purges in the Polish party leadership.

The ageing of the Soviet Politburo led to weak national leadership between the late 1970s and 1985. The senile Brezhnev gave way to Andropov and his dialysis machine and he in turn to the emphysemic Chernenko and his renal machine. After Brezhnev's death Andropov was the most able man vying for leadership but given his state of health he should never have become Party leader. Chernenko, given his state of health, should also never have been made Party leader. The mechanism for choosing a new leader ensured that it was the interests of the majority of the Politburo – all old men – which took precedence over the needs of the country. Crisp, decisive leadership was necessary but was notably absent. When Vyacheslav Molotov, at 90 years of age, was rehabilitated and readmitted to the Communist Party in 1984, a wit remarked that Chernenko was grooming his successor!

All this changed with Chernenko's death. Given the fact that he was clearly a dying man there was ample time to choose a successor. When Chernenko died on 10 March 1985 the transition to Gorbachev as Party leader proceeded with breathtaking speed. Forewarned was evidently forearmed. The fact that Chernenko was allowed to die in office when it was quite clear that he was quite incapable of performing his duties underlines once again that the Party elite is unwilling to countenance any measure aimed at the removal of an incompetent or senile leader. The fear appears to be that if such rules were laid down, they might be misused. If a medical certificate were enough to remove an incumbent leader, the group of doctors looking after Politburo members' health would become a feared body of men!

Gorbachev's election breaks new ground. Despite the fact that when Chernenko died five of the ten full members of the Politburo were 70 years old or more the youngest man, Gorbachev, was chosen. The circle of old men electing old men has been broken. The promotion of Gorbachev can be looked at from another angle. Andropov's election was a reaction to the immobility of the late Brezhnev years but the dynamism of the first months of Andropov's rule lead to a reaction. So Chernenko came in — Brezhnevism without Brezhnev. Chernenko's inactivity in turn caused another reaction. So in came Gorbachev – Andropovism without Andropov. On a more flippant note there is the hirsute theory. The bald Lenin was followed by the hirsute Stalin. He in turn was succeeded by the bald Khrushchev. He gave way to the hairy Brezhnev. Then came Andropov and his bald pate followed by Chernenko and his full head of hair. Since both Romanov and Grishin had plenty of hair the succession had to go to the bald Gorbachev!

What of the future of communist states? Stephen White is optimistic about the powers of adaptability of communist systems. The political development of these states and their relative stability has coincided with their numbers increasing world-wide, with Zimbabwe the latest adherent. Alexander Zinoviev (1984) has pointed out that such states with their 'communality' or collective conservatism are strong. The citizen in such a society may well know that he is politically impotent but he will therefore tend to concentrate on his private life and to develop areas of private initiative or enterprise which are permitted by the authorities. Society may thus be relatively stable provided the coercive apparatus is loyal to the regime and intermediate group cohesiveness – such as Solidarity in Poland – cannot take place. Ideology is quite adaptable to its present conservative, legitimating role, especially if modified by nationalism in some meaningful form, and if the standard of living is tolerable and shows signs of getting better.

A communist regime faced with declining economic performance has at its disposal some means of adaptation and consultation, as Stephen White shows. But this collection does indicate that leadership succession is a weak spot until new and more regularised procedures can be instituted. With the possible exception of Yugoslavia, no country here considered has yet shown any convincing way of solving this fundamental problem. What tentative conclusions can be drawn from these case studies?

(1) The head of the Communist Party is the country's main political actor.

(2) A new Party leader, to all intents and purposes, is elected for life. On election he is a member of a collective leadership but attempts to strengthen his position by moving his nominees into leading Party and state bureaucratic posts. As his 'tail' or '*Seilschaft*' grows so does his political influence, but he must satisfy the aspirations of his supporters.

(3) To become a national leader the Party leader needs a great state office, for example Prime Minister or President. In the USSR it is the presidency.

An exceptions to this is Kádár (Hungary) who, although clearly a national leader, only heads the Communist Party.

Collective leadership is the norm at the beginning and end of an incumbency. The greatest influence on policy tends to be exercised during the middle period in office. Communist systems appear to favour collective leadership but there is a marked impulse to generate a strong national leader. Sometimes he does not emerge – for instance, Andropov and Chernenko (USSR), Kania (Poland) – either because he has too little time or he lacks ability as a politician. It is becoming more difficult to become a strong national leader in a developed country, such as the USSR.

(4) The older the revolution, the older the political leadership. The exceptions are Poland, and the Soviet Union since 1985. Due to the longevity in office the Politburo tends to fall into two groups: the old men and the younger men. The generation in power seeks to retain power: for example, Brezhnev to Andropov to Chernenko. This may break down, as in the Soviet Union, when the Politburo runs out of credible, old men to succeed.

(5)   Infrequent leadership change is the norm: for example, six in the Soviet Union, three in Czechoslovakia, one in the GDR and Albania. Poland again is the exception.

(6)   There is no mechanism for the removal of an incompetent or senile leader. If possible he is allowed to die in office. Honourable retirement has still to be introduced.

(7)   As the revolution matures so the leadership role of women declines. Women are sometimes to be found in important positions when power is secured – they may be married to leading Party officials – but lose their position afterwards as the revolution is institutionalised. Full Politburo members are now almost exclusively male. There is one full Politburo member in each of Poland, Hungary, Albania, Romania and China who is female.
        It is common now for the wife of the national leader to play no overt political role. She may become almost invisible. Exceptions are Mme Ceauşescu (Romania) and Margot Honecker (GDR). However, the latter is not a full or candidate member of the Politburo; she is Minister of Education. Very exceptionally a daughter may play an important role, such as Lyudmila Zhivkova (Bulgaria).
        No Communist Party has ever been led by a woman and the likelihood of this happening this century is very remote.

(8)   The cult of the personality appears to be endemic to communist systems. Exceptions are Andropov (USSR) and Kádár (Hungary).

(9)   The Stalinist heritage has been sloughed off by all communist countries except Romania and Albania. Both states can be seen as being run by a clan. In Albania political change may be attended by violence. It is still common to accuse defeated opponents of being agents of British and US imperialism. This practice went out in the USSR in 1953. Hence Albania is still the most Stalinist.

(10)   The Party leader is Commander-in-Chief of the Armed Forces; most states have a National Defence Council, or its equivalent, of which he is chairman. The Minister of Defence is always a member of the Politburo and is sometimes a professional soldier. The closest links between the Party and

the military are in China, Yugoslavia and Albania. Military leaders who have become Party leaders have previously been partisans: Mao Zedong and Tito. Jaruzelski (Poland) is the first professional soldier to head a Party. Party – military relations are often a source of tension.

(11) Under Stalin the head of the security police played a key role. After 1953 Party leaders sought to re-establish their domination and succeeded. Being head of the security police normally excludes its holder from succession except when he ceases to be head and enters the Secretariat: for instance, Andropov (USSR).

(12) The mechanism for choosing a new Party leader is very unclear. In the USSR an 'electoral college' selects him but it is still too early to say that this has been institutionalised. There have been too few successions in most states for precedents to have emerged. The military and the security police have increased their influence in most states, and this applies to the succession.

(13) Leadership and succession in communist states is now very diverse. As communist systems mature they evolve different types.

(14) Incipient institutionalisation of leadership and succession appears to be under way in most communist states, with Yugoslavia the most prominent exponent of this at the present time.

National leaderships as of July 1985, have been appended to Chapters 2, 4, 5, 6, 7, 8, 9, 10 and 11.

1 The Soviet Union

PETER FRANK

Political regimes see the social order as being eternal and sacred and their prime duty as being the maintenance of the social order. In contrast, revolutionary movements are intent upon the destruction of the prevailing social order; yet, once in office, they, too, consider themselves to be guardians of the eternal, sacred, *new* social order.

The Bolsheviks were no exception to this general rule. Dedicated to the overthrow of Tsarist autocracy and, after that, to the elimination of nascent bourgeois democracy, after October 1917 they embarked upon the calculated destruction of the existing political order, social structure and economic system. To a very large degree (although not, perhaps, so thoroughly as they had wished) they accomplished this task, and so inaugurated a new social order, an order centred upon the creation of 'the new Soviet man and woman'.

A vital ideological component of the new society was collectivism, and the extent to which the elements of the new social order are collectivist is striking: the working class, *narod* (the people), the Party, the soviets. Again, if we consider the new institutions, then they, too, are collectivist: the Party Congress, the Central Committee, the Politburo, 'collective leadership'. Indeed, the official ideology scorned the role of the individual in history, and the institutions of the new Soviet state reflected that view.

Yet from the outset there was a disjunction between theory and practice, for towering above the revolution, the very creator and inspiration of the Bolshevik Party, was Lenin. Even allowing for the extravagent claims of Soviet hagiography, there can be no doubting the role of the individual, as personified by Lenin, in the Russian revolution. This disjunction of theory and practice still persists in the Soviet political process, and is particularly bothersome in matters to do with leadership and succession, as was made manifest as early as Lenin's last illness preceding his death in January 1924.

16

Realising that the end was imminent, Lenin became preoccupied with the question of who should succeed him as leader. Reading his 'Testament', it is immediately obvious that he is not concerned with the collectivist institutions of leadership, but with *individuals*. It is individuals' strengths and weaknesses, foibles and frailties that he is concerned about. Such potential successors as Bukharin, Stalin and Trotsky are assessed in isolation from any institutional office (except that Lenin is obviously acutely aware of the great bureaucratic power that Stalin has accumulated as Secretary General – though this office, significantly, is an individual appointment). Lenin's dilemma is exemplified by his proposed solution to the problem: enlarge the membership of the (collectivist) Central Committee. Anything less likely to succeed, or more likely to play into the hands of Secretary General Stalin (given his control of appointment), is hard to imagine; yet it expresses neatly the paradox of an ostensibly collectivist political system, rooted in a collectivist ideology, throwing up strong charismatic leaders.

Since the system does not formally recognise personalised, individual leadership, yet at the same time is characterised by precisely that phenomenon, every change of leader in the USSR is in some sense irregular. In any political system there are certain costs relating to succession that the social order must bear. These may, at a mundane level, be tangible, financial costs arising out of, for example, the election campaign. More importantly, leadership change effected by election may, by heightening awareness, highlight and exacerbate social tensions. But successions may benefit the social order, too. Government may be reinvigorated; there is the possibility of changing persons and policies (or not, as the electorate prefers), and all this may be done speedily and without damaging the social order. To the extent that participation involving choice tends to legitimate regimes, it could be argued that the social order is both ratified and strengthened. In other words, embodied in this kind of leadership succession are elements of both continuity and change.

To accommodate the twin objectives of continuity and change (contradictory though they may appear to be), political systems try to devise means of reconciling them in an orderly, regular, legitimate and legitimising fashion. This is done by creating *technical mechanisms* to ensure smooth succession, mechanisms that will cope with change of leadership *and* with the reinforcement and continuation of the social order. An instance of a simple technical mechanism is encapsulated in the formula 'The King is dead; long live the King!' A more complicated example is the election of an American president, where there are clear rules concerning such matters as fixed-term elections, not serving for more than two terms, and so on. We shall refer to such mechanisms as *technical content*.

In those systems where technical content is high, there is little or no ambiguity about how a leader is to be appointed or who that leader is. Thus, if we say that Reagan is President, what we mean is that Reagan is President because he has properly fulfilled certain technical requirements of the American political system. In short, leadership is defined by the office, and not by the personality.

Technical mechanisms are to do with change, with installing a leader. What about continuity? Obviously, that is also reinforced by virtue of there having been a regular, orderly, legitimate succession. But systems also often tend to try to enhance the legitimacy and continuity of the social order by the use of ritual. Few actually see an incoming British Prime Minister kissing the reigning monarch's hands, nor, in practical terms, does it have much force; but it symbolises nonetheless the continuity of the system and the social order. Similarly, there is no constitutional requirement that an outgoing American president should be present at the inauguration ceremony of his successor, yet this custom has powerful ritualistic and symbolic force in emphasising that, despite the strains imposed by the recently-fought election campaign, the system – the social order – is intact. Ritual in countries such as Britain and the United States is relatively weak, and its effect, when linked with the technical content of succession, is to enhance the status, dignity, legitimacy and the authority of the incumbent leader and to emphasise the continuity of the social order. In other words, ritual supplements and enhances technical content; it is not a substitute for it.

In the Soviet Union, technical content in leadership succession is low. Taking the Soviet period as a whole, there appears to be no orderly, established, regular and well understood mechanism for changing leaders. In so far as technical content exists at all, it relates to collectivist institutions; in fact, *individual* leadership is not formally recognised. Therefore, as a substitute for technical content, what is often referred to as ritual becomes salient, and must serve both the social order and the individual leader.

An early example of the use of 'ritual' in the succession process is the 'Lenin enrolment' of 1924. Lenin, despite his charisma, never held specific office within the Party. He would have disdained the General Secretaryship, and there was (and is) no such office as

Chairman or President of the Party. Instead, after 1917, he was head of the government: more precisely, chairman of the Council of People's Commissars, Sovnarkom. When Lenin died, Stalin (and all the other aspirants) were not in the least interested in occupying this post. It was an office which, so far as supreme leadership was concerned, had very little power. In other words, so long as Lenin was chairman of Sovnarkom it was important; once he went it was not. Similarly, Stalin had perceived the potential of the General Secretaryship; he rose to dictatorial pre-eminence via that post; and skilfully used it as an instrument in the struggle for power. Stalin invested the General Secretaryship with power; not the other way round.

Still, matters were not cut and dried in 1924 when Lenin died, and as a device to enhance his chances Stalin proposed that the Party should swell its ranks with a special 'Lenin enrolment' in honour of the deceased leader. It was an astute move. How could Trotsky or Bukharin resist such a suggestion: to have done so would have seemed disloyal to the great Lenin, and place-seeking to boot. But who would be responsible for the enrolment? Who would decide who was admitted to the Party? The Secretary General, of course; and if the new members soon swamped the old, Leninist membership, who might be far less pliant, so much the better.

However, devices such as the Lenin enrolment are not ritual. Ritual suggests something regular and unvarying. To take church ritual as an example: each week the service is read in a particular order and each component of the service has its particular meaning, yet is part of the whole. The Lenin enrolment, on the other hand, was a once-for-all device to gain political advantage in the leadership contest. It was an opportunistic symbolic act intended to facilitate a particular contestant's (Stalin's) succession. For convenience, we shall refer to other, similar devices as *facilitating symbolism*.

Stalin's death in March 1953 and the ensuing succession struggle once again exemplify the low technical content and the use of facilitating symbolism. By the time he died, Stalin was both Party leader and Prime Minister. He had risen to supreme leadership by exploiting the power potential of the Party post, but in later years he had ruled through the organs of the state, notably the agencies of physical repression, and the Party had paid a particularly heavy toll in the mass purges of the 1930s. By 1953 it was by no means self-evidently obvious that the Party was still the main locus of political power in the Soviet Union. To begin with, Malenkov was the main contender to succeed. A Party Secretary, he also assumed the premiership: the same two offices that Stalin had occupied. Then, shortly after Stalin's death there appeared on the front page of *Pravda* a photograph purporting to show Mao, Stalin and Malenkov posing together. The symbolism was obvious. Here is the new leader, the successor to Stalin and the colleague of Mao. The picture was designed to facilitate and fortify Malenkov's succession. The picture was a fake! The point is obvious: had the system had a sufficient degree of technical content no subterfuge would have been necessary.

In the contest that ensued, such was the uncertainty and ambiguity surrounding the leadership office that, faced with having to make a choice, Malenkov relinquished the Party post and retained the premiership. It was Khrushchev's skill as a politician, his manipulation of the Party Secretaryship and his policy of rehabilitating the Party generally that had the important effect of making the Party First (or General) Secretaryship the senior position within the Soviet collective leadership. He also renounced terror as a weapon in the succession struggle, so that, since the execution of Beria in 1953, violence has not been used when changing leaders. As a general rule, we can say that, since Khrushchev, *the occupancy of the Party office has been the necessary (but not in itself the sufficient) pre-condition for attaining national leadership status*.

Khrushchev, as a leader, was more politician than bureaucrat: he led from the front. Ebullient, impetuous, expansive, bullying, sentimental, he was given to experimentation and innovation. Inspired by praiseworthy motives, if things did not go his way he would change tack and try something else. The 'virgin lands' campaign, abolition of ministries and creation of *sovnarkhozy*, bifurcation of the party and soviet apparatuses – these were the kinds of arbitrary 'hare-brained schemes' that were to bring about his political demise in 1964. Before that, following the defeat of the so-called 'anti-Party group' in 1957, he had, like Stalin before him, added the premiership to his Party Secretaryship. The result was that, following his ousting, it was stated that never again would both these offices be embodied in the same person.

This was a protective ruling (designed to obviate too great a concentration of power in one person's hands) and it had the effect of making attainment of national leadership even more difficult. By 1964, there could be no doubt but that the Party Secretaryship was the senior position in the Soviet political system. Yet considerations of personal ambition plus the exigencies of rule seemed to impel

Soviet leaders towards acquiring the government office, too (which is how we would define 'national leadership', as distinct from 'senior position'). But with the 1964 ruling in place, how would this now be possible?

It is remarkable how firmly established, both within and without the USSR, has become the notion that the state presidency goes with the Party post. Yet these two offices were linked in the USSR for the first time only in 1977. Now it is commonplace to read phrases such as 'It took Brezhnev thirteen years to become President . . .' Such a formulation seems to imply that, with the premiership closed to him, Brezhnev from 1964 to 1977 was patiently wheeling and dealing, so that eventually he 'managed' to secure the presidency. I do not think that it was like that at all.

The presidency in the Soviet Union had never hitherto been regarded as being important or influential. But Brezhnev had himself served as President between May 1960 and July 1964, while from June 1963 he was simultaneously a member of the CPSU Secretariat, so the utility of linking the Party and the state offices may have had its genesis in that experience. Also, this institutional linkage had become quite common by the 1970s in several Soviet-type political systems. Moreover, Brezhnev was extremely active in the foreign policy realm in his early years in office, and this brought him into contact with foreign leaders bearing the title of President.

The crucial point in the evolution of the institutionalisation of the Soviet leadership was reached in August 1975 when Brezhnev went to Helsinki to sign the Final Act on behalf of the USSR. On the document he designated himself:

Secretary General of the Central Committee of the Communist Party of the Soviet Union [and] head of the delegation of the USSR at the concluding stage of the conference.

Later, this was changed to simply: 'Secretary General CC CPSU'. Whether the redesignation occurred for purely protocol reasons, or whether it was because his colleagues objected to the original description, is not known. But with thirty-five heads of state or government present (no fewer than six of them leaders of Soviet-type systems) it was embarrassing both personally and from a national standpoint not to be able to ratify an important international document in a way which reflects the status and dignity of the signatory.

Confirmation of the correctness of this analysis is to be found in the speech made by Suslov to the USSR Supreme Soviet on 16 June 1977 when he proposed Brezhnev for the state presidency (that is, the chairmanship of the presidium of the USSR Supreme Soviet). First, Suslov emphasised that the decision to link the two offices had been taken at a plenary session of the CPSU Central Committee on 24 May, thus emphasising the primacy of the Party, and, by extension, of the Party post, over the state office. Secondly, he linked this new development with considerations of foreign policy; Brezhnev, he said, 'worthily represents our Party, the entire Soviet people, and our great socialist state in the world arena. And it is significant', he continued, 'that on international documents having vital meaning not only for our country, but also for the relaxation of international tension and strengthening the cause of peace, there stands the signature of L. I. Brezhnev.' And thirdly, Suslov reminded his audience that Brezhnev had for many years already been *de facto* 'the most authoritative representative of the Communist Party and the Soviet socialist state'.

It is more accurate, therefore, to say that it took Brezhnev two years, from August 1975 to June 1977, to gain the presidency. Why so long? There was, of course, an incumbent president, Podgorny, and he was no political lightweight. To that extent, it is again remarkable that Brezhnev, given the constraints of working within a collective leadership, managed to oust Podgorny and assume his title in so short a time. Since then, because the incumbent President has been simultaneously Party Secretary General, the death of the national leader has automatically left the presidency vacant and this has greatly simplified the process of succession. Incidentally, Brezhnev departed for France for talks with President Giscard d'Estaing on 20 June 1977, only four days after the meeting of the Supreme Soviet.

While *raisons d'état* and personal vanity were no doubt prime considerations in the Party-state linkage, there were other benefits, too. The national leader, as the embodiment of Party and state, has his own legitimacy enhanced, which in turn helps to reinforce the legitimacy of the social order. It may also in certain circumstances be a protection against attempts to unseat him, precisely because his legitimacy is so much stronger. And, symbolically, the linkage becomes part of a tradition in communist systems that includes charismatic giants such as Mao, Ho Chi Minh and Tito.

There is another, perhaps originally unanticipated consequence. By 1964, Soviet society and the Soviet economy had become so large and complex as to be beyond the capacity of any individual to manage effectively and indefinitely. To that extent, it would have been of doubtful benefit for a leader to be chairman of the Council of Ministers (premier) as well as Party Secretary. Yet, in order to feel secure, a Soviet leader needs to be able to control the government administration without being directly responsible and accountable for it. Once more, historical accident was fortuitous.

In 1961 Khrushchev had announced the setting-up of a commission to draft a new constitution for the USSR. Thereafter nothing happened until it was learned that Brezhnev had inherited the chairmanship of the drafting commission. Once more, nothing happened. Then, at the Plenum of 24 May 1977 (the same meeting that approved Brezhnev's appointment to the presidency) a new draft constitution was considered. The text of the draft was published in *Pravda* and other newspapers on 4 June, twelve days later Brezhnev became President, and on 7 October 1977 the USSR Supreme Soviet formally adopted the new constitution. Article 130 of the Constitution states that:

> The Council of Ministers of the USSR shall be responsible and accountable to the Supreme Soviet of the USSR and, between sessions of the Supreme Soviet of the USSR, to the Presidium of the Supreme Soviet of the USSR.

Now, this formulation is not a whit different from that which appeared in the previous constitution. But what *is* different is Article 6 of the new constitution which clearly and unambiguously specifies the CPSU as being the 'leading and directing core' of Soviet society. As President, therefore, Brezhnev now had authority without responsibility for the government administration: it was a substantial political gain that appears, *inter alia*, to have had the effect of institutionalising the linking of Party and state posts to form a pattern of national leadership office-holding.

There remain still the questions as to how a contestant is selected for the senior leadership position and then how that leader becomes national leader. In November 1982, in February 1984 and again in March 1985 observers were surprised by the smoothness and speed with which the new leader was installed following the deaths of Brezhnev, Andropov and Chernenko. The successors, Andropov, Chernenko and Gorbachev were drawn from the full membership of the Politburo, all three were Central Committee secretaries, and all were named as heading the burial commission for their predecessors.

But beyond that, give or take a few rumours as to how the Politburo voted, we know virtually nothing. Certainly, the Central Committee played no role other than that of ratifying the Politburo's choice (although that is not to say that the Politburo did not take into account the supposed views of groupings within the Central Committee). Technical content appears to have been minimal.

Once the new Secretary General has been installed, the immediate next step is to make him chairman of the USSR Defence Council. Because of the somewhat secret nature of this body, there has not, so far, been a formal public announcement; but apparently casual reference or leaks have enabled observers to deduce that incumbency of this office follows quickly upon succession to the General Secretaryship and is linked with that post, and not with the state presidency.

Seven months elapsed between Andropov's succeeding to the General Secretaryship in November 1982 and his becoming President in June the following year. Again, the 'delay' is easily explicable, not in terms of power struggle, but because Andropov was not even a member of the USSR Supreme Soviet presidium in November 1982 (an omission that was rectified at the next session of the Supreme Soviet in December), and, concerned as Andropov was to eschew a cult of the individual and observe proper procedures, he then waited until the next Supreme Soviet meeting in June 1983 before assuming the presidency.

Similarly, when Chernenko succeeded Andropov as Secretary General in February 1984 a general election campaign for the USSR Supreme Soviet was already in full swing. Chernenko simply let matters take their constitutional course and was duly elected to the presidium and then to be its chairman in April 1984 following the general election on 4 March.

On the basis of three precedents, it appears safe to assert that national leadership in the USSR now consists of appointment to the CPSU General Secretaryship, followed by the chairmanship of the Defence Council and the state presidency (in that order). However, formal technical content remains low and it is uncertain how firm these precedents are. The attendant benefits of this linkage, as has been argued, are substantial, and it would appear to be in the system's interest to make the convention hold. The election of Gromyko as President in July 1985 would not appear to invalidate this state of affairs since it is reasonable to assume that Gorbachev's eventual aim is to become President.

The signs are that the Soviet collective leadership *is* aware of the utility of maintaining the system that seems to have evolved. When Chernenko proposed Andropov as President on 16 June 1983 he used much the same formula as that stated by Suslov six years earlier. It was a plenum of the CPSU Central Committee that had decided unanimously that Andropov should be President, and it had been found 'expedient' that the Secretary General should 'hold concurrently' the state presidency, one reason being that 'our foreign friends see in him an outstanding leader of the Leninist type'. When fifteen months later Tikhonov proposed Chernenko as Secretary General he referred to him as being 'a prominent leader of the Communist Party *and the Soviet state* [emphasis added: this was before Chernenko's accession to the presidency], a true associate of such Leninist-type leaders as Leonid Ilyich Brezhnev and Yury Vladimirovich Andropov were', a formulation that less than three weeks later had become 'an outstanding figure of the Communist Party and the Soviet state, a leader of the Leninist type'! These nuances are attempts to use symbols to facilitate succession by creating an aura of continuity and legitimacy around the incoming leader.

The USSR appears to be edging towards an established succession procedure. The combination of offices and their order of precedence seem to be settled, although we have little idea as to how the actual choice of successor is made. Such rules as there are (the primacy of Congress and the Central Committee) are ignored (despite the optimism generated by the crises of 1957 and, to a lesser degree, by 1964), and the precedent amounts so far to only three successions. Nor is the problem confined just to putting a new leader in place. Equally important is the question of how to replace (or re-endorse) incumbent leaders. Brezhnev continued to rule until well beyond his physical and mental capacities, with the system, literally, waiting for him to die. When at last he did go, his successor (the ablest of the contestants for the leadership) was himself already mortally ill. Such a pattern may suit the vested interests of the Party–state bureaucracies, and it would be incredibly difficult to systematise and regularise leadership selection and re-endorsement without encroaching upon some of the fundamental tenets of Communist Party rule (democratic centralism, unanimity, the ban of factionalism). But unless and until there is a technical mechanism for changing leaders, as well as replacing them once they die, the Soviet political system is bound to oscillate between periods of relative dynamism and prolonged inertia. It may be that the oligarchical leadership is aware of this, and is willing to pay the price. Anything else would impose too great a strain upon the social order, and that, they would argue, is sacred and eternal. The election of Gorbachev has postponed the need to agree on a mechanism for changing leaders since he may hold office for at least two decades. Since there is no guarantee that he will enjoy good health during his full term of office, this basic weakness remains.

THE PRESENT SOVIET LEADERSHIP

Politburo	Function
Gorbachev, Mikhail (1931)	Secretary General; Chairman, Defence Council
Aliev, Geidar (1923)	First Deputy Chairman, USSR Council of Ministers
Vorotnikov, Vitaly (1926)	Chairman, RSFSR Council of Ministers
Grishin, Viktor (1914)	First Secretary, Moscow city Party
Gromyko, Andrei (1909)	Chairman, USSR Supreme Soviet
Kunaev, Dinmukhamed (1912)	First Secretary, CP of Kazakhstan
Ligachev, Egor (1920)	CC Secretary, Organisational Party Work
Ryzhkov, Nikolai (1929)	CC Secretary, Economic Department
Shevardnadze, Eduard (1928)	USSR Minister of Foreign Affairs
Solomentsev, Mikhail (1913)	Chairman, Party Control Commission
Tikhonov, Nikolai (1905)	Chairman, USSR Council of Ministers
Chebrikov, Viktor General (1923)	Chairman, KGB

Shcherbitsky, Vladimir (1918) First Secretary, CP of Ukraine

Candidate Members

Demichev, Pyotr (1918) USSR Minister of Culture

Dolgikh, Vladimir (1924) CC Secretary, Heavy Industry, Power

Kuznetsov, Vasily (1901) First Deputy Chairman, USSR Supreme Soviet

Ponomarev, Boris (1905) CC Secretary, International Department

Sokolov, Sergei Marshal (1911) USSR Minister of Defence

Secretariat

Gorbachev, Mikhail Secretary General

Dolgikh, Vladimir as above

Eltsin, B. N. Head, Construction

Zaikov, L. N. Head,, Machine Building

Zimyanin, Mikhail (1914) Head, Propaganda, Culture

Kapitonov, Ivan (1915) Head, Consumer Goods, Food

Ligachev, Egor as above

Nikonov, Viktor (1929) Head, agriculture

Ponomarev, Boris as above

Rusakov, Konstantin (1909) Head, Relations with Communist Parties of Socialist Countries

Ryzhkov, Nikolai as above

USSR Council of Ministers

Tikhonov, Nikolai Prime Minister

Aliev, Geidar First Deputy Chairman

USSR Council of Defence

Gorbachev, Mikhail	Chairman
Sokolov, Sergei Marshal	USSR Minister of Defence
Akhromeev, Sergei Marshal (1923)	Chief of Staff
Tikhonov, Nikolai	Prime Minister

USSR Supreme Soviet Presidium

Gromyko, Andrei	Chairman (President)
Kuznetsov, Vasily	First Deputy Chairman

2 Soviet Leadership Profiles

STEPHEN CARTER

Between November 1982, and March 1985, there were three leadership successions in the Soviet Union. This unprecedented sequence of events, which occasioned an almost annual pilgrimage of world leaders to funerals in Moscow, seems at last to have settled the post-Brezhnev succession with the elevation of Mikhail Sergeevich Gorbachev to the post of Secretary General of the Party.

The interim period was characterised by a sequence of almost embarrassing events for the Soviet leadership: Brezhnev's evident ill-health, especially after the summer of 1982, was followed in mid August of 1983 by the complete disappearance of Andropov from public life. Despite frequent articles signed by Andropov in the central Soviet press, portraits, claims that Andropov had a 'cold', and so on, the great man did not appear and his death, for acute renal deficiency and other conditions, was announced in February 1984. Then, after 54 days' absence from the scene in the summer of 1984, Chernenko appeared in public only rarely: His emphysema had been evident from an early as the funeral of Andropov. The 'cult of personality' continued, important articles under Chernenko's name (such as that in *Kommunist*, 18, 1984) appeared, and he was even revived sufficiently to vote in the Supreme Soviet elections of February 1985; but his health was self-evidently flagging. Despite the elaborate deception, few were surprised when the death of Chernenko was announced on 11 March 1985.

Such events inevitably gave rise to jokes at the expense of the political system. The Soviet Union, it was said, not only has the corpse of its founder, Lenin, in the Red Square Mausoleum: It also has some corpses in high political office! Perhaps some of the figures on the Red Square reviewing platform were cardboard cut-outs? Chernenko's collective leadership was compared to a troika with a dead driver. And so it went on. A chronic weakness of the Soviet

29

system was clearly exposed, and its lack of accountability to the public, its low 'technical content' as a self-appointing oligarchy, and something of its essential nature were revealed.

Political succession is a two-stage process: It requires, (1), removal of the existing encumbent, and (2), his replacement by a new leader. It is evident that the Soviet stage (1) is carried out in a very unsatisfactory and old-fashioned way. In a manner which can be compared only with medieval monarchies, Soviet leaders can apparently be removed by death (Lenin, Stalin, Brezhnev, Andropov, Chernenko), or, exceptionally, by a highly risky 'palace revolt' (Khrushchev). However, the Soviet stage (2) is now achieved fairly smoothly. It seems that the Politburo can agree on a candidate for the office of Secretary General quite quickly, by majority vote and subsequent unanimous endorsement, followed by formal Central Committee ratification. Andropov was confirmed by his colleagues within two days of Brezhnev's death, and was proposed for office by his defeated rival, Chernenko, who paused only to stress 'collective leadership'. In his turn, Chernenko was endorsed, probably after Gromyko and Ustinov had intervened in a previously split vote, after about four days, and was in position to receive foreign visitors at Andropov's funeral. It is possible that Gorbachev was identified as Second Secretary even at this early stage. Certainly, Gorbachev's endorsement was remarkably swift, occurring on the same day as the announcement of Chernenko's death (11 March 1985).

As T. H. Rigby has observed: 'Formal positions have, of course, been vital as means to and channels of personal authority, but there is none in the Soviet Union which suffices to impart it. Except for Lenin, leaders have had to work and fight for it *after* appointment to high office' (Rigby, Brown and Reddaway, 1980, p. 16). This is true because the new Secretary General 'inherits' a Politburo, Secretariat, and Central Committee. It will take him time to promote supporters into crucial posts in the hierarchy, and McCauley has suggested that a typical time period for such a consolidation of power would be five years (McCauley, 1983b, p. 13). As Peter Frank indicates above, the 'incipient institutionalisation' of the Soviet system since Brezhnev suggests that a Secretary General tends to acquire the posts of Chairman of the Defence Council and of President of the Presidium of the USSR Supreme Soviet. The Presidency gives the new leader added legitimacy and protocol status, while the Chairmanship of the Defence Council makes him Commander-in-Chief. Andropov achieved these posts between November 1982 and 16 June 1983.

Chernenko's acquisition was even quicker, a period of 7 weeks between February and April 1984.

However, Chernenko's rapid acquisition of the 'institutionalised' posts did not, apparently, enhance his power: He was unable to make any appointments to the slowly diminishing Politburo, or to the Secretariat, and apart from possible influence on the decision to reopen negotiations with the USA at Geneva in 1985, appears to have had little impact of any kind. Conversely, Andropov's ascetic and energetic personality stamped itself on events quite soon after his accession: Measures to enforce improved labour discipline were in force by December 1982, and he succeeded in appointing Ligachev to the Secretariat, and Chebrikov and Vorotnikov to the Politburo, the following December, only a few weeks before he died.

Assuming that Gorbachev eventually accrues all the traditional offices of a Secretary General, he is well placed to make a quick impact on appointments: Already, several changes have been announced in the State apparatus, and the XXVIIth Congress of the Party is scheduled for February 1986. This will be the occasion at which the old, discredited 'Khrushchev' Party Programme of 1961 will be replaced, some new Party Rules will be introduced, a new Five Year Plan willl be adopted, and a new Central Committee will be elected. Other things being equal, the new Secretary General will find this timing fortuitously to his advantage. At the time of writing, it would seem that the post-Brezhnev succession, and possibly the most significant Soviet succession since the death of Stalin, is well on the way to consolidation.

However, the policy implications of this succession are much more difficult to predict. In Soviet conditions, there are three 'general' reasons for this: First, a Secretary General today does not wield the power of a Stalin or even of a Khrushchev. A recent paper by Graeme Gill (BBC Caris Report, 15,85) analyses with clarity the arguments for emphasising 'collective leadership' and the checks on the powers of the Secretary General. Secondly, in order to be selected by his Politburo colleagues, the would-be Secretary General cannot afford to appear either too conservative or too radical. Above all, he must be tactful and restrained. Even after accession to power, but before his consolidation, he may use policy debates more as a political weapon to outwit his rivals than to clarify his true position. Stalin's support for the 'centre' during NEP, and Khrushchev's attack on Malenkov's consumer goods programme as a 'belching up of the Rightist deviation' will be remembered by students of Soviet history.

Thirdly, in contrast to the adversarial politics of Western democracies, Soviet 'monolithism' and the ban on factionalism in the Party makes policy differentiation between leaders somewhat arcane: One is dealing with subtle emphases and matters of degree rather than of kind.

Nevertheless, a descriptive account of the historical background to the post-Brezhnev successions, and the political profiles of those involved, together with a tentative hypothesis of their apparent policy priorities, may help to indicate the issues and choices involved.

The long 'Brezhnev years', 1964–82 (during which the USA had five Presidents, while the UK had six governments and five parliaments), were a period of 'stability of cadres' after the frantic innovations of the Khrushchev period. Brezhnev's political system, perhaps best encapsulated in the 1977 Constitution of the USSR, which established the leading role of the Party (Article 6), suffered from an elderly leadership which was almost visibly decaying into immobility and corruption during its last years. This immobility was symbolised at the XXVIth Congress in 1981 by a failure to either promote or demote the top echelons of the Party. In 1982 the whiff of scandal touched the Brezhnev family itself when Brezhnev's daughter Galina was involved in bribe-taking circles, such as that of 'Boris the Gypsy', which were under KGB investigation. The passing of the Brezhnev era seemed to be prefigured in the death of its 'eminence grise', Mikhail Suslov, in early 1982. His place in the Central Committee Secretariat was taken by the former KGB chief, Yuri Vladimirovich Andropov, then 68 years old.

Andropov's political profile was an unusual one. Active as a Party boss in Karelia in the forties, he transferred to the centre in 1954, after which he was ambassador in Hungary. He was elevated to the Central Committee Secretariat in 1957, and to the KGB chairmanship in 1967. An effective and ruthless man, qualities demonstrated by his handling of the Hungarian crisis of 1956, and by his restoration of morale and status to the KGB 1967–82, he was widely feared and respected. In retrospect, his initiatives in home policy have continued to exert influence, while foreign policy, symbolised by the ever-present Gromyko, has also shown continuity rather than change. Only Andropov's terminal ill-health after August 1983, coincided with a worsening of the international atmosphere after the downing of Korean Airlines 007, and the Soviet mishandling of arms negotiations after the installation of medium-range missiles in Europe later that year.

Andropov's domestic policies seemed to include a resolute attack on corruption in high places, an emphasis of labour discipline in general, and limited technocratic reform in the Party and the economy. Andropov's pace of activity was formidable: Mikhail Gorbachev was in charge of the Party elections in 1983, during which 22.6 per cent of all oblast (province) and krai (area) first secretaries were replaced. About half the departments of the Central Committee were reorganised, and in the summer of 1983, Grigory Romanov was brought into the Secretariat in Moscow from Leningrad. In this sense, is Gorbachev was and Romanov an 'Andropovite'.

Significantly, Romanov was replaced, not by his deputy, but by the Chairman of the Leningrad *gorispolkom* (executive committee of the city soviet), L. N. Zaikov. Promotions to top Party posts of former Soviet officials are by no means unprecedented, but Andropov did seem to de-emphasise Party privilege. Similarly, 'localism' (*mestnichestvo*) was attacked by elevating second secretaries from 'foreign' oblasts or republics. For example, G. V. Kolbin, former second secretary of the Georgian Party, became first secretary of the Ulyanovsk *obkom*. Finally, new blood was introduced, as when Vitaly Vorotnikov was posted from service overseas to take over from S. F. Medunov in Krasnodar krai and then rose to Politburo status as Chairman of the RSFSR Council of Ministers. N. N. Slyunkov, who was then not even a member of the Central Committee, replaced Kiselev in Belorussia. The Party Control Committee, which has atrophied under the octogenarian Pelshe, was given a new lease of life under Solomentsev, and the KGB's Chebrikov was awarded Politburo candidate status. Andropov also promoted members of the 'military industrial complex' to the Central Committee, and created three new Marshals of the Soviet Union, including Sergei Akhromeev.

In brief, a lot of highly placed officials, used to the privilege, security, and status of their positions under Brezhnev, may have been severely shaken by the Andropov regime. The selection of Chernenko, a man closely associated with the Brezhnev style, seemed to reflect that unease. Chernenko's political profile clearly indicates his dependence on Brezhnev and his affiliations with the Party *apparatchiki*. Born in 1911, Chernenko was a peasant's son from Krasnoyarsk, and became a full member of the Party in 1931, two years after the inauguration of the collectivisation drive. From the point of view of the military establishment, he had a relatively undistinguished career, serving briefly only with the Border Guards, and although he volunteered for the front in the Great Patriotic War, he was a member of the 'chairborne division' in Siberia. Later, he went to Penza, and then to the Moldavian Party, where he associated with Brezhnev in the late forties and early fifties. Chernenko was in charge of agitation and propaganda in Moldavia, and he has a strongly ideological experience of Party work. (It is surely significant that a strong attack on the Moldavian Party, and its first secretary Semyon Grossu, appeared in *Pravda* on 15 December 1983, under Andropov, only to be countered by a rehabilitation the following spring, under Chernenko.)

Chernenko followed Brezhnev to Moscow, gaining experience in the Central Committee Secretariat, and the Secretariat of the Presidium of the USSR Supreme Soviet from 1960. From 1965, he was Head of Department in the General Department of the Secretariat, the Department which deals with the Politburo agenda. A careful and sycophantic Party functionary, Chernenko was rewarded in 1976 with elevation to the status of Secretary of the Central Committee, apparently over the head of Kirilenko. He achieved Politburo membership in 1978.

Chernenko was thus clearly associated with 'Brezhnevism', the older generation, conservatism, and respect for tried and tested methods of work. However, Chernenko's weak health and personality prevented this 'Brezhnevite' conservatism from doing more than slowing down the pace of reform. For example, under Chernenko, Yuri Sokolov, manager of Gastronom No. 1, a man close to the Brezhnev family, and who had been condemned under Andropov for corruption, was in fact executed. He might well have expected reprieve from Brezhnev's protegé. Reformist articles continued to appear in journals such as *Voprosi Istorii*, which seemed to indicate that some important debates were going on without Chernenko: And in a final indignity, a reformist article, ostensibly written by Chernenko himself, but in fact almost certainly drafted in his name by others, appeared in *Kommunist* in December 1984. The pace of change and external pressures, too much for Chernenko's physical health or intellect, now confronted his successor. On the surface, there was continuity. But the accession of Gorbachev surely indicates change.

Mikhail Sergeevich Gorbachev is Russian, born on 2 March 1931, in the village of Privolnoe in Krasnogvardeisky Raion in Stavropol Krai. His parents, like those of Chernenko and Romanov, were peasants. In 1946, he had a part time job at a machine tractor station.

At 19, already decorated with the Order of the Red Banner, he entered the law faculty of Moscow University, joining the Party in 1952, and graduating in 1955. Clearly, Gorbachev was a man of exceptional ability, and possibly enjoyed some kind of influence, at an early age. He proved a capable Komsomol organiser at university, and in 1956 was appointed first secretary of the Stavropol city Komsomol Committee. In 1958, he was deputy head of the department of agitation and propaganda of the Stavropol krai Komsomol Committee, and in the same year he was elevated to first secretary of the Komsomol there. Gorbachev had proven himself a high flyer by the end of his twenties, and a man of wide experience, which included practical knowledge of agriculture as well as legal training from the prestigious Moscow University.

In 1960, Fyodor Kulakov, one of Khrushchev's leading agricultural experts, was appointed first secretary of the Stavropol krai Party Committee. This connection aided Gorbachev, for he rose quickly in the Stavropol city Party Committee (1966) and the Krai Party Committee (1970). The next year, Gorbachev was elected to the Central Committee, and in 1978, he succeeded his former boss Kulakov as CC Secretary in charge of Agriculture. In 1979, Gorbachev was elected candidate member, and in 1980 a full member, of the Politburo.

Following the XXVIth Congress in 1981, Gorbachev's name appeared directly after Chernenko's in the list of CC Secretaries, but his greatest career boost occurred in 1982, when after the deaths of Suslov and Brezhnev, and Kirilenko's retirement, Gorbachev appeared in third place in the hierarchy after Andropov and Chernenko.

In April 1984, Gorbachev acquired the chair of the Foreign Affairs Commission of the Supreme Soviet's Council of the Union, which enabled him to influence foreign policy and to meet foreign delegations at both Party and State level. Gorbachev, accompanied by his wife Raisa, made a very favourable impression during a visit to Britain in December 1984.

Following the demotion of Marshal Ogarkov in September 1984, and the death of Marshal Ustinov later that year, the influence of the military in the top leadership seemed to be waning. Marshal Sokolov (73), the new Minister of Defence, was not then awarded a Politburo position. Seweryn Bialer (*Time*, 25 March 85, p. 10) has argued, 'It was very fortunate for Gorbachev that the military was put in its place before he took power.' When Gorbachev made his speech at

Chernenko's funeral, he was accompanied by Politburo colleagues and representatives of civilian life, and the military were confined to a separate reviewing stand. These facts have led some analysts to conclude that Gorbachev came to power with the aid of Gromyko (who proposed Gorbachev in glowing terms), the KGB, the economic managers, and the younger generation of the Party. He is seen as a reformer, an enlightened 'Westerniser', even a 'liberal', in contrast to the older generation. This would surely be an oversimplification: Gorbachev is an 'Andropovite', formidable politicians with an eye to needed reforms in the interests of strengthening the Soviet Union and improving economic performance.

Gorbachev's speeches and writings have not been collectively published at the time of writing, and so in summarising some of Gorbachev's stated views, I rely largely on recent speeches, such as that given at an Ideological Conference in December 1984, his electoral address of February 1985, his funeral oration in March 1985, and recent analyses made by Julian Cooper and Stephen White at the annual NASEES Conference in March 1985 held at Cambridge, England.

In recent years, there has been much speculation about ways to improve the Soviet planning system: The malaise, the need for modernisation, 'intensification' of industry and agriculture, of better allocation of scarce resources and labour, and a more rational 'economic mechanism', are clearly perceived. Debates between Soviet economists have been sharp, and there is some impatience with professional economists and social scientists in top Party circles. Several 'experiments' have been proposed and carried out. These include:

1. *The 'Brigade' or 'Link' system in agriculture.* This gave autonomy to production teams at the local level, who were rewarded according to fulfilment of previously nominated targets. Some successes have been recorded, but poor harvests have continued for about 6 years to 1985.
2. *The Leningrad Experiment.* This involved a plan to 'shake out' excess labour, and reward the more efficient work force with higher pay. From January 1985, this scheme has been extended to more enterprises in 8 Industrial Ministries, indicating some success.
3. *The Poti Experiment in Georgia.* This involves the administration

of municipal economic activity led by self-financing (*khozraschet*) territorial associations.

4. *The Belorussian Experiment*. This involves new methods of paying for completed construction projects: A reward for satisfactory *results* in a notoriously weak area of the system.

5. *Consumer services*. In retail distribution in the RSFSR, there has been a pilot scheme to reduce drastically the number of 'Plan Indicators' which store managers are required to fulfil. This simplifies the administrative tasks locally, and reduces the flow of information to the centre, without diminishing central control.

6. *The 'Large Scale Economic Experiment in Industry'*. From January 1984, 700 enterprises of 5 Ministries were given both greater independence and greater responsibility in plan and contract fulfilment. This scheme does seem to have improved both fulfilment of delivery quotas and labour productivity. As from January 1985, about 6 per cent of all enterprises, accounting for some 12 per cent of all production, have gone over to this system.

Overall, these experiments do not amount to radical reform on either the Chinese or Hungarian 'market socialism' models: They seem to be designed to cut out bureaucratism in planning, to cash in on local initiative, to reward diligence and punish idleness, without loosening central controls.

The future direction of Soviet policy and ideology will become much clearer with the publication of the new Party Programme, which will be drafted under Gorbachev's influence with the aid of an editorial board which consists of: Gorbachev, Ponomarev, Zimyanin, Stukalin, V. A. Medvedev, Kosolapov (editor of *Kommunist*), and Afanasev (editor of *Pravda*). The contents of this Programme may have been prefigured in Gorbachev's ideological speech of 10 December 84.

The improvement of 'developed socialism', now seen as a protracted historical period without any of the Khrushchevian schemes about the attainment of an egalitarian communism, is to be the goal of ideological activity among the people. But Gorbachev is not primarily an ideologist: He demands 'unity of words and deed', and above all, 'effectiveness' in the country's 'overall labour rhythm'. The Party, he said, had launched a struggle to establish order, organisation, and discipline, and to heighten responsibility of cadres at all levels of management. The aim must be higher growth rates and an improvement in the moral and political atmosphere. Patriotic and atheist propaganda work must go ahead, while a profound transformation in 'the entire system of social relations', and the qualitatively higher standard of living, are envisaged. This might require new solutions from social scientists and economists, improved mass news media, *glasnost* (publicity), and development of new means of participation by the people, 'socialist self-government'. 'Lenin never counterposed Soviet state power of self-government by the people.' However, it is clear that Gorbachev does not intend to slacken the Party's hold over this process, since this is needed to 'ensure unity and cohesion'.

The major area of concentration will be the scientific-technical and organisational improvement of the economy, in order to achieve modenisation and 'intensification of social production'. Educational reform was mentioned in this context. As regards management, the 'large-scale economic experiment in industry' came in for praise, and will be extended. Social justice, the elimination of corruption, 'distributive justice' and the improvement of the social wage, including the Health Service, and cultural facilities, were mentioned.

In countering 'capitalist propaganda', which is clearly seen as dangerous and effective, Gorbachev asked for 'creative and aggressive' self-confidence in the socialist system and aims of peace and social progress. Gorbachev praised Party workers who achieved results, and did not rely on a formal-bureaucratic approach, arrogance towards the masses, nepotism, and favouritism. He made reassuring gestures in the direction of the creative intelligentsia. In the end, Gorbachev creates an impression of impatience and practicality: 'Businesslike efficiency', 'boldness and persistence', 'order, organisation, and discipline', and the 'labour rhythm' are the typical phrases of Gorbachevism.

The apparent contradictions between socialist self-government or 'participation' and Party control; between initiative or responsibility at the local level and nationwide labour discipline and *poryadok* (order); between a creative approach to social or economic problems and ideological conformity; are unresolved. However, one feels that the new Soviet leadership will demand, above all, not discussion but practical *results*. The minimum reforms required to achieve these results will be enforced, but no radical changes, it seems, can be expected. The same would seem to apply in foreign affairs, where President Gromyko still looms large: Gorbachev's approach to the crucial relationship with the USA will surely remain consistent with past policies. In this respect he will try to exploit differences between the USA and her allies, and weaknesses in US policy. Foreign Minister Shevardnadze is as yet an unknown quantity.

To summarise, Gorbachev is in a good position to make extensive personnel changes and to consolidate his position politically. Reforms will be pragmatic and effective rather than radical. Gorbachev seems to be an Andropovite, and should not be seen as a 'liberal'. He will pursue Soviet interests with ruthlessness and intelligence: But his task is gigantic, and he faces some rivalry as well as the inherent contradictions and inertia of the system.

3 Poland

GEORGE SANFORD

The character of Polish communist leadership has been conditioned by the overwhelming problems faced by the Polish United Workers' Party (PZPR, the widely-used Polish initials) in establishing itself in Polish society. The Polish case has been marked by the extent as well as the longevity of the continuing interplay between normal Soviet-type 'closed' internal Party mechanisms and more 'open' ones produced by forces external to the PZPR, notably the pressures of a far-from-controlled Polish society (on the latter, see Lane and Kolankiewicz, 1973). Specifically Polish conditions have not only had a greater impact on the communist leadership élite than elsewhere during succession crises but they have also influenced leaders' subsequent policies, factional conflict within the PZPR and the First Secretary's capacity to build up his power within the PZPR and his political legitimacy in the eyes of society. There has also been a complex relationship between the Soviet and Polish leaderships which, since 1956, cannot be characterised wholly in terms of Kremlin domination. Something close to a triangular interplay, involving different power balances, political strategies and alliances between them and Polish society has emerged in various ways at different times.

It is widely accepted that the originality of the Polish case lies primarily in the difficulties experienced by the PZPR hard-core and its Soviet allies in building socialism in a fairly large (36 millions in 1984), homogeneously Polish and Roman Catholic population with anti-state, strong pro-Western and some anti-Russian traditions and inclinations (Kolankiewicz and Taras, 1977). This historical inheritance has complicated the PZPR's efforts to control and to benefit from the postwar socio-economic processes of industrialisation, urbanisation, and the building of a modern, socially differentiated, demographically young society with high educational standards and growing professional and economic aspirations (Szczepański, 1973). These social realities have consequently divided the Polish leadership class over the speed and intensity at which it should attempt to build socialism in Poland; a key issue has always been the extent to which the Soviet model should be followed or whether national forms taking Polish conditions and peculiarities should prevail (Sanford 1980, p. 563).

The challenge posed to the Party–state–society balance established in 1956, by Solidarity in 1980–1, eventually impelled the PZPR élite to call in the military, headed by General Wojciech Jaruzelski, who imposed the State of War in December 1981. But traditional forms of resticted and closed intra-Party politics had earlier prevailed for long periods; the novel Polish features of socio-economic crisis leading to PZPR leadership change in October 1956, December 1970 and August–September 1980, have therefore been counterbalanced by many normal Soviet-type features. After discussing the above pattern this chapter will examine the character of the Jaruzelski regime and the likely prospects for its evolution.

The detailed political history of Polish communism in power has been covered elsewhere (Dziewanowski, 1976; de Weydenthal, 1978; for documentary sources Sanford, 1982). One might note the following background comments on the peculiarities of Poland's postwar development here. The establishment of a fully-blown Soviet communist dictatorship was preceded in 1945–7 by a qualified form of political and social pluralism which saw the increasing domination of the Polish Workers' Party (PPR), formed in 1942, the successor to the interwar Polish Communist Party (KPP) dissolved by Stalin in 1938. This transitional period was presided over by a mixed communist leadership in terms of wartime experiences and loyalties. (See Polonsky and Drukier, 1980, pp. 1–139). The 'Nativists', symbolised by PPR Secretary General, Władysław Gomułka, who had spent the war in Poland and the 'Muscovites', led by Bolesław Bierut, who had spent the war in the USSR or fought in the Soviet sponsored Berling Army, were never clearly organised factions at this time; nevertheless they had different political attitudes. The former were purged and the latter dominated the relatively short Stalinist period from 1948–54 which set up the formal shell of the Soviet type of communist rule and a centralised, heavy industry-dominated, planning system. Great transformations took place but Polish society, far from being refashioned in a totalitarian mould, reverted to a traditional Polish political culture response, formed by the nineteenth-century experience of resistance to the partitioning powers – that of nationwide opposition to what was perceived as a hostile and foreign-dominated Polish state. First intellectuals, then workers and finally (as a result of factional Party conflict over who should be scapegoated and who should advance) younger, domesticist and more reformist communists challenged the indecisive and weakly-established Stalinist leadership. The crisis culminated in the sweeping away of the Old Stalinists, the defeat of the pro-Soviet faction and the return of Gomułka to the leadership in October 1956 (Kozik, 1982; Syrop, 1957).

A novel and fundamentally revised communist system then emerged. Gomułka refashioned a more balanced relationship with society, based on private ownership of the bulk of the land, coexistence with the Roman Catholic Church and above all the concession by the Kremlin of some domestic autonomy to the Warsaw leadership (Stehle, 1965). Gomułka re-established the PZPR hegemony in a slightly looser form, forswearing the general use of police terror. He maintained orthodox democratic centralist methods, investment priorities and centralised economic mechanisms. Conflict was therefore built into the hybrid and unstable 1956–80 system. Polish leaders had to develop novel skills as crisis managers (Pirages, 1972; Bauman, in Janos, 1976). The system had, however, sufficient safety valves to ride out periodic confrontations with social and religious groups and maintained itself by sacrificing Gomułka in December 1970 after the Baltic seacoast riots. Gierek's more pragmatic, less ideological, consumer-oriented technocracy, however, overheated the economy and lost control of its foreign debts. Gierek failed to respond adequately to the failure of his attempt to raise food prices in 1976. He neither improved the economy's performance nor damped down society's expectations. In particular he was unable to allay the discontents of a more self-confident and mature working class. Its industrial action in the summer of 1980 not only overthrew him and his team, but far-reaching political and economic demands, including the right to strike and to form self-managing trade unions (NSZZ), also buried the 1956–80 system.

Although it has been suggested above that Poland's postwar political history can best be regarded as going through four distinct phases (1944–8, 1948–56, 1956–80 and 1980 – the present day) the periodisation which most usefully serves our discussion of Polish leadership and succession is naturally that of the individual leaders' terms of office. These are always highly significant chronological milestones in communist politics (For a short official overview see Jarema Maciszewski in *Polska*, 1974, pp. 126–40).

POLITICAL SUCCESSION

There have been six successions to the office of communist First Secretary since 1948. (1) Gomułka–Bierut in September 1948, although technically a succession within the PPR was, however, part of the unification proceedings which formed the PZPR out of the merger of the PPR with the Polish Socialist Party (PPS). Like (2) Bierut–Ochab in 1956 it was a 'closed' succession; in both cases the main interest lay in Soviet pressure, even direction, but the second was also affected by political unrest. The next three successions – (3) Ochab–Gomułka in October 1956, (4) Gomułka–Gierek in December 1970 and (5) Gierek–Kania in September 1980 – were more 'open' PZPR responses to social discontent. The leader's fall was caused by social pressures but the internal party, including Soviet processes, determined which individual would succeed to the top office. The latest, (6) Kania–Jaruzelski succession in October 1981, although caused by Kania's failure to pacify society and to re-establish the PZPR's leading role, was nevertheless a more closed affair.

(1) The normal Soviet type of wholly internal party changeover

Gomułka, as PPR Secretary General, had become identified with the strategy that the building of communism in Poland required tactical adjustments to national conditions, especially in agriculture (Bethell, 1969, pp. 139–62). He was therefore a victim of Stalin's Cold War tack, marked by the establishment of the Cominform and the repercussions of the Soviet–Yugoslav dispute (Kołomejczyk and Szyzdek, 1971, pp. 236–42; see Andrzej Werblan on significance of 1948, *Polityka*, 12 June 1982). Gomułka's fall and replacement by Bierut was therefore initiated by Stalin in order to concentrate power in the hands of his more dependable Muscovite agents who set about Stalinising and Sovietising Poland to an accelerated degree (Staar 1962).

TABLE 3.1 *PZPR First Secretaries*

Name	Year of Birth	Term as First Secretary	Politburo Membership (Dates as candidate in brackets)	Other Functions
Bierut, Bolesław	1892	Dec. 1948– Mar. 1956	1948–56	President of Republic 1947–52 Chairman Council of Ministers 1952–4
Ochab, Edward	1906	Mar.–Oct. 1956	1954–68	CC Sec 1950–4, 1956–7, 1960–4. Minister of Agriculture 1957–9
Gomułka, Władysław	1905	Oct. 1956–Dec. 1970	1956–70	Secretary General PPR 1943–8 Deputy Premier 1944–9
Gierek, Edward	1913	Dec. 1970– Sept. 1980	1956, 1959–80	First Secretary, Katowice Province 1957–70 CC Secretary Mar. 1956–64
Kania, Stanisław	1927	Sept. 1980–Oct. 1981	1971–81 (1971–5)	CC Secretary 1971–80 M. Council of State 1982–
Jaruzelski, Wojciech	1923	Oct. 1981–	December 1970– (1970–1)	Minister of Defence 1968–83 Chairman Council of Ministers Feb. 1981–

M = Member

PPR First Secretaries were Marceli Nowotko (Jan.–Nov. 1942), Paweł Finder (Nov. 1942 – Nov. 1943), Władysław Gomułka (Nov. 1943 – Sept. 1948) and Bolesław Bierut (Aug. – Dec. 1948).

(2) Death in office

Bierut died on 12 March 1956 while attending the Twentieth CPSU Congress in Moscow. The convenient death of the Polish 'mini-Stalin' came at a time of political thaw and ferment which had accelerated during 1955. The Poles had introduced their own 'New Course' very slowly after Stalin's death in March 1953. The police apparatus was disciplined and returned to Party control. Investment priorities were re-adjusted slightly and the PZPR inner-core split gradually into the pro-Soviet *Natolin* and more domestic-reformist *Puławy* factions. Much is still unclear about the PZPR Sixth Plenum of 20 March 1956 but it is probable that there was behind-the-scenes consideration of the candidatures of Khrushchev's preferred first choices, Zenon Nowak or Franciszek Mazur, and of the ex-Stalinist CC Secretary, Roman Zambrowski, who later posed as a liberal and had it whispered that he was blackballed solely because of his Jewish origins. In the end the CC compromised on the highly experienced and ideologically reliable Old Bolshevik and CC Secretary, Edward Ochab, who was acceptable to all the warring factions in Moscow.

(3) The PZPR leadership balances between Polish society and Soviet power

Ochab lacked the dominant personality, luck, skill and time neces-sary to pacify society and to unite the PZPR. Gomułka's arrest and disgrace gained him the reputation of being a principled man who had suffered for a Polish Road to Socialism. He therefore became an invaluable political symbol in 1956. The PZPR leaders knew, how-ever, that he was a reliable communist. His rehabilitation was deter-mined by pragmatic centrists such as Ochab and Premier Cyrankie-wicz who, in spite of Soviet pressure, drew reformist conclusions from the Poznań Uprising of 28 June at the Seventh Plenum of 18–28 July. Having decided on Gomułka's return to power they were supported by the whole nation in facing up to the top level CPSU delegation, headed by Khrushchev, which descended on Warsaw and threatened armed intervention. The Eighth Plenum of 19–21 October 1956 nevertheless appointed Gomułka as First Secretary in 'a genu-ine election by secret ballot' (Skilling 1966, p. 82). He managed to reassure the Russians after a dramatic confrontation (Syrop 1957, pp. 81–146). The *Natolinists* were dropped from the Politburo, notably

Defence Minister, Marshal Konstanty Rokossowski. Gomułka's programme set out in his plenum speech of 20 October was approved
amidst widespread popular enthusiasm. (The whole Eighth Plenum
proceedings were reproduced in *Nowe Drogi*, October 1956.) Gomułka was not a real socialist reformer, however. He merely confirmed the gains of 'October'. His coming to power signalled the end
of the political and social pluralism and PZPR paralysis which had
made them possible (cf. Round Table discussion, *Polityka*, 24 October 1981). Gomułka's first priority was to rebuild the PZPR's
hegemony on a wider and more national basis; but this did not mean
implementing the 'October' ideas of socialist democracy and economic decentralisation which he increasingly denounced as revisionist
(Góra 1976, ch. IV).

(4) Leadership and policy change defuses regional revolt

Gomułka's position had been weakened by the onslaught of an
authoritarian-minded faction of national communists dubbed the
Partisans, led by Mieczysław Moczar, Minister of the Interior
(1964–8), and by the student demonstrations and PZPR counter-
reaction of Spring 1968. He was therefore a tired and discredited old
man when he was brought down by demonstrations by the Baltic
seacoast workers against the food price increases of 13 December 1970
(see Pelczynski, in Bromke and Strong, 1973; Rakowski 1981; Kubiak Report, *Nowe Drogi*, special edition 1983, pp. 39–48). The week
long riots which caused an officially admitted count of 44 deaths and
1164 serious injuries, were finally halted when the PZPR central
aktyw decided against the use of force. Gomułka was replaced by
Edward Gierek, the long-established First Secretary in Katowice
province (1957–70). Gierek gradually defused the situation during
1971 through economic concessions and his direct man-to-man approach. He promised reform and economic prosperity while criticising Gomułka's autocratic and 'faulty style' of leadership (Eighth
Plenum speech, *Nowe Drogi*, May 1971). Gierek had been widely
regarded as the PZPR Crown Prince from its Fourth Congress in
1964. He was now the obvious choice.

(5) A national workers' revolt overthrows Gierek

Gierek strengthened his leadership position at the PZPR Eight
Congress. He demoted his main potential rival, Stefan Olszowski,

from the Politburo and Secretariat and exiled him as ambassador to the GDR. Other autonomous figures such as the ex-*Partisan*, Jósef Kępa and the capable liberal Jósef Tejchma were also dropped. This effort to produce strong, united leadership, however, proved irrelevant to the wave of workers' strikes which built up after the covert raising of meat prices on 1 July 1980. They culminated in the occupation strike in the Lenin shipyard in Gdańsk and the dramatic confrontations between the regime and the workers which produced the social agreements of Gdańsk, Szczecin and Jastrzębie (Kemp-Welch, 1983).

Gierek's fall took place in two stages. His failure to resolve the strike situation by bread and butter concessions on an individual factory basis and the ruling out of the use of force because of the size and intensity of the revolutionary outburst caused him to lose his closest Politburo and Secretariat supporters (Babiuch, Łukasiewicz, Szydlak, Wrzaszczyk, Pyka and Zandarowski) at the Fourth Plenum of 24 August while Babiuch was replaced as Premier by Pinkowski. (RPiG, 1980, p. 112) Gierek himself was not replaced by Stanisław Kania until the Sixth Plenum of 5 September. Kania, a rural youth and agricultural functionary, originally hailing from backward southeast Poland, had been in both the Politburo and Secretariat since 1971, with special responsibility for security. He gave the reports to the Fourth and Fifth Plena and became the spokesman of the pragmatic centrists at this time. The Soviet leaders, through Ambassador Aristov, were undoubtedly instrumental in advising his appointment. He was a tried and tested, ideologically reliable and totally unimaginative, although tactically flexible, generalist Party functionary who could be relied upon not to succumb to reformist ideas and pressures. His main rival, ex-Foreign Minister and CC Secretary, Olszowski, did not return to the PZPR seats of power in the Politburo and Secretariat until the Fourth Plenum. His promises of an efficiently executed reform programme, to be implemented from above, did not convince his colleagues, while the Kremlin remembered his political flirting with the *Partisans* in the late 1960s.

(6) Time for the general

By Autumn 1981 Kania had succeeded in renewing the PZPR leadership personnel at every level and in democratising it internally within the controlled Leninist limits, which culminated in the PZPR's Extraordinary Ninth Congress in July 1981 (Sanford, 1983). This rallying and renewal of the main inner-ring of Party membership was not accompanied by much success in either pacifying society or in remedying the economic diaster through the programme of Socialist Renewal (Myant, 1982). The PZPR leaders and their Soviet patrons had never really accepted NSZZs and the unlimited right to strike. They probably never reconciled themselves to the permanent existence of Solidarity as a massive national force, partly trade union and partly political and social movement. Kania's great achievement, in Soviet terms, had been to out-manœuvre the genuine reformist elements within the PZPR who were willing to make the post-1980 system work. He prevented even loyal reform-communists like the provincial Party First Secretaries, Tadeusz Fiszbach from Gdańsk and Krystyn Dąbrowa from Kraków, from taking over real power within the PZPR Central Party Apparatus (CPA – defined as Politburo, Secretariat, CC Department Heads); he also successfully prevented reformists from infiltrating the main props of communist rule in Poland – the police, procuracy, mass-media, army and above all the CPA itself. The Ninth Congresss Politburo, although entirely new apart from Kania, Barcikowski, Jaruzelski and Olszowski, was however, determined to impose its own version of a Front of National Understanding on society and on Solidarity which had meanwhile, become programmatically and organisationally more determined at its September 1981 Congress. In order to do so it relied increasingly on the army whose commander, Jaruzelski, had become Premier in February 1981 while remaining Minister of Defence. The Ninth Congress strategy was now viewed as a political fiasco in terms of pacifying society or breaking Solidarity up. Preparations for martial law had accelerated during the Autumn (Sanford, 1984). Above all the PZPR outer-ring membership, 700 000 of whom at most joined Solidarity and which had organised a Horizontal Movement to counteract the CPA's vertical lines of control, was still highly volatile and leaving the Party in droves. Jaruzelski was therefore elected First Secretary, by 180 votes against 4, at the Fourth Plenum in October 1981, in order to save the communist system (*Nowe Drogi*, November 1981).

The mechanisms within the PZPR for producing First Secretaries have therefore functioned in somewhat unorthodox ways at times. Soviet influence took varying forms, the magic circle of candidates was often wider than in other communist states and the final choice sometimes lay formally with the whole CC, but on occasion with the more restricted CPA (cf. Farrell, 1970; Beck, 1973; Skilling, 1966). Only Ochab and Kania, the least successful First Secretaries, fitted the current truism drawn from recent Soviet experience, that a leadership candidate has to be in the Politburo and Secretariat prior to accession. Kania, however, was re-elected by a two-to-one majority in a straight fight against Barcikowski at the Ninth Congress, which also elected the Politburo Secretariat and CC in a free vote. Bierut and Jaruzelski had state posts. Gierek was a provincial chieftain although he had previously been a CC Secretary as well (1956–64). Gomułka was not even in the Politburo in October 1956, although he had admittedly been the PPR Secretary General (1943–8). On the other hand the CC faced real political alternatives and voted far from unanimously in October 1956. Special crisis conditions placed effective choice within the PZPR central *aktyw* (defined as CPA plus some provincial party bosses) in both December 1970 and September 1980 while the CC was little more than a rubber-stamp in September 1947 and, in a different way, in October 1981 (on Soviet intervention in East European successions see Korbonski, 1976, pp. 10–12).

PATTERNS OF TOP OFFICE-HOLDING

Let us now examine the influence of changes in the top Party post on the chairmanships of the Council of Ministers (colloquially Premier) and of the Council of State (on central Polish institutions see Sanford, 1981). Significantly the first three Party successions in the first half of People's Poland history did not affect the other two posts. The ex-PPS leader, Józef Cyrankiewicz, showed outstanding political skill and adaptability and considerable administrative and oratorical talent in protecting his position as Premier from February 1947 to December 1970, with a short break from November 1952 to March 1954 when Bierut combined the top Party and state jobs. Even then Cyrankiewicz remained as a deputy Premier. One should also note that, as a purely symbolic sop to the ex-PPS element within the PZPR, Cyrankiewicz was also a member of the CC Secretariat from 1948–54. However, when Bierut relinquished the Premier's post to Cyrankiewicz he formally limited his power by surrounding him with two autonomous First Deputy Chairmen of the Council of Ministers, Hilary Minc and Zenon Nowak, from March 1954 to October 1956. This was the only occasion when this Soviet practice was applied in Poland. The Premier has normally dominated the state apparatus (cf. Wojciech Sokolewicz, 'Rząd w Remoncie' in *Prawo i Zycie*, 26 July

1981). The post of the Chairman of the collegial Council of State was less prestigious than the Presidency of the Republic filled by Bierut from 1947 to 1952. His successor as the new type of Head of State until his death in 1964 was the Old Bolshevik, Aleksander Zawadzki. His political prestige and good standing with the Kremlin ensured that there was no question of Gomułka replacing him. Ochab was rewarded with his post but he was replaced in disgrace in April 1968 by Gomułka's close supporter, Marshal Marian Spychalski (Defence Minister, 1956–68). Gomułka's fall in December 1970 entailed Cyrankiewicz being 'kicked upstairs' to the Council of State post until his honourable retirement in March 1972. His successor, the much respected Warsaw University historian and ex-Education Minister, Henryk Jabłoński, was still in office in summer 1984. On the other hand, although Gierek maintained Piotr Jaroszewicz as Premier throughout the 1970s, he made him the regime scapegoat for the economic crisis in February 1980. Gierek's main lieutenant, Edward Babiuch, only lasted as Premier till August 1980, when he was replaced by Józef Pińkowski, a colourless CC Economic Secretary. Pińkowski's indecision and inability to tackle the problems of the post-August period in turn led to his unprecedented replacement by the military chief, Jaruzelski, in February 1981.

The Polish pattern of incumbency has therefore been for these top posts normally to be kept separate. Only Bierut ever combined these offices before Jaruzelski. Bierut was President of the Republic 1947–52, Party chief, 1948–56 and Premier 1952–4. Gomułka had, since the war, been a deputy Premier and Minister for the Recovered Territories as well as PPR Secretary General but he never held a ministerial post after 1956. On the other hand Gierek's strenuous efforts to institute and to occupy a powerful Presidency were successfully resisted in the mid-1970s. Like Gomułka (1957–71) he had to be content with ordinary membership of the Council of State (1976–80). The political crisis of 1980–1, however, led to the centralisation of Party and state power in Jaruzelski's hands. Although he ceded the defence ministry to General Florian Siwicki (previously Chief of Staff) in October 1983, he retained his full powers as Commander-in-Chief through his chairmanship of the up-graded Committee for the Defence of the Country (KOK).

The narrow and centralised basis of the postwar Polish communist leadership can be illustrated as follows. Only fourteen different individuals have ever held any of the three top posts since 1944, but of the twenty-two incumbencies in these posts no less than thirteen

TABLE 3.2 *Heads of State*

Name	Year of Birth	Term of Office	Politburo Membership	Other functions
Chairman: Krajowa Rada Narodowa (KRN – National Council for the Homeland)				
Bierut, Bolesław	1892	Nov. 1944– Feb. 1947	PPR 1944–8	Secretary General PPR Aug.–Dec. 1948 Chairman CC PZPR 1948–Mar. 1954 1st Secretary PZPR 1954 – Mar. 1956
President of Republic				
Bierut, Bolesław	1892	Feb. 1947– Nov. 1952	1948–56	
Chairman of Council of State				
Zawadzki, Aleksander	1899	Nov. 1952– Aug. 1964	1948–64 (PPR 1944–8)	PPR CC Secretary 1944–8 Deputy Chairman Council of Ministers 1950–2
Ochab, Edward	1906	Aug. 1964– Apr. 1968	1954–68	First Secretary PZPR 1956
Spychalski, Marian	1906	Apr. 1968– Dec. 1970	1959–70	Minister of Defence, 1956–68
Cyrankiewicz, Józef	1911	Dec. 1970– Mar. 1972	1948–71	Chairman of Council of Ministers, 1947–52, 1954–70
Jabłoński, Henryk	1909	Mar. 1972–	Dec. 1970– Jul. 1981 (1970–1)	Minister of Education, 1965–72

M = Member

TABLE 3.3   Chairmen of the Council of Ministers

Name	Year of Birth	Politburo Membership	Term as Premier	Other functions
Osóbka-Morawski, Edward	1909	PPS	Jul.1944–Feb. 1947	Minister of Public Administration 1947–8
Cyrankiewicz, Józef	1911	1948–71	Feb.1947–Nov. 1952	CC Secretary 1948–54
Bierut, Bolesław	1892	1948–56	Nov. 1952–Mar. 1954	PZPR First Secretary 1948–56 President 1947–52
Cyrankiewicz, Józef	1911	1948–71	Mar. 1954–Dec. 1970	Chairman Council of State 1970–2
Jaroszewicz, Piotr	1909	1970–Feb 1980 (1964–70)	Dec. 1970–Feb. 1980	Deputy Chairman Council of Ministers 1952–70
Babiuch, Edward	1927	1970–80	Feb–Aug. 1980	CC Secretary 1970–80 M. Council of State 1972–80
Pińkowski, Józef	1929	Aug. 1980–Apr. 1981– (Feb.–Aug. 1980)	Aug. 1980–Feb. 1981	CC Secretary 1974–80
Jaruzelski, Wojciech	1923	Dec. 1970– (1970–1)	Feb. 1981–	PZPR First Secretary Oct. 1981– Minister of Defence 1968–83

M = Member

have been monopolised by five individuals (Bierut, Gomułka, Cyrankiewicz, Ochab and Jaruzelski) while the remaining nine individuals have only ever held a single office for a single period. But paradoxically, one of the most striking features of the composition of the top level communist leadership, in spite of Poland's turbulent postwar development, has been long periods of leadership stability and strikingly long incumbencies in major offices just below the very top ones. Since 1948 there have admittedly been five different Heads of State, six different Chairmen of the Council of Ministers and six different PZPR First Secretaries, three of them since 1980. These figures testify to a greater degree of political instability than in any of the other East European states, notably in 1955–7, 1968–71 and 1980–2. But individuals like Gierek and Cyrankiewicz had more than twenty years in the PZPR Politburo, and at present (1984) Jaruzelski and Olszowski (with a short break) have been there since 1970 and Barcikowski since 1971. Various individuals had terms of over ten years in the CC Secretariat, notably Gierek 18 years, Gomułka 14 years, Zambrowski 14 years, Kliszko 13 years and Ochab, Kania, Babiuch, Łukasiewicz and Strzelecki between 9 and 11 years. The Council of Ministers was until 1980 characterised by long incumbencies, testifying to a pattern of stability and specialisation in the largely administrative preparation and execution of CPA policies (cf. Jerzy Stembrowicz in *Państwo i Prawo*, Aug.–Sept. 1970). Noteworthy individuals with Soviet-length periods of office proliferate and are headed by the following: Cyrankiewicz (1946–70), Jaroszewicz (1950–80, deputy premier 1952–70 and premier 1970–80), Mieczysław Jagielski (1959–81), Jaruzelski (1968–83 as Minister of Defence, 1981 to present as premier) and Stefan Jędrychowski, who, apart from a break in 1947–9, held ministerial office continually from the first cabinet of 1944 until his honourable retirement in 1974 (Mołdawa, 1971).

BUILDING UP LEADERSHIP POWER WITHIN THE PZPR

We now move on to see how PZPR leaders, once elected, built up their power within the party on a secure basis. Both Ochab and Kania failed to do so partly because of their undominating personalities but mainly because of the scale of the social explosions of 1956 and 1980–1 and their divisive effects on the PZPR. On the surface Bierut appears to be the closest Polish equivalent to the more widespread

Soviet bloc type of Stalinist party-dictator. But although he symbolised the 1948–56 system he formed a leadership *troika* with Minc, the economic planner and Berman, the ideology chief. Other personalities also played important roles, for example, Zambrowski in the Secretariat, Radkiewicz in the police and Rokossowski in the military sector. Bierut, a rather mousy and colourless functionary, never developed a personally dominant leadership, unlike Rákosi in Hungary. Bierut was a figurehead executing Stalin's direct orders, and his control of the CPA and of the main offices depended entirely on Stalin's *fiat*. Bierut forced through the preliminary stages of building a totalitarian society but, lacking sufficient personally committed CPA supporters (Dworakowski, Chełchowski, Matuszewski), he was increasingly abandoned by the younger, less committed Stalinists during the New Course. Only Bierut's timely death saved him from being swept away by social unrest and party factionalism in 1956.

Gomułka and Gierek, although very different in their personalities, policies and leadership styles, do however, share some common features in how they came to power, how they built up their authority and how they lost office. This is the protest–consolidation–upheaval cycle which many observers have discerned in post-1956 Polish politics (Bieńkowski 1969). Both were brought to power and displaced by social upheavals. On both occasions the dominant section of the PZPR central *aktyw* viewed them as 'providential' figures who would defuse social unrest and rally the party. But Gomułka needed from October 1956 till the Third Congress in March 1959 before he established his leadership team on a stable majority basis through the co-option of his main lieutenant, Zenon Kliszko, and other supporters such as Gierek, Stefan Jędrychowski and Adam Rapacki. Gomułka took a centrist Leninist position between revisionism and dogmatism as he defined them but he increasingly tilted against the former. Too-reformist figures such as Jerzy Morawski and Władysław Matwin were therefore replaced by middle-of-the-road CC Secretaries like Ryszard Strzelecki and Artur Starewicz and even some second-rank Stalinists. They helped Gomułka to ride out the storms of the *Partisan* offensive. Gomułka, however, proved exceptionally bad at managing the top PZPR echelons in the late 1960s. The 1968 crisis initiated a very considerable process of Party-state instability and personnel turnover, which was not rounded off by Gierek until early 1972. Gomułka was primarily concerned to suppress any Dubček-like movement at birth in Poland, through the cowing of students and the intelligentsia and the carrying through of an apparently anti-Zionist purge of the Party. Although his position was shored up by Brezhnev at the Fifth Congress in October 1968, Gomułka's economic priorities and mistakes linked with his old-mannish and autocratic leadership style led to the mishandling of food price-increases in December 1970. The Baltic outburst was sufficient inducement for the PZPR to change its leader and its policies.

Gierek gained control of the PZPR much more quickly and efficiently than Gomułka. The Seventh and Eighth Plena of December 1970 and February 1971 cleared out Gomułka's inner-circle (Jaszczuk, Kliszko, Strzelecki, Spychalski and Loga-Sowiński). They were replaced either by Gierek's lieutenants (Babiuch, Barcikowski, Szydlak gave him an immediate Secretariat majority) or with Politburo notables who had ensured his election (Jabłoński, Jagielski, Jaroszewicz and Jaruzelski). Gierek dismissed Moczar from the Secretariat in June 1971 and relegated him to the reserve post of chairman of the Supreme Control Chamber (NIK) for the entire 1970s. The Sixth Congress in December 1971 appointed a loyal Politburo, Secretariat and CC and showed how rapidly Gierek had gained control of all the Party–state power levers. (See Bromke in *Problems of Communism*, Sept.–Oct. 1972, pp. 3–6). After that Gierek's functionaries such as Łukasiewicz, Żabiński, Pyka or Żandarowski ascended the bureaucratic ladder step-by-step during the 1970s, while Gierek himself merely shrugged off Szlachcic's challenge in 1974. Unlike Gomułka, Gierek's *forte* lay in managing the party. At the end of his regime he consolidated his leadership team very skilfully at the Eighth Congress in February 1980, thus ensuring that no challenge could emerge from within the Party ('Nowe Władze Partii', *Polityka*, 23 February 1980). It therefore took an external development, nothing less than the Workers' upsurge, to shift him and his leadership team. But even then their posts were merely filled by equally reliable second-rankers, colloquially dubbed Gierek's pall-bearers, who moved up (Pińkowski, Waszczuk, Wojtaszek). This proved the dominant factor in the PZPR's response to the social crisis as the CPA stood firm under Kania. It delayed the Ninth Congress and the implementation of reforms until the economic crisis had worn down Polish society and time had revealed Solidarity's weaknesses and divisions (see chapters by Blazyca, Kolankiewicz and Sanford, in Woodall, 1982).

THE ELUSIVE SEARCH FOR LEGITIMACY

Since assuming power in Poland the communists have sought to establish an accepted and legitimate basis for their authority by presenting the following programmes. First, they have offered the Poles the Marxist–Leninist conception of building socialism and a just egalitarian society without exploitation in various stages. This ideal only carried conviction until de-Stalinisation. After that the bulk of the population accepted general socialist ideals but became over-critical, particularly in 1980–1, of the clash between theory and reality, especially of social inequality and élite privilege. Polish Marxism–Leninism lost most of its operational value as a mobilising ideology.

The ideological appeal was largely replaced by the second theme of the modernisation of a backward country. By 1980 the leadership élite claimed that industrialisation and urbanisation was the PZPR's main historical achievement in building the basis for 'Developed Socialism' (cf. Woodall, in Woodall, 1982). Critics naturally pointed to its costly, unbalanced and incomplete character and the structural political-economic consequences which have ensued. The Marxist –Leninist and modernising socialist appeals were naturally the main themes of Bierut's regime.

Thirdly, the PZPR under Gomułka became more domestic–national in its vocabulary, symbols and traditional forms. The PZPR attempted to utilise its newly gained domestic autonomy to identify the party completely with the now extremely homogeneous ethnic Polish core. In addition, Gomułka accentuated the *motif* applied by all PZPR leaders that the country's postwar frontiers and international situation, guaranteed by the Soviet alliance and communist neighbours, was the most secure and stable one that the Poles could hope for in their particularly difficult geographical position.

Fourthly, the PZPR's ideological weakness, partial success in socio-economic modernisation and nationalist inclinations under Gomułka only left Gierek with the Khrushchevite option of promising consumer prosperity and some Hungarian-type reforms, although he quickly reneged on the latter. But he went further. He suggested that the 'Second Poland' would be a far more meritocratic society and that the university educated service stratum would have easier access into the PZPR *nomenklatura*. This attempt at inclusionary politics reflected a genuine shift away from a mobilising to a more integrationist form of political rule, but it was insufficiently applied to smooth out all the varied stresses of the 1970s (Bielasek, in Simon and Kanet, 1981). The post-1976 economic collapse, however, ensured that the system was overloaded with too many demands.

The emergence of a more mature, demanding and discontented working class, whose summer 1980 revolt also sparked off contestation by a wider range of social groups, forced the PZPR into its fifth programme. This was Kania's controlled strategy of genuine Leninist democratic centralism within the party and national renewal led by a revitalised Party membership.

The sixth programme of a pluralist, political system with autonomous political and social groups, a socialist market economy and a shrinkage of the PZPR's leading role to 51 per cent, first partially mooted in 1956, and presented with renewed vigour during Solidarity's heyday, affected the PZPR grassroots membership but was rejected by the inner-ring membership and the Party élites, whose sticking-point was the fifth programme. Even that was to be imposed from the top after the opposition had been broken by repression in 1982, thus ruling out western social contract type conceptions. The Polish experience therefore demonstrates, yet again, the Soviet–Leninist priority of maintaining the Communist Party hegemony intact. On the other hand, Polish policy-making and governmental practices have been much neglected in the West in favour of sociological and economic analysis (cf. Sanford, 1981).

LEADERSHIP CHANGE AS A SURROGATE FOR REFORM

The PZPR, since 1956, has always tended to hope that new leaders and new polices would obviate the need for basic structural changes. Consequently there has been open and bitter conflict between individuals within the leadership as to who should bear the political consequences and who should advance. But one should note that the 'revolutionary generation' was not wholly removed in 1956, only the most discredited pro-Soviet Stalinists. The personnel turnover of 1968–71 was considerable and unparalleled (see Pirages, in Farrell, 1970, pp. 259–62) but it was only a pale precursor of the hurricane which hit the communist functionary class in 1980–2. Kania, Moczar and Grabski attempted to divert social discontent away from demands for structural reforms by jettisoning Gierek's leadership cohort and by blaming its mistakes and corruption for the crisis in what was termed a 'settlement of accounts'. (On the anti-corruption drive, see *Nowe Drogi*, August 1981, pp. 102–11.) But Kania succeeded in controlling the pre-Ninth Congress democratisation drive so well that the Party renewal failed to produce any qualitative changes. Power was decentralised down to an equally reliable layer of second rank PZPR militants who found themselves promoted. But the quantitative scale of leadership change was dramatic (chronicled in *Polityka*, 20 Feb. 1982, 30 Oct. 1982, 1 Jan. 1983). At the Ninth Congress only four pre-July incumbents out of sixteen were retained on the Politburo, three out of nine in the CC Secretariat and twenty-three out of 220 CC members. Forty-six out of forty-nine provincial First Secretaries had gone, while between 38 per cent and more than 50 per cent of the provincial, municipal, factory and basic cell committees and their executives were new (Sanford, 1983, ch. 6).

Earlier studies, such as Carl Beck's, showed the tendency towards a more university-educated, more professional leadership in Poland, with an increasingly unified set of central party–state career–experience patterns; these toned down the revolutionary and ideological qualities of the earlier KPP/PPR/Soviet wartime leadership cohort which was shaken in 1956 and largely pensioned off in 1968–71 (Beck, in Beck, 1973, pp. 103–13, 124–44). Although the Polish political landscape and the leadership class has been transformed to an unprecedented degree by the shocks of the early 1980s, the university educated and political élites in Poland seem to be increasingly fused together. There has been a striking emphasis on higher educational qualifications and a remarkable number of academics have been co-opted by the more flexible political processes and the military regime into directing political positions since 1980 (for example, Messner, Porębski, Kubiak, Orzechowski). Even less than in the past do ideological reliability and personal loyalty to the *apparat*, as typified by Kania himself, prove sufficient qualities for political success. Various other skills such as personal character, intellect and professional ability also seem to be at an additional premium in Poland, particularly when crisis conditions produce a freer, competitive element (Wiatr and Ostrowski 1967, pp. 147ff.; Farrell 1970, pp. 88–107). In terms of personal qualities and skills, Gomułka, Gierek and Jaruzelski and their supporting teams compare well with other communist leaders so it is not the least of Polish paradoxes that social discontent should have produced such strong critiques of Polish leadership.

THE JARUZELSKI REGIME: PENETRATION OR SUBSTITUTION?

Although the Polish military, headed by Jaruzelski, took over real power from the PZPR Politburo and shifted it to the Military Council of National Salvation (WRON) during the State of War the actual extent of the military penetration of the Party–state was more significant in qualitative than in purely quantitive terms. According to General Dziekan, Head of the CC Cadres Department, only 103 officers had been granted formal leave of absence to assume top-level directing positions, notably six in the Council of Ministers, two as PZPR provincial First Secretaries, ten as provincial governors, fourteen as large enterprise directors, while twenty-two had become CC functionaries like Dziekan himself (*Polityka*, 19 Nov. 1983). The picture presented here is of only a slight shift from civil to military functionaries; but it underestimates, intentionally, the factor of reserve officers and above all the crucial role played by Jaruzelski himself and of Generals in the top state institutions such as Czesław Kiszczak, the Minister of the Interior, Piotrowski at Mining, Hupałowski (now NIK) and then Oliwa at Public Administration and the very important functions of Janiszewski as deputy Minister in charge of the Bureau of the Council of Ministers (URM). Having said that, one should note that the military have only one full member of the Politburo (Jaruzelski) plus two candidates (Kiszczak, Siwicki) while they have never had a representative in the Communist 'holy of holies', the CC Secretariat, apart from Jaruzelski.

Although Military Commissioners oversaw directly, the state and local administrations as well as the 190-odd largest enterprises during the State of War they were then withdrawn. WRON was the formal seat of key decisions in 1982 but the evidence suggests that Jaruzelski now governs largely through the traditional institutions of communist rule. There has been the occasional reversion to Operational Army Groups, first used in Autumn 1981, for various tasks, but this has been a subsidiary factor. The impression of a novel system is heightened intentionally by the appearance of fresh institutions such as the new trade unions, built from the bottom upwards, after Solidarity's dissolution in Autumn 1982, but this is a mistaken view. The Patriotic Movement for National Rebirth (PRON) is not all that different from the previous FJN, while even Jaruzelski's greater use of the Sejm (National Assembly) for announcing and legitimising decisions is largely a tactical shift. Jaruzelski now rules in traditional Soviet–Leninist

ways through the Party apparatus. He has been supported very ably
by the previously mentioned Generals, plus others such as Jósef
Baryła, the Head of the Main Political Department (GZP); but the
CPA and the Council of Ministers are run mainly by the new civil
functionaries promoted by Jaruzelski. Key roles have been played in
the large, but fluid, Secretariat by Józef Czyrek, Tadeusz Porębski,
Zbigniew Messner, Marian Woźniak, Marian Orzechowski and
Włodzimierz Mokrzyszczak. Some have also brought order to the
key provincial parties (Messner in Katowice, Porębski in Wrocław,
Woźniak in Warsaw city and Bejger in Gdańsk) while others have
animated the state ministries (Messner as deputy Premier in charge
of the economy, Manfred Gorywoda as Chairman of the Planning
Commission). Orzechowski (PRON Secretary General) has emerged
as the regime's ideological spokesman, while Messner and Porębski
in 1984 appeared to be overlords of the economic and general
political sectors. The Ninth Congress figures most associated with the
1980–1 period, such as the Kraków University sociology professor,
Hieronym Kubiak and Jan Łabęcki, the Gdańsk shipyard Party
spokesman lost influence while Olszowski was moved away from the
CC Secretariat to the Ministry of Foreign Affairs.

TABLE 3.4   *PZPR Politburo*

Name	Year of Birth	Politburo Term	Other functions
Barcikowski, Kazimierz	1927	Candidate 1971–80 Full Sept. 1980–	CC Secretary Oct. 1980–
Czechowicz, Tadeusz	1935	Jul. 1981–	First Secretary Łódź Province
Czyrek, Józef	1928	Jul. 1981–	CC Secretary Jul. 1981– Minister of Foreign Affairs 1980–2
Grzyb, Zofia (f)	1928	Jul. 1981–	Radom Leather Worker
Jaruzelski, Wojciech	1923	Candidate 1970–1 Full 1971–	Chairman Council of Ministers Feb. 1981–

Kałlkus, Stanisław	1933	Jul. 1982–	Poznań Worker/Local Activist
Kubiak, Hieronim	1934	Jul. 1981–	CC Secretary 1981–2
Messner, Zbigniew	1929	Jul. 1981–	Deputy Premier Nov. 1983
Milewski, Mirosław	1928	Jul. 1981–	Minister of the Interior 1980–1
Olszowski, Stefan	1931	1970–Feb. 1980 Aug. 1980–	CC Secretary 1968–71, 1976–Feb. 1980, Aug. 1980–Jul. 1982 Minister of Foreign Affairs, 1982–
Opałko, Stanisław	1911	Jul. 1981–	First Secretary Tarnów Province
Porębski, Tadeusz	1931	Jul. 1981–	First Secretary Wrocław Province 1980–3
Romanik, Jerzy	1931	Jul. 1981–	Silesian Coal miner
Siwak, Albin	1933	Jul. 1981–	Warsaw Building Worker-Activist
Woźniak, Marian	1936	Candidate Feb–Jul. 1982 Full Jul. 1982–	First Secretary Warsaw City, Jun. 1981– CC Secretary 1981–2
Candidates			
Bejger, Stanisław	1929	Jul. 1982–	First Secretary Gdańsk Province Jan. 1982–
Glowczyk, Jan	1927	Jul. 1981–	CC Secretary Jul. 1982–
Kiszczak, Czesław	1925	Feb. 1982–	Minister of the Interior 1981–
Mokrzyszczak, Włodzimierz	1938	Jul. 1981–	First Secretary, Olsztyn Province 1981–
Orzechowski, Marian	1931	Nov. 1983–	CC Secretary 1981–3 PRON Secretary General Dec. 1982–
Siwicki, Florian	1925	Oct. 1981–	Chief of Gen Staff 1973–83 Minister of Defence Nov 1983–

(f)   female

TABLE 3.5   *PZPR CC Secretariat*

Name	Born	Secretariat Term
Barcikowski, Kazimierz	1927	Oct. 1980 –
Bednarski, Henryk	1934	Nov. 1983 –
Czyrek, Józef	1928	Jul. 1981 –
Główczyk, Jan	1927	Jul. 1982 –
Jaruzelski, Wojciech	1923	Oct. 1981 –
Michałek, Zbigniew	1935	Jul. 1981 –
Milewski, Mirosław	1928	Jul. 1981 –
Mokrzyszczak, Włodzimierz	1938	Oct.1981 –
Porębski, Tadeusz	1931	Nov. 1983 –
Świrgon, Waldemar	1953	Oct. 1982 –

FUTURE PROSPECTS?

The continuing tension between Polish society and the communist state makes it particularly hazardous to attempt to forecast future prospects. However, there are indicators such as the regime's relative success in achieving a 75 per cent turnout in the June 1984 local government elections (*Trybuna Ludu*, 20 June 1984) that Jaruzelski has gone a long way towards rebuilding the bases of communist power. Jaruzelski may have to await the death of Marshal Rola-Żymierski (born 1890) before the Kremlin will agree to his Marshal's baton, but a possible short-term scenario is that he would institute and occupy a powerful Romanian type of Presidency, while ceding the premiership to a loyal civil adviser such as Czyrek or Messner.

Jaruzelski is unlikely to resign voluntarily as PZPR First Secretary. Two contrary scenarios can be envisaged. Either Jaruzelski achieves a degree of economic recovery by the mid-1980s, which enables him to recruit another million PZPR members to replace those lost since 1980. If political and economic stabilisation results one could then accept the validity of comparing contemporary Poland with Hungary 1956–61, as is often done in Poland, and foresee the emergence of Kádár-type reforms and compromises. These might then provide the basis for a long period of rule by Jaruzelski (born 1923). Or, on the other hand, another social outburst, or even Soviet pressure at the end of the consolidation phase, might lead to Jaruzelski's downfall, the reassertion of the civil communist apparatus and the blaming of the rigours of the 1980s upon the army. It would then be well-nigh impossible to foresee where the new leader would emerge from, but it is unlikely not to be one of the Politburo and Secretariat members listed in Tables 3.4 and 3.5. In the direst extremities a 'lost leader' such as Kania might be wheeled out as a providential saviour of the system or more incredibly an ambitious, younger figure like Żabiński or the ambassador to the USSR, Kociołek. In 1984 it appeared likely that Jaruzelski's departure was only a theoretical possibility. In such an event the PZPR central *aktyw* would probably reject a militay successor such as Kiszczak or Siwicki. It would not spend too long on old faces such as Olszowski and Barcikowski before choosing one of Czyrek, Messner, Porębski or Woźniak in descending order of probability.

In Poland, as in the USSR, one can discern a pattern of co-option and growing influence in the military's relations with the party (Korbonski, in Adelman, 1982). Growing Soviet Party dependence on its repressive forces aided Andropov's rise to power but in the incomparably greater Polish communist crisis the civil apparatus relinquished its key positions voluntarily to military individuals. In that sense there was no civil-military conflict in 1981–3. A real symbiosis took place, despite the public grumbles of displaced functionaries, such as Grabski and the private thoughts of the likes of Olszowski. This symbiosis makes it possible for Jaruzelski, subject to unforseeable circumstances, to abandon his military uniform, whenever necessary, and to turn into a fully fledged, and therefore long-term, civil Party leader.

4   The German Democratic Republic

MARTIN McCAULEY

INTRODUCTION

There have only been two Party leaders in the GDR since 1945, Walter Ulbricht and Erich Honecker (Martin McCauley, 1979 and 1983a; Childs, 1983). Hence there has only been one succession and it was anything but smooth. Ulbricht had caused Brezhnev and the Soviet leadership offence over his stand on the Berlin question. Moscow was keen to secure a Berlin Agreement without which the process of *détente* in Europe could not develop. Berlin was a necessary stage on the road which eventually led to the Helsinki Final Act in 1975. The decision to unseat Ulbricht may have been taken at the Twenty-Fourth Congress of the Communist Party of the Soviet Union (CPSU) in Moscow in March–April 1971. Brezhnev had no doubts about the identity of the new man. *Kronprinz* Erich Honecker had assumed that role for several years. Moscow made its intentions clear in a telegram congratulating the Socialist Unity Party (SED) on the twenty-fifth anniversary of its founding. Instead of Brezhnev, Secretary General of the CPSU, sending fraternal greetings to Ulbricht, First Secretary of the SED, the telegram was unsigned and was from the CC, CPSU to the CC, SED. It spoke highly of the roles played by Wilhelm Pieck and Otto Grotewohl in building up the SED. The main architect of the SED's rise to power, Walter Ulbricht, was not even mentioned. Clearly Ulbricht had to go. In his resignation speech on 3 May 1971 he conceded that the decision to step down had been a difficult one, Ulbricht evidently believed that he would be allowed to resign with honour and agreed to address the Eighth Congress of the SED on 15 June 1971. He looked forward to being thanked for his lifelong devotion to the communist cause.

Instead, the evening before an emissary from the CC presented him with the text of his speech and also that of Honecker's. Ulbricht took such umbrage at both that he refused to appear, and in the event his speech was read for him. The SED also leaked an abrasive account of his resignation to the *New York Times* (22 June 1971), one which was highly uncomplimentary to the former First Secretary. A major reason for the ungracious exit of Ulbricht was that the SED had decided to change more than its leader – it was also going to change its policies. The Congress was the ideal platform from which to present the new line and this involved destroying the former First Secretary's reputation and standing.

When Ulbricht resigned the SED invented a new honorary post for him, 'in honour of his services'. He became chairman of the Party and remained in the Politburo. However he also held two key state positions: he was chairman of the GDR National Council of Defence and chairman of the GDR State Council (President). He was quickly eased out of the Defence Council and replaced by Erich Honecker. He was permitted to retain high position as head of state, but by the time he died on 1 August 1973 the job involved little more than ceremonial duties. After he died the SED did not know what to do with his ashes. Finally after 48 days they were given a modest burial with no foreign mourners reported present.

Ulbricht's downfall underlined one of the key variables in the east German leadership stakes: the Soviet connection. Hitherto Ulbricht's almost legendary flexibility *vis-à-vis* Moscow had served him well, but during the late 1960s he greatly overestimated his room for manœuvre towards the CPSU. He had clearly lost Brezhnev's confidence by 1971. However, tension between the leader and Moscow would not necessarily be enough to bring him down. Other factors play a part, such as the confidence of the Party apparatus and society in his leadership. Economic success is an important source of legitimacy but here the GDR was in difficulties after promising so much in the mid-1960s. The Party apparatus, especially the ideologists, were unhappy with the course the country was taking. Since there had never been a succession in the SED (this assumes that Ulbricht was always more important than Pieck in the KPD–SED) there was bound to be uncertainty about how it should be managed. Hence a factor which carried some weight was the need to have an heir apparent waiting in the wings. Ulbricht had allowed Honecker to be cast in this role and this contributed to Ulbricht's own undoing. Which factor was accorded greatest weight is impossible to say but

Ulbricht's failure to satisfy several key constituencies by 1971 proved fatal.

ULBRICHT'S RISE TO POWER

Although Ulbricht can be identified as the main political actor as early as 1945 his power was limited both by the role of the Soviet Military Administration in Germany (SMAD) – the centre of power in the Soviet Zone of Occupation between 1945 and 1949 – and its successor and by the ambivalent position of the Soviet Union on the question of a unified Germany. Since a Soviet command economy model ill-suited the GDR he was also under pressure from others in the apparatus who favoured greater use of the market mechanism.

The most serious threat to Ulbricht's political career occurred in June 1953 when workers spearheaded demonstrations in East Berlin and many other cities in the GDR. The main grievances were economic, with the labour force unwilling to make the sacrifices demanded of it by the plan to build socialism in the GDR, launched the previous year.

All communist leaders have to satisfy at least three constituencies: the Soviets, the party apparatus and society. The June uprising underlined the fact that Ulbricht had failed to satisfy all three. Moscow, in the wake of Stalin's death, had counselled a softer economic line, and been ignored. The uprising, paradoxically, saved him. Had it not occurred his opponents in the Party apparatus would have replaced him with one of their members more in favour of a slow march to socialism. The fall of Beria in Moscow was also a contributory factor in saving Ulbricht.

The decision by Moscow to accept the division of Germany in 1955 strengthened Ulbricht's hand. One of the arguments employed by his Party opponents was that his economic policies were widening the gulf between the two parts of Germany, but by late 1958 Ulbricht had emerged the victor. In his early years he had patiently built up his authority but by 1958 he was able to go over to the offensive and use confrontational tactics. Only in late 1958 can one call him the undisputed national leader. This put him in a position to acquire more state offices. When Pieck died in September 1960 the presidency was abolished and the GDR Council of State was instituted. Ulbricht became its chairman, and thus in effect President. At the same time he ceased to be deputy Prime Minister. Also in 1960 the GDR

Council of National Defence was established and Ulbricht became chairman of that as well. Hence in 1960 he was head of the Party, the Council of National Defence and the Council of State – he was visibly the national leader. When Otto Grotewohl died in September 1964 the post of Prime Minister passed to Willi Stoph. This did not, in fact, mean a weakening of Ulbricht's power. On the contrary it was enhanced by the fact that the Council of State became the most significant state institution during the years 1963–70 and this was given substance in the 1968 Constitution. It then became formally more important than the government.

A leader may build up his authority in various ways: success in economic and foreign policy, being seen to be innovative in ideology and developing a cult of his own personality. A leader is very fortunate if he achieves all these goals.

Ulbricht's economic policies before 1961 were geared towards securing the victory of the socialist relations of production. This meant bringing all key industrial enterprises into the state sector and carrying out the collectivisation of agriculture. The building of the Berlin Wall in August 1961 was vital to this strategy since the leadership had reached the sombre conclusion that socialism could not be built while the Berlin frontier remained open. This had been driven home in the late 1950s when the attempt to catch up with the West German level of labour productivity and living standards failed. With the Berlin Wall in place Ulbricht could engage in a controlled economic experiment and the New Economic System was introduced in 1963, later to become the Economic System of Socialism. The green light for experimentation had been given in 1962 when Evsei Liberman, a Kharkov economist, had argued in the pages of *Pravada*, for more decision-making at the enterprise level, among other things. At the same time Ulbricht became very enthusiastic about the gains the scientific-technical revolution could bring to GDR industry and society. Given German technical expertise it seemed possible for the GDR at last to outstrip West Germany and to become a model advanced industrial society. Among the disciplines which were accorded high status were systems theory and cybernetics. They held out the prospect of a self-regulating economic system. The word 'system' became a new code word for 'progress'.

The 1960s saw considerable innovation in the field of ideology. Ulbricht, on the occasion of the 100th anniversary of the publication of Karl Marx's *Das Kapital*, in September 1967, presented his understanding of socialism. It should not be seen as a 'short, transition

phase in the development of society . . . but [as] a relatively independent socio-economic formation during the historical epoch of the
transition from capitalism to communism' (Ulbricht 1967, p. 38).
Shortly afterwards Günter Mittag, the leading economic brain behind
the economic reform, went one step further and claimed that socialism developed on its own base. The GDR was experiencing the
'formation of the developed social system of socialism'. The scientific
management of society appeared feasible in the not too distant
future.

The SED was very aware of the fact that socialism in the GDR had
been built on a solid industrial foundation, inherited from capitalism.
Hence the GDR was different from all other socialist states, with the
exception of part of Czechoslovakia. It prided itself that it was the
first country to demonstrate that socialism could be built in a highly
industrialised state. This proved, so it was claimed, that the argument
that socialism was a form of social organisation which was only
suitable for countries at a low level of industrial development was
untrue.

The concept of the socialist human community also evolved during
the 1960s. It smudged the boundaries of class. The concept of the
people's state, formulated by Khrushchev, was also understood diffe-
rently by Ulbricht and the SED leadership.

Ulbricht did attempt to foster a cult of his own personality. However his bald head, goatee beard, glasses and squeaky Saxon voice
militated against it. Ulbricht, in the event, gambled too heavily on
the scientific-technical revolution solving the economic and social ills
of the GDR. In late 1970 experimentation came to an end and more
orthodox central planning methods returned. Failure in the economic
field was compounded by the resentment of the professional ideologists who had been shoved aside during the late 1960s. Digging in his
heels to secure a better deal for the GDR during the negotiations
which led to the Berlin Agreement sealed Ulbricht's fate.

HONECKER ASSERTS HIS AUTHORITY

As the clear favourite to step into Ulbricht's shoes as Party leader,
Honecker had had time and opportunity to prepare himself for the
post. Nevertheless his experience of affairs was limited. He had been
the first leader of the Free German Youth (FDJ) movement, and the
finishing touches to his party education were applied during study in

the Soviet Union in 1956–7. A year later he became CC Secretary for Security. Thus when he took over in May 1971 he had never held a top government post or had any experience of economic or technical questions. However, he was a member of the two bodies from which new Party leaders normally emerge, the Politburo and the Secretariat.

His most formidable opponent was Willi Stoph, Prime Minister since 1964. Also a member of the Politburo, Stoph was an army General and had been Minister for National Defence between 1956 and 1960. As a former Minister of the Interior Stoph had amassed his own experience of security and military affairs, but through government.

The situation in the GDR paralleled that of the Soviet Union where Brezhnev headed the Party and Kosygin the government. In Berlin, just as in Moscow, the Party leader proved to be the more astute politician. An incoming Party leader always seeks to place his supporters in key positions. This is one way he can build up his authority. At the Eight Party Congress in June 1971 Honecker was able to advance Werner Lamberz and Werner Krolikowski to full membership of the Politburo. The latter's promotion was quite remarkable in that he had previously only been a member of the Central Committee. Harry Tisch, first secretary of Bezirk Rostock and Colonel-General Erich Mielke, Minister of State Security, became candidate members. More significantly five of the fifteen Bezirk First Secretaries were replaced after the Congress and four of the new appointees had had notable careers in the FDJ.

After becoming First Secretary in May 1971 Honecker replaced Ulbricht as chairman of the Council of National Defence the following month. In November 1971 he was made a member of the GDR Council of State. Hence he held two of the top four offices in the Party and state. However, further progress was blocked by Ulbricht, chairman of the Council of State – in effect President – and by Stoph, the Prime Minister.

The next move by Honecker was to enhance the role of the Party at the expense of the other two institutions. The Council of State was the first to come under attack. In 1971 it was the leading state institution. However three *démarches* greatly reduced its power. In 1972 a new law on the Council of Ministers was promulgated and new rules of procedure for the Volkskammer, the parliament, were also adopted. The finishing touch was applied by the amendments to the constitution of 7 March 1974.

Honecker's authority was great enough by October 1973 to enable him to remove Stoph as Prime Minister and make him chairman of the Council of State, a clear demotion. At the same time Günter Mittag, the architect of the economic reforms of the 1960s, lost his place as CC secretary for the economy and became first deputy chairman of the Council of Ministers, again a clear demotion. Horst Sindermann became Prime Minister and Werner Krolikowski took Mittag's position in the Secretariat.

Hence by October 1973 one can identify Honecker as the national leader. It had only taken him just over two years to advance from Party to national leader. The period of power-sharing with Stoph was clearly over. Unfortunately for Honecker at precisely this moment the explosion in the price of hydrocarbons occurred and this was to have momentous consequences for the GDR economy. The GDR's terms of trade gradually worsened – it had to export more to import the same amount of goods – and as time passed it became palpably clear that the Sindermann–Krolikowski team was sinking under the burden of these problems. In October 1976 Sindermann and Krolikowski were sacked and Stoph and Mittag returned to their old jobs. Administrative and technical expertise had triumphed over Party expertise. However, by an astute move Honecker had reduced Stoph's authority as Prime Minister shortly before he reverted to his old post. New Party statutes were adopted in 1976. In the former 1963 statutes it was laid down that Party organs in state institutions could not exercise controlling functions. This was in conformity with the ethos of the scientific-technical revolution when technical expertise was to be given its head. In the new Party statutes, Party organs in state institutions were to exercise controlling functions. Hence the balance between the Party and the government was neatly tilted in favour of the Party.

To underline his national position Honecker replaced Stoph as chairman of the Council of State. Thus in October 1976 he occupied three of the four key posts in Party and state. The Ninth Party Congress in May 1976 had confirmed his commanding position. Besides becoming Secretary General at the Congress (thus following in Brezhnev's footsteps) he was able to promote six men to either full or candidate Politburo status. Of the twenty-eight full and candidate members of the new Politburo nine had been FDJ functionaries. The first demotion under Honecker occurred at the Tenth Party Congress in June 1981 when Albert Norden, CC secretary for agitation and propaganda, was dropped. The only addition to the Politburo was Günter Schabowski, the chief editor of *Neues Deutschland* (*ND*), who became a candidate member at the Congress. Before the Congress he had not even been a member of the Central Committee but there is a tradition in the SED that the chief editor of the Party organ sits in the Politburo. The only other person to join the Politburo, first as a candidate and then as a full member, between 1976 and 1984 was Egon Krenz. He also became a CC secretary. This remarkable stability of Politburo membership may have meant that since Honecker's rapid promotion to national leader in the early 1970s his power had declined and that a collective leadership, with the Secretary General as *primus inter pares*, had taken over.

Then in May 1984 Werner Jarowinsky, Günther Kleiber and Günter Schabowski were promoted from candidate to full membership of the Politburo. Herbert Häber was also made a full member. Whereas Jarowinsky had remained a candidate member for 21 years, Häber became a full member without passing through this stage. Häber and Konrad Naumann became CC secretaries at the same time. The promotion of Jarowinsky and Kleiber raises the level of economic expertise among the full Politburo members. Häber is the leading SED specialist on East–West German relations.

The style of leadership changed after Honecker's succession. After 1958 Ulbricht, clearly led from the front and the criticisms of him at the Eighth Party Congress in 1971 revealed the frustration his colleagues often felt about his style of rule. He was accused of being unresponsive to criticism, of lacking concern for collective leadership and of overweening self-confidence. Honecker dissociated himself from all this, and became the epitome of the consensus politician. Honecker's public persona, on the other hand, was that of a sombre, serious man. Perhaps his years in the Secretariat dealing with security and military affairs had strengthened these traits, but to be quickly accepted as national leader he would have to learn to smile and to create a relaxed atmosphere wherever he went.

The rhetoric, bombast, high-flown phrases and impossible goals of the Ulbricht era were dropped and a business-like approach was adopted. Experimentation in state and society became a thing of the past. Since Honecker's goal was to reassert Party pre-eminence, economic orthodoxy became the order of the day. The Economic System of Socialism with its special role for the scientific-technical intelligentsia was laid to rest.

In the field of ideology the guidelines for the Honecker era were actually laid down just before Ulbricht was forced to step down. On 15 April 1971 the SED Politburo stated that the directives of the

Twenty-Fourth CPSU Congress, which had met in Moscow in March–April 1971, were of 'general theoretical and political importance'. They were 'binding' on the SED in its search for solutions to the 'basic questions of the creation of developed socialist society in the GDR' (*Einheit*, May 1971, pp. 499–500). Thus ended the divergence between the SED's interpretation of Marxism–Leninism and that of the CPSU, evident since the 1960s. Socialism as a 'relatively independent socio-economic formation' which developed on its own base, the 'developed social system of socialism' and the 'socialist human community' – concepts which had originated with Ulbricht – were brushed aside. The 'developed social system of socialism' ceded primacy to 'developed socialist society'. The expression 'real existing socialism' – the hallmark of the Honecker era – made its first appearance in 1973.

Viewing society as a system, adopted at the Ninth Party Congress, was thus explicitly rejected. The harmonious concept of the 'socialist human communtiy' in which class differences were almost obliterated was superceded by a 'class society of a special type' while the state retained the 'birthpangs of the old society', although they were gradually disappearing. In resurrecting the class nature of GDR society the SED was emphasising the leading role of the working class and by extension its vanguard, the Party. The emphasis on systems theory in the late Ulbricht era magnified the significance of the Council of Ministers and the Council of State as regulators of economic and social life and in so doing downgraded the Party to an increasingly supervisory role. As previously mentioned the relationship between the Party and the state under Honecker has been neatly reversed.

In communist states a new leader seeks to add to his authority by denigrating the record of his predecessor. Hence Ulbricht's name appeared less and less frequently and Honecker spoke of a new 'social phase' beginning under his leadership. The 'chief task' was to ensure an all-around growth in economic and social wellbeing. This, in turn, would flow from 'increasing efficiency, scientific-technical progress and higher labour productivity'. (The scientific-technical revolution of the 1960s became scientific-technical progress in the 1970s.) The riots in Poland in December 1970 had brought home to the SED the necessity of paying greater attention to the living standards of the average person. The gulf in living standards between those with technical skills and those without, which had widened so much during the 1960s, had to be closed.

The Party brought science and technology increasingly under its wing. A whole range of scientific councils attached to the GDR Academy of Sciences, the Academy of Sciences of the CC, SED and other central and Party organisations have come into being. This allows the SED to plan, co-ordinate and supervise the subject matter and results of research much more competently, and so the Party becomes the main integrative force.

Honecker made it very clear when he took over that the role of the SED would increase. There was 'no alternative' to the rising influence of the Party. This, in turn, meant that more pressure was being applied on the four non-socialist parties. Under developed socialism one might have expected these parties to fade away. Although all the non-socialist parties acknowledge the leading role of the SED and declare the building of communism as their goal, their membership has grown throughout the Honecker era. One of the reasons for this is that party membership is required for an increasing number of GDR posts. Also political parties are a valuable source of information on political, economic and social matters. The expansion of the other parties testifies to their usefulness as transmission belts for SED policies.

The SED leadership entertained very high hopes in the early 1970s about the contribution writers and artists could make to the development of socialism. In December 1971 Honecker went so far as to say: 'In my opinion there can be no taboos in the realm of culture and literature, providing one starts from a resolutely socialist point of view.' The Party was taken aback by some of the material which was published, but it was not until 17 November 1976 that it lost patience. On that day it deprived Wolf Biermann, a folk singer and baladeer, of his GDR citizenship when he was on tour in West Germany. Many other writers and artists followed Biermann into exile or were given long-term exit visas to the West. The currents of discontent within Party ranks surfaced in a fierce attack on the SED by Rudolf Bahro. He chose a West German publisher to give vent to his exasperation at the 'incompetent' rule of the 'Politburocracy'. Imprisoned in the GDR, he was later expelled to West Germany.

The SED's treatment of cultural and political dissent provides insights into the concept of 'real, existing socialism'. The present order of things is seen as the highest development of socialism yet achieved in the GDR. No other analysis will be tolerated.

A noticeable feature of the Honecker era has been the creeping militarisation of society. This phenomenon parallels a similar tendency in the Soviet Union. New directives about socialist military training in schools were issued in 1972 and 1973. A direct result of this has been the rising significance of the National People's Army (NVA).

The Honecker era has seen an increase in the influence of the instruments of coercion, the civil and political police and the military, and they are now consuming an ever growing proportion of national income. This would suggest that those in the leadership connected with security and defence have increased their influence. It is instructive that all this happened at a time when the SED's position in the state is unassailable. Therefore it is not a product of the Party's weakness but has paralleled its accretion of influence.

THE SUCCESSION

Honecker's best years were those just after he took over as Party leader from Ulbricht. By the end of 1973 he had moved from Party to national leader. However, the terms of trade began to turn against the GDR at precisely this moment. This eventually led to the recall of Mittag and Stoph in 1976. Since then it has been an uphill struggle for Honecker and the GDR and one result of this has been the reversal of policy towards the Federal Republic. On 11 December 1970 he had warned the population to be on its guard to meet the coming confrontation with West Germany, a conflict which the GDR had to win since the West German goal was to subordinate the GDR to its will and then to liquidate it as a state (*Neues Deutschland*, 12 December 1970). However, on 12 December 1981 Honecker struck quite a different note during his talks with Helmut Schmidt, the West German Chancellor. He stressed the mutual responsibility of the two German states for the maintenance of peace. 'Whatever political or social differences exist between our countries', Honecker said, 'we cannot and must not permit ourselves to be detached from this responsibility to the people of Europe and to history itself' (*Neues Deutschland*, 14 December, 1981). He committed himself to doing everything in his power to ensure that the GDR retained close ties with the Federal Republic in the future. *Abgrenzung* or separation had given way to *Annäherung* (or *rapprochement*) with Bonn. This improving relationship has even survived the stationing of Pershing II missiles in West Germany.

The present state of East–West German relations testifies to the weaknesses and strengths of the present GDR state. On the one hand the economic imperative is such that practically any policy which helps the GDR economy to keep afloat, especially to meet its hard currency debt servicing, is acceptable. On the other hand the state is at present strong enough to suppress social discontent, and anyway it has the Soviet Army to back it up.

However, the GDR is facing formidable problems. On the positive side the economy is capable of growing steadily. National income growth of 3 per cent, industrial growth of 4 per cent and agricultural growth of one per cent, all annually, are all quite feasible during the rest of the 1980s. But on the negative side living standards have been stagnating since 1980 and are unlikely to show any appreciable improvement during the rest of this dacade. Then there is the military burden. The increase in annual military expenditure has exceeded that of national income every year since 1970. Honecker has bluntly stated that 'sacrifices' have to be made. The regime is acutely aware of the risk of social tension and immediately acts to defuse the situation. An example of this was the Politburo decision of 20 October 1982 concerning the supply of certain consumer goods during the last quarter of the year (*Neues Deutschland*, 27–28 November 1982). Large quantities of West German consumer goods were immediately imported to meet shortfalls in the GDR. This had become necessary since women had taken to queueing in the morning to secure goods which would not be available in the afternoon. The early shift thus lost many of its workers.

The need to produce a scientific-technical super-élite, so as to achieve competitiveness in world markets is bound to be divisive. Ideology is lacklustre at present and indeed Honecker has been very scathing about officials who are only capable of repeating Party directives. Success for a Party official increasingly means an ability to suggest solutions to economic problems and thereby to raise productivity.

Do all these problems make Honecker's position insecure? He has little economic expertise so he must rely on Mittag, Stoph and to a lesser extent on Jarowinsky and Kleiber. The influence of the instruments of coercion has steadily grown. Hence there are those in the Politburo over whom he has only limited influence since they either possess expertise which is desperately needed or because they have good lines of communication with Moscow. These include Hager, CC secretary for ideology, Hoffmann, the Minister of National Security and Mielke, the Minister of State Security.

In the late Brezhnev period East Berlin saw Chernenko as the next Soviet leader and awarded him two Karl Marx Orders. Andropov was given nothing. Nevertheless under Andropov Honecker became the first East European leader to pay a state visit to Moscow, (in May 1983) and it is reasonable to assume that while there he discussed the difficulties of his relationship with the abrasive Pyotr Abrasimov, the Soviet ambassador to the GDR. The outcome was that Abrasimov was replaced by Vyacheslav Kochemasov whom the SED leader had known since the 1950s. Honecker grew more self-confident in his relations with the CPSU under Andropov and when the latter died *Neues Deutschland* merely printed his obituary. In contrast Brezhnev's obituary was accompanied by pages of praise.

The need of the new Secretary General to build up his power base in the CPSU will mean that less attention can be paid to Eastern Europe. Hence if there is a succession struggle in the SED it might be determined almost entirely in East Berlin with Gorbachev accepting the new incumbent.

Although Honecker does not appear to be under threat at present there are various scenarios which could undermine his position. One would be economic failure in the GDR. This could come about through a slowdown in growth coupled with mounting hard currency indebtedness. The point might be reached where it was no longer feasible to import West German goods to cope with lacunæ in GDR domestic supplies. Then the relationship with West Germany could go sour, cutting off much needed credits.

Who is his most likely successor? It goes without saying that he would have to be acceptable to three constituencies: the Soviets, the Party apparatus and society. Besides Honecker there are now twenty full members of the Politburo. They break down into two age groups. Hager (born 1912), Hoffmann (1910), Mielke (1907) Mückenberger (1910) and Neumann (1909) all appear too old. Then there is Sindermann (1915) who would appear to belong to this group, though he has had a large black mark against his name since he failed as Prime Minister between 1973 and 1976. Stoph (1914), the Prime Minister, may also be too old, although his lines of communication with Moscow must very good given his years in military and security affairs. Axen (1916) may also be too long in the tooth. Then there is Dohlus (1925), but his experience is limited. He has been secretary for Party organs since 1960. Krolikowski (1928) would appear to belong to the right age cohort but he failed as CC secretary for the economy between 1973 and 1976. That leaves Felfe (1928), CC secretary for agriculture; Häber (1930), CC secretary; Herrmann

(1928), CC secretary for agitation and propaganda; Jarowinsky (1927); Kleiber (1931); Mittag (1926), CC secretary for the economy; Naumann (1928), CC secretary; Schabowski (1929); and Tisch (1927), head of the trade union organisation, FDGB. Then there is Krenz (1937), who is the CC secretary for security. The probability of a candidate member succeeding Honecker appears to be nil.

Applying the criterion that those in the Secretariat and the Politburo stand the best chance of becoming the next Secretary General, Axen, Dohlus, Felfe, Häber, Hager, Herrmann, Krenz, Mittag and Naumann fall into this category. Mittag's best chance of succeeding Honecker would be an economic crisis. His supporters would argue that only he could lead the country out of the mess it was in. Under more normal circumstances it would appear unlikely that an economist would be elected Secretary General. Another criterion which could be applied would be to list those who had been colleagues in the FDJ. Into this category would come Axen, Felfe, Herrmann, Krenz and Naumann. This pedigree has already produced one Secretary General, Honecker. Another group would consist of those responsible for security and military affairs. This cohort would consist of Hoffmann, Krenz, Mielke and Stoph. Here again there is a precedent, Honecker.

If all the criteria are added up there is only one person who is a full member of the Politburo, a CC secretary with an FDJ background and involved in security affairs – Krenz (1937). However, he appears too young and inexperienced. On the other hand he was a member of the SED delegation at Andropov's funeral and at the Comecon summit in June 1984. His chances have improved since he replaced the ailing Verner as CC secretary for security in November 1983. If Honecker remained until the end of the decade Krenz's chances would look very rosy. He is not a very impressive public speaker but this defect did not prevent Chernenko becoming Secretary General of the CPSU.

If there is no economic crisis and Honecker goes quickly who would succeed him? With Mittag and Krenz at a considerable disadvantage the way would be open for Herrmann and Naumann. As CC secretary for agitation and propaganda Herrmann is the Chernenko of the SED. Naumann is known as a hard, ambitious *apparatchik* who as First Secretary of Bezirk Berlin runs the GDR capital effectively. He has been especially severe on the cultural intelligentsia and in this respect behaved rather like Romanov when the latter was First Secretary of Leningrad *oblast*.

Under normal circumstances the Party can look forward to a

smooth handover of power from Honecker to his successor. However the increase in the number of GDR citizens wishing to emigrate to West Germany must be causing concern. The SED is in a quandary: if it makes it easier to leave this will encourage more to apply, but if it reduces opportunities social pressures will build up within the country. The desire of Frau Inge Berg, the niece of Willi Stoph, the Prime Minister, and her family to emigrate is alarming. Given that she belongs to a powerful and privileged GDR family, if she is discontented she may be just the tip of an iceberg. A situation could develop where economic stagnation and less co-operative attitude on the part of the West German government – which is paying large sums for exit visas for the East Germans – could lead to a tense internal situation. This scenario would strengthen the influence of the political police and the military. This is the milieu which produced Jaruzelski and the other generals in Poland who came to the rescue of the civilian Party. At present only Hoffmann is in the Politburo but there are two deparments in the CC Secretariat which are headed by military men: Colonel General Herbert Scheibe is in charge of security questions and Colonel Werner Hübner is head of socialist military training and military-political education. However, neither is a CC secretary. These are the type of men who could advance rapidly if the SED found itself in a difficult internal position.

Are there any signs of opposition to Honecker's leadership at present which might put him under pressure? There appears to be one issue over which he could be challenged, the volte-face in relations with West Germany. Konrad Naumann has made the point that the GDR should rely on its own resources instead of becoming increasingly enmeshed with West Germany. Others may sympathise, but at present this is not a viable option. Hence the greatest threat to Honecker's leadership is economic, and he may find himself under increasing pressure as time passes.

THE PRESENT LEADERSHIP OF THE GDR

Politburo	Function
Honecker, Erich (1912)	Secretary General, chairman, National Defence Council, chairman, Council of State

Axen, Hermann (1916)	CC Secretary for international relations
Dohlus, Horst (1925)	CC Secretary for party organs
Felfe, Werner (1928)	CC Secretary for agriculture
Häber, Herbert (1930)	CC Secretary, Intra-German relations
Hager, Kurt (1912)	CC Secretary for culture and science
Herrmann, Joachim (1928)	CC Secretary for agitation and propaganda
Hoffmann, General Heinz (1910)	Minister of National Defence
Jarowinsky, Werner (1927)	CC Secretary for trade and supply, churches
Kleiber, Günther (1931)	Deputy Prime Minister
Krenz, Egon (1937)	CC Secretary for security, youth and sport
Krolikowski, Werner (1928)	First Deputy Prime Minister
Mielke, General Erich (1907)	Minister of State Security
Mittag, Günter (1926)	CC Secretary for the economy
Mückenberger, Erich (1910)	Chairman, Party Central Control Commission
Naumann, Konrad (1928)	CC Secretary
Neumann, Alfred (1909)	First Deputy Prime Minister
Schabowski, Günter (1929)	Chief editor, *Neues Deutschland*
Sindermann, Horst (1915)	President, *Volkskammer*
Stoph, Willi (1914)	Prime Minister
Tisch, Harry (1927)	Chairman, FDGB

Candidate Members

Lange, Ingeburg (1927)	CC Secretary for women
Müller, Margarete (1931)	Member, Council of State
Schürer, Gerhard (1921)	Chairman, State Planning Commission
Walde, Werner (1926)	First Secretary, Bezirk Cottbus

Secretariat

Honecker, Erich	Herrmann, Joachim
Axen, Hermann	Jarowinsky, Werner
Dohlus, Horst	Krenz, Egon
Felfe, Werner	Lange, Ingeburg
Häber, Herbert	Mittag, Günter
Hager, Kurt	Naumann, Konrad

National Defence Council

Honecker, Erich	Chairman
Streletz, Colonel General Fritz (1926)	Secretary, NVA Chief of Staff

Council of Ministers

Stoph, Willi	Chairman
Krolikowski, Werner	First deputy
Neumann, Alfred	First deputy

Council of State

Honecker, Erich	Chairman (President)

5 Czechoslovakia

GORDON WIGHTMAN

Since the imposition of effective one-party rule in Czechoslovakia in February 1948, there have been four undisputed leaders, but it is only since the mid-1950s that the leading position has been identified with the post of First or Secretary General of the Communist Party (CPCz). The pre-eminence of the first communist ruler, Klement Gottwald, may be attributed to his combination of the top post within the Party – he was then CPCz Chairman – with high state office. He had been Prime Minister since March 1946 and his transition to the presidency of the republic, following the resignation of Edvard Beneš in June 1948, suggested that political authority continued to be associated with state positions rather than Party posts even after the communist *coup*. That would explain why the senior figure in the Party after Gottwald's death in March 1953, Antonín Zápotocký, became President and allowed the newly established post of First Secretary of the CPCz Central Committee to go to the relatively unknown Antonín Novotný in September 1953.

Novotný's emergence as the leading figure in Czechoslovakia after an ambiguous period of 'dual leadership' indicated the primacy of the Party Secretaryship over the headship of state and the pre-eminence of his successors in that post – Alexander Dubček who became First Secretary in January 1968 and Gustáv Husák who replaced Dubček in April 1969 (and adopted the title of Secretary General two years later) – has been unquestioned. Nevertheless, Zápotocký's choice of the presidency is not without interest, since it conforms with a pattern that distinguishes Czechoslovak practice from that in the Soviet Union. No CPCz leader since Gottwald has sought to combine leadership of the Party with the post of Prime Minister. Dubček acquired no state position during his fifteen months as First Secretary but both Novotný and Husák, the former in 1957, four years after

81

becoming CPCz leader, the latter in 1975, six years after his election as head of the Party, preferred the presidency to the government post.

LEGITIMACY

It is clear that the Czechoslovak presidency confers on the Party leader advantages similar to those his Soviet counterparts have obtained through election to a state post (Brown, 1980, pp. 141–3; Frank, 1980, pp. 99–100). The headship of state gives him a legitimate authority within Czechoslovakia he would otherwise lack and, on the international stage, his real power is demonstrated in a form familiar to foreign leaders (which it is not by his Party position alone). However, any explanation for the consistency with which CPCz leaders have opted for the presidency since 1948 rather than the post of Prime Minister (preferred notably by Khrushchev) must take into account distinctive features of the office. In that respect, great weight must be attached to the prestige associated with the Czechoslovak presidency. As Edward Taborsky has explained:

> Held formerly by such giants as Thomas Masaryk and Edvard Beneš, the Presidency had acquired in Czechoslovakia a stature and a value, both symbolic and political, beyond and above those accruing to similar institutions in other parliamentary regimes. (Taborsky, 1961, p. 170)

That consideration would certainly appear to have been in Novotný's mind when he justified retention of a single-man presidency in the new socialist Constitution, adopted in 1960, on the grounds that it had become 'a characteristic trait of the Czechoslovak state in the eyes of the working people' and passed over the opportunity to replace it with a collective head-of-state, as in other communist countries (Taborsky, 1961, p. 183). It is worth noting, too, that a similar note was struck by Peter Colotka, the Slovak Prime Minister, when Husák was nominated for a second presidential term on 20 May 1980. Although he went no further back than the first communist incumbent of that office for his precedents, Colotka stressed that 'comrade Husák embodies the best traditions of the presidential office, Gottwald's socialist traditions . . .' (*Život strany*, 1980, 12, p. 5).

The prestige of the presidency, however, seems unlikely to have been the sole factor which has persuaded CPCz leaders to prefer that post. Successive Czechoslovak Constitutions have conferred on the President rights of intervention in government not possessed by his Soviet counterpart (see, for example, Article 62 of the 1960 Constitution, which empowers him 'to take the chair at meetings of the Government, to request reports from the Government and its individual members, and to discuss with the Government or its members matters requiring action'). These provisions may fall short of the comprehensive control acquisition of the chairmanship of the USSR Council of Ministers gave Khrushchev (Brown, 1980, p. 140), but it would be unwise to dismiss the significance to a CPCz leader of the additional power they provide over government ministries. The combination of the top Party post with the presidency was seen by Novotný's opponents in 1968 as a source of his excessive power (comparable by implication with Khrushchev's simultaneous occupancy of the top Party and government posts in the Soviet Union) and for that reason Dubček was unlikely ever to add the presidency (or any other state post) to the First Secretaryship even if he had held the latter for longer than fifteen months.

The two occasions when the presidency has not been occupied by the Party leader (between 1953 and 1957 and from 1968 to 1975) provide some support for the view that the powers of the head of state in Czechoslovakia are such as to make an incumbent First Secretary, at the very least, reluctant to permit a vacancy in the presidential chair to be filled by another eminent member of the leadership. The assumption of the presidency on Gottwald's death in March 1953 by Antonín Zápotocký, and his failure to secure a place at the same time in the Secretariat, may have been based on a miscalculation as to the locus of real power, comparable to Malenkov's retention of the chairmanship of the USSR Council of Ministers and resignation from the CPSU Secretariat (Frank, 1980, p. 93). Nevertheless, the prediction of one Czech émigré, writing in 1954, that no one else in the leadership could become 'master of the regime . . . as long as Zápotocký remains President of the Republic: the prerogatives reserved to the head of state by the Czechoslovak Constitution are too important' (Barton, 1954, p. 223), proved justified. That period of 'dual leadership' under Novotný and Zápotocký is reported to have been a time of recurring conflicts between the First Secretary and President (*Život strany*, 1968, 15, pp. 12–13), finally ended by the latter's death in 1957.

The risk that appointment to the presidency of a major political figure could work to the leader's disadvantage is also demonstrated by the second example of a President who was not simultaneously First Secretary. When Ludvík Svoboda was elected head of state in March 1968, he was chosen as a man who would restore the dignity of that office and at the same time remain aloof from political struggles within the CPCz. 'This post,' Zdeněk Mlynář (who became a member of the Central Committee Secretariat in April 1968) recalled in his political memoirs,

> was no longer to be linked with a high party post: the CPCz leadership instinctively longed for an 'above-party' President who would awaken a little a feeling of continuity with the Presidents of the First, pre-war Republic. (Mlynář, 1978, p. 141)

However, that attempt to limit the role of the President – made explicit by Svoboda's exclusion from the party Presidium (as the CPCz's leading body has been called since 1962) – proved untenable under the pressure of events. Soviet recognition of the President's constitutional authority, following the Warsaw Pact invasion of Czechoslovakia in August 1968, brought Svoboda into the political arena and led to his co-option to the Presidium at the end of that month. Moscow's recognition undoubtedly contributed to Svoboda's emergence as a key political figure in the subsequent political struggle when his voice was added to those favouring concessions to Soviet demands for the curtailment of the 1968 reform programme, but his increased influence also owed a great deal to acceptance within the leadership that the views of the President could not be ignored.

Husák's assumption of the presidency in 1975 may thus be seen as a means to avoiding not only, as Kusin has suggested, the elevation of a Presidium member whose 'lack of charisma' made him unsuited to that prestigious post (Kusin, 1978, p. 193), but also the appointment of a strong political figure whose influence might have been increased at the Secretary General's expense – as much as to a desire on Husák's part to acquire the advantages of a state post, outlined earlier. Nevertheless, the decision once more to combine the top Party post with the headship of state caused some embarrassment within a leadership which had shared the view of reformists in 1968 that Novotný's tenure of both positions had contributed to his accumulation of excessive power. It felt compelled to provide some explanation for that volte-face and in May 1975, the Party's theoretical journal, *Nová mysl*, reported that

The Central Committee considered the experience of past years and reached the conclusion that the question of the relationship between the office of President of the Republic and a leading official of the Party, of their combination in one person or their division between two people, is always dependent on the concrete situation and on evaluation of all the optimal needs of the further development of the Party and of socialist society.

It was convinced, the report said, that Husák's candidature for the presidency was 'in accord with the concrete conditions and needs of the present stage of development of our Party and society'.

INSTRUMENTS OF POWER

The CPCz leader's assumption of the presidency, despite the advantages it may subsequently bring, should not be taken to indicate his emergence as the dominant figure within the leadership. Whereas in the Soviet Union Khrushchev's acquisition of the chairmanship of the USSR Council of Ministers in 1958 and Brezhnev's appointment as Chairman of the Presidium of the USSR Supreme Soviet in 1977 reflected their ascendancy in the CPSU Politburo, the elections of Novotný and Husák to the Czechoslovak presidency were not consequent on previous establishment of their supremacy within the CPCz Presidium. A better indicator of a Party leader's power, in Czechoslovakia as in other communist states, is his ability to form a Presidium in which a majority owe their inclusion to the First Secretary's patronage. That was not the case either at the time of Novotný's election to the presidency or that of Husák. For the first six years of Novotný's tenure of the presidential office, he continued to share power with men who, for the most part, had reached leading positions before Novotný's accession to the top Party post. His dominance within the CPCz was established only after 1963, when, following the belated adoption of a policy of de-Stalinisation, those members of the Presidium most closely implicated in the political repression of the early 1950s were removed and replaced by men dependent on the First Secretary for their promotion (Wightman, 1981, pp. 403–4).

In that respect, Husák has signally failed to emulate Novotný even in the years since his accession to the presidency. As Mlynář has put it

Husák has not been able to carry out any operation reinforcing his own personal position, although such operations, always demonstrating the role of the most powerful personality have been carried out by every Party chief in the Soviet bloc in the post-Stalin era. (Mlynář, 1982, p. 28)

Husák's absence from the political scene between his imprisonment in the 1950s and his re-emergence in 1968 no doubt put him at a disadvantage in terms of building up a network of supporters within the Party-state bureaucracy from whom to select candidates for key positions. A more crucial factor underlying his failure to promote his 'clients' to the CPCz Presidium, however, was the desire on the part of the Soviet leadership to ensure the presence within that body of men whose loyalty to Moscow and commitment to the Soviet model of socialism were beyond doubt. Although the Presidium underwent a radical transformation between Husák's election as Party leader in April 1969 and the Fourteenth CPCz Congress in May 1971, the body which emerged (and which has not been fundamentally changed since that time) consisted not of men dependent on Husák's patronage but of men whose loyalty to Moscow had been demonstrated – in some cases by their antipathy to the 1968 reforms and willingness at the time of the invasion to participate in their suppression, and in others by their readiness, despite their earlier involvement in the Prague Spring, to come to terms with Soviet demands for a return to orthodoxy.

Paradoxically, Dubček, the one leader not to combine the top Party post with the presidency, had greater success in forming 'his own' leadership, only three months after his election as First Secretary. Both the Presidium and Central Committee Secretariat, set up in April 1968, were dominated by men who had links of a personal or professional nature with Dubček or with two other members of a key triumvirate within the Presidium: Oldřich Černík, the newly appointed Prime Minister, and Drahomír Kolder, a Secretary of the Central Committee (Mlynář, 1978, p. 134). In some instances – those of Viliam Šalgovič as the Deputy Minister of the Interior responsible for the security police and Miloš Jakeš as Chairman of the party's Central Control and Auditing Commission – Dubček pushed through their appointment despite objections within the Presidium, in the belief that their antipathy to the reformist course would be overriden by personal loyalty to him (Mlynář, 1978, pp. 120, 145).

The successful exercise of patronage and the formation by the

Party leader of 'his own' Presidium, however, have proved to be neither a guarantee of security of tenure nor of leadership unity. By December 1967, Novotný no longer retained the support of a majority within the Presidium when his authority was challenged on the floor of the Central Committee – despite having appointed eight of its ten full members. Clientelism, moreover, was a weak basis for maintenance of unity within the Dubček leadership at a time when pressure for more radical reform from Party rank and file and the public exacerbated differences in attitude within the Presidium.

On the other hand, Husák's failure to bring his own associates into the Presidium should not be seen as a source of disunity or a threat to his survival. As Kusin put it in 1978

> While it is undoubtedly true that there have been and still are diverse opinions in the leadership, mainly but not solely along the dividing line between advocates of hard and not-so-hard policies, the leadership has over the years established a *modus vivendi* which suits all members. (Kusin, 1978, p. 191)

Although the Secretary General has been unable to increase his power *vis-à-vis* his colleagues, a number of factors operate in his favour. Moscow's continued backing for his occupancy of the top Party post is an important political resource and, it may be noted, the absence of that support was crucial when both Novotný and Dubček lost office. Despite the constraints on his power of appointment, Husák has ensured that some key positions have gone to his associates. The Central Committee Secretary in charge of party organs, Mikuláš Beňo, is, like the Party leader, a Slovak whose career can be linked with Husák's in the 1970s (He became the head of the Secretary General's private office in 1973 before his promotion to the position of Secretary in 1977). The Minister of the Interior between 1973 and 1984, Jaromír Obzina, like his immediate predecessor, Radko Kaska, has been described as a Husák supporter (Kusin, 1978, p. 192). The promotion to candidate membership of the Presidium in November 1982 of Josef Haman (who served in the Secretariat of the Secretary General from 1973 to 1976 and then became head of the President's Chancellery until his appointment as a Central Committee Secretary in 1978) suggests that Husák's capacity to influence appointments outside the ranks of voting members of the Presidium, though weaker than that of his predecessors, should not be wholly discounted.

Nevertheless, the paucity of changes among full members of that body in recent years suggests that a balance has been achieved which the leadership is wary of upsetting. Since the promotion to full membership of Miloš Jakeš following the party's Sixteenth Congress in April 1981, the Presidium has avoided, as far as possible, any change in the composition of that group. Even when two full members, Josef Kempný and Václav Hůla, lost in June 1981 the posts (as Secretary of the Central Committee and Chairman of the State Planning Commission, respectively) which justified their inclusion within the Presidium, neither was dropped. Hůla's continuation as a Deputy Prime Minister (until his death in 1983) made his survival in the Presidium less remarkable than that of Kempný, who was demoted to the relatively insignificant chairmanship of the Czech National Front (the umbrella organisation embracing all political parties and social organisations, chaired at the federal level by the Secretary General). The presence within the Presidium of individuals who do not simultaneously hold another important post is not unprecedented (Jaromír Dolanský's membership of that body between 1966 and 1968 is a case in point) but it remains unusual.

Hůla's death at the age of fifty-eight illustrates the precariousness of the balance within a leadership whose average age in 1984 was sixty-three. Although Husák has managed 'to hold the party Presidium in a state of uneasy equilibrium' (Kusin, 1982, p. 136) so far, there is no guarantee that this will continue for much longer. Ill-health or death might force further changes, whatever the leadership might wish, in the near future. Whether or not they would be to Husák's advantage is unpredictable, but his failure, fifteen years after becoming Party leader, to achieve that increase in power over time which Novotný in Czechoslovakia and CPSU leaders, up to and including Brezhnev, have attained (Brown, 1980, p. 136), does not suggest that they would be in his favour.

INSTRUMENTS OF COERCION

When a CPCz leader has simultaneously been head of state, he has had an advantage in also being commander-in-chief of the armed forces. However, even when the First Secretary has not been President, he has attempted to ensure his control over the military, as well as the security police, through subordination to him of the supervisory Central Committee unit – the Eighth Department or Department

of State Administration. The responsibility of that same section of
the apparatus (except between July 1968 and July 1969) for the
judiciary provides the leader with an important resource for the
suppression of political dissent as well as preventing use of the forces
of coercion by his colleagues against him. On the other hand, on the
one occasion when military aid has been sought at a time of leadership crisis, in December 1967, the armed forces failed to come to the
First Secretary's assistance (For an account of those events, see
Skilling, 1976, pp. 172–4).

While the influence of the military and the security police in
internal politics cannot be ignored, neither has attained the level of
institutional representation that has been the case in the Soviet
Union, notably since the early 1970s. The Minister of Defence has
not been included in the Party Presidium since 1956 and the last
Minister of the Interior (to whom the security police are responsible)
to hold a post in that body, Rudolf Barák, was removed in 1962 on
embezzlement charges – reportedly after trying to use his position to
undermine Novotný (Skilling, 1976, pp. 40–1).

KEY POLITICAL INSTITUTIONS

Although Czechoslovak practice has not conformed exactly with that
in other Soviet-type systems, the light thrown on the relationship
between the three most important political institutions – the Party
Presidium, the Central Committee Secretariat and the federal Government – by evidence from the 1960s is relevant not only to subsequent developments in Czechoslovakia but to the functions of
equivalent bodies in other communist countries. As in other socialist
states, the pre-eminence of the Party Presidium may be attributed to
a number of factors. The Party leader's survival in office depends on
maintenance of majority support within it and policy decisions require its (often only formal) approval. Its importance also derives
from its composition. In addition to the First or Secretary General
and a number of other Central Committee Secretaries (currently
four, one more than the norm in the 1960s and 1970s), the CPCz
Presidium has come to include the holders of a range of other posts
which make it the focal point of the political system as a whole. The
Prime Minister, the Chairman of parliament, the Slovak Prime
Minister and (since 1969) his Czech counterpart have invariably been
members. Except between April and August 1968, the presidency

(when not held by the Party leader) has brought Presidium membership, as has the post of Leading Secretary of the Prague City Party committee. Except in 1968, the Slovak Party has had two representatives – the Slovak First Secretary and a second Slovak official who has combined membership of the Slovak Presidium with a Secretaryship of the Slovak Central Committee.

Czechoslovak practice has, however, differed from that followed in the Soviet Union and at least some other communist states as far as Presidium membership is concerned, insofar as the Chairman of the Party's disciplinary body, the Central Control and Auditing Commission, is not formally included in its ranks. While his exclusion may have been intended to conform with attempts at a separation of powers between the Commission and executive bodies of the Party (Wightman, 1981, pp. 406–7), his attendance in practice at Presidium meetings makes that departure from the norm largely meaningless. The role of the Commission in purging reformists from the Party in 1970 made clear its function as an executant of leadership policy rather than that of an impartial arbitrator between the Presidium and the membership (implied in its election, not by the Central Committee, but by the Party Congress).

Any attempt to assess the relative influence of the Central Committee Secretariat and the Government must take into account a further departure from practice in other communist states. Within the CPCz, a distinction has traditionally been made between Secretaries of the Central Committee who have responsibility for particular areas of Party policy and supervise sections of the apparatus, and members of the Secretariat who do not (currently, Marie Kabrhelová, the chairwoman of the women's movement, is in the latter category – as was Oldřich Švestka, the editor-in-chief of the Party newspaper, *Rudé právo*, until his death in 1983). Zdeněk Mlynář has testified that the absence of a power base within the Party apparatus during his two months as an ordinary member of the Secretariat without Secretary status was a disadvantage (Mlynář, 1978, p. 140) and it is clear that that group remains the least influential of Secretariat members. The influence of those Secretaries who are simultaneously members of the Presidium is clear, but the presence of all Secretariat members at Presidium meetings gives them an advantage over most Government members beyond those derived from its role as the Party's supervisory agency and its control over appointments in all institutions. Access to the Party's authoritative decision-making body for most ministers remains indirect – either through the Secretariat (as Brown has stressed with regard to the CPSU; Brown, 1984, p. 81) or those few Government members in the Presidium – the three Prime Ministers, noted above, and usually a Deputy Prime Minister (who is often also Chairman of the State Planning Commission).

Yet, while it may be concluded that in general terms the influence of the Secretariat is greater than that of the Government, there are grounds for expecting greater variation than that overall picture suggests. As Brown noted for Czechoslovakia in the 1960s, ministries' 'specialized knowledge puts them in a position where they are often the initiators of major policy, even if they seldom have the last word' (Brown, 1966, p. 469). Although insistence on ideological orthodoxy since the Prague Spring acts as a severe constraint on all sectors, greater scope for government ministers to exert influence may be anticipated in those areas where expertise is at a premium (the economy or technological development) than in other more politically sensitive sectors (such as culture or the mass media).

On the other hand, evidence from 1968 suggests that the influence of the Secretariat is further enhanced by the ineffectiveness of the Presidium as the party's supreme policy-making body. Under both Novotný and Dubček, serious examination of issues under discussion was hindered by the amount of business put before it (Šik, *Kulturní noviny*, 29 March 1968; Mlynář, 1978, p. 176). Mlynář, who attended its meetings first as a member of the Secretariat and then as a Central Committee Secretary after April 1968, has testified that discussions in the Presidium often remained so general or strayed so far from the point that its decisions, almost inevitably, reflected the original recommendations prepared by the apparatus rather than the consensus arrived at by argument and debate (Mlynář, 1978, pp. 174–7).

It seems unlikely that Presidium deliberations have improved since the Prague Spring, given the increased centralisation of subsequent years and the continuation in leading positions of some members of the 1968 Presidium. Nevertheless, it remains the body in which the Party leader has to maintain majority support if his survival in office is to be assured.

POLICY-MAKING

Although Husák's failure to form 'his own' Presidium suggests his individual power over policy is weaker than that of his two predecessors as Party leader, the scope for policy initiative was in any case limited after 1969 by his acceptance of Soviet demands that the reforms of the Prague Spring be dismantled. The policy of 'normal-isation' pursued after Husák's election as First Secretary outlawed not only departures from orthodoxy in the political sphere but also the kind of reforms in the economy which had been linked in the 1960s with political democratisation.

Nevertheless, 'normalisation' also brought advantages for the lead-ership, for it removed other, domestic constraints which had been apparent not only in 1968, but also, in some cases, during the last years of Novotný's rule. Condemnation of reformist ideas as re-visionism and right-wing opportunism precluded discussion of change except within limits acceptable to the leadership. A purge of the CPCz membership, completed in December 1970, removed from the Party unrepentant supporters of reform and eliminated those sections of the intelligentsia, in particular, which, throughout the 1960s, had brought pressure to bear on the leadership in favour of change, in some cases through participation as advisers to the Party apparatus and in others through contributions to the mass media, scholarship and the arts. While the reimposition of censorship in 1969 prevented the continuing dissemination of heterodox ideas (except through the restricted channels of *samizdat*), it also silenced public opinion which during the Prague Spring had been both an important resource for Dubček in overcoming resistance to reform within the Presidium and a factor which at times pushed him along a more radical path than he might otherwise have taken. 'Normalisation', however, also permit-ted accommodation of another group active in the 1960s. The intro-duction of a federal state system in January 1969 (which gave Slovaks formal equality with the Czechs), parity in appointments to central posts and Husák's personal identification with Slovak nationalism throughout his career, have combined to remove those grievances which made Slovak discontentment an issue in internal politics in the past.

Husák's readiness to conform with Soviet wishes and his success in neutralising or accommodating those groups within the CPCz which combined to challenge Novotný in the autumn of 1967 suggests his position, barring unforeseeable events, is secure. In the past, the CPCz leader has been most vulnerable when his Presidium colleagues have been able to distance themselves from discredited policies with which the First Secretary was personally identified – Novotný's hostility to Slovak aspirations and his attempts in 1967 to reverse progress towards reform, or Dubček's efforts to resist 'normalisation' after the 1968 invasion. In that respect, Husák's colleagues are as closely identified with post-1969 policy and as vulnerable to a change of direction (unlikely though that may be) as the Secretary General. Economic failure seems unlikely to affect Husák directly. Economic problems early in the 1980s rebounded, not on the Secretary General, but on Kempný and Hůla, two Presidium members more closely involved in that policy area.

SUCCESSION

Previous leadership changes offer some guidance on factors which will influence the choice of a new leader when Husák leaves the political scene, even though the circumstances in which he will be chosen are likely to be markedly different to those prevailing when Dubček was elected First Secretary in January 1968 or when Husák replaced him in April 1969. On both those occasions the Central Committee was a much less docile body than it is in the 1980s and the candidate had to be acceptable to those groups represented within it which had challenged Novotný's position and were active during the Prague Spring. The need to obtain support from Slovak members, a crucial factor both in 1968 and 1969, seems likely to be a less critical consideration (though by no means a negligible one, since a leader whose hostility to Slovaks might revive discontent within that national group would be an unwise choice). The expulsion of advocates of reform removed another interest which had to be taken into account not only in January 1968 but also at the time Husák's nomination, when he was seen as the politician most likely to preserve some of the reforms.

Contenders for the succession have to be full members of the Party Presidium, but evidence from 1968 and 1969 suggests that, as distinct from recent practice in the CPSU, the candidate does not have to be a Secretary of the Central Committee. Both Dubček and Husák were First Secretary of the Slovak party at the time of their promotion to the top post. However, while experience in the Party apparatus would seem likely to be a prerequisite, those members of the leadership who combine full membership of the Presidium with a non-Party post remain eligible for the post of Secretary General. Mlynář has testified that in January 1968 Oldřich Černík, then Chairman of the State Planning Commission, was a serious contender for the succession to Novotný along with Dubček and Jiří Hendrych, at that time a

Central Committee Secretary (Mlynář, 1978, p. 119). Nevertheless, those members of the present Presidium, such as the Czech and Slovak Prime Ministers, Josef Korčák and Peter Colotka, whose political careers have been almost exclusively in government, or Karel Hoffman, the Chairman of the trade union organisation, who last held a post within the Party bureaucracy in 1959, would seem to have little chance of becoming Party leader.

The successful candidate has to win majority support within the Presidium and, in present circumstances, has therefore to be acceptable both to its ideologically hardline members and those of a more pragmatic disposition. The longer Husák remains in office, the greater the possibility that the balance between those two groups will shift and affect the chances of individuals who at present seem strong contenders. Moreover, any change of leadership in Moscow could affect the outcome of a succession struggle within the CPCz insofar as the latter attempted to select a candidate who would be more responsive to any change of direction in the USSR.

Given the uncertainties about the circumstances and the time of Husák's departure from the leadership, predicting his successor is highly risky. At best, those whose claims to the post of Secretary General seem strongest at the present time may be identified, partly through a process of elimination. Besides Korčák, Colotka and Hoffman, whose experience would count against them, Josef Kempný's prospects of becoming leader would appear to be ruled out by his demotion from the Secretariat in 1981. Vasil Bilák's age (he was sixty-seven in 1984) seems likely to reduce his chances in a Presidium whose average age is sixty-three, and his hardline views would scarcely appeal to more moderate Presidium members. The past association of the Prague Secretary, Antonín Kapek, with neo-Stalinist groups would make him even less attractive to more pragmatic leaders, while the identification of Alois Indra, the present Chairman of the Federal Assembly, with Czech nationalism must remain an obstacle to his promotion in a Party which cannot wholly ignore Slovak opinion.

Of the three remaining full members of the Presidium – Lubomír Štrougal, the federal Prime Minister, Jozef Lenárt, the Slovak First Secretary, and Miloš Jakeš, who combines that position with a Secretaryship of the Central Committee – Jakeš' claims appear strongest – especially if rumours of Štrougal's ill health are true. All three have had experience in government and the Party bureaucracy, but where Štrougal's commitment to reform during the Prague Spring may make him suspect to hardline members of the leadership, the loyalty of Jakeš and Lenárt to the Soviet Union in 1968 does not make them unacceptable to more pragmatic Presidium members. As Prime Minister between 1963 and early 1968, Lenárt was identified with the attempts at reform during the last years of Novotný's rule and would seem favourably disposed towards technocratic change. Although Jakeš has consistently been identified with a strongly pro-Soviet position and a hardline policy on membership during his tenure as Chairman of the Party Central Control and Auditing Commission between 1968 and 1977, his willingness, as Central Committee Secretary responsible for economic policy since June 1981, to countenance technocratic reform would seem likely to help him appeal beyond those hardliners in the Presidium, from whom support might be expected for his candidacy, to those of a more pragmatic persuasion. If Jakeš' claims seem stronger than those of Lenárt, that is at least partly because, while Lenárt's career has been one of survival over the past two decades rather than steady advancement, Jakeš' rise to prominence in recent years has been rapid. From the chairmanship of the Control Commission to a Secretaryship of the Central Committee and candidate membership of the Presidium in 1977 he rose to full membership of that body four years later, shortly before his assumption of secretarial responsibility for the economy.

Whatever the outcome of the succession, it will be interesting to see whether the new leader continues to combine the presidency with the top Party post, or whether Czechoslovakia will again depart from recent Soviet practice and, at least for a time, keep those offices separate.

THE CZECHOSLOVAK LEADERSHIP

Presidium	Function
Husák, Gustáv (1913)	Secretary General; President; Chairman, Czechoslovak National Front
Bilák, Vasil (1917)	CC Secretary for international Relations

Colotka, Peter (1925)	Prime Minister, Slovak Government
Hoffman, Karel (1924)	Chairman, Trades Union Movement
Indra, Alois (1921)	Chairman, Federal Assembly
Jakeš, Miloš (1922)	CC Secretary for the Economy
Kapek, Antonín (1922)	Leading Secretary, Prague City Committee
Kempný, Josef (1921)	Chairman, Czech National Front
Korčák, Josef (1921)	Prime Minister, Czech Government
Lenárt, Jozef (1923)	First Secretary, Communist Party of Slovakia
Štrougal, Lubomir (1924)	Prime Minister, Federal Government

Candidate Members

Hruškovič, Miloslav (1925)	Members of Slovak Party Presidium; Secretary of Slovak CC
Fojtík, Jan (1928)	CC Secretary for Ideology and Mass Media
Haman, Josef (1933)	CC Secretary for Industry

Secretariat

Secretaries

Husák, Gustáv	as above
Beňo, Mikuláš (1930)	CC Secretary for Party Organs

Bilák, Vasil	as above
Fojtík, Jan	as above
Haman, Josef	as above
Havlín, Josef	CC Secretary for Education and Culture
Jakeš, Miloš	as above
Pitra, František (1932)	CC Secretary for Agriculture
Poledník, Jindřich (1937)	CC Secretary for Social Organisations

Member of the Secretariat

Kabrhelová, Marie (1925)	Chairwoman, Czechoslovak Women's Association

Central Control and Auditing Commission

Hajn, Jaroslav (1919)	Chairman

President of the Republic

Husák, Gustáv

Federal Government

Štrougal, Lubomír	Prime Minister
Colotka, Peter	Deputy Prime Minister; Prime Minister, Slovak Government
Korčák, Josef	Deputy Prime Minister; Prime Minister, Czech Government
Gerle, Ladislav (1936)	Deputy Prime Minister (responsible for energy and heavy industry)

Laco, Karol (1921)	Deputy Prime Minister (responsible for legal/state questions)
Lučán, Matej (1928)	Deputy Prime Minister (responsible for culture)
Obzina, Jaromír (1929)	Deputy Prime Minister; Chairman, State Commission for Scientific, Technical and Investment Development
Potáč, Svatopluk (1925)	Deputy Prime Minister; Chairman, State Planning Commission
Rohlíček, Rudolf (1929)	Deputy Prime Minister (responsible for relations with CMEA)
Vaclavik, Milan ( )	Minister of National Defence
Chňoupek, Bohuslav (1925)	Minister of Foreign Affairs
Vajnar, Vratislav (1930)	Minister of the Interior

Federal Assembly

Indra, Alois	Chairman

6 Hungary

GEORGE SCHÖPFLIN

There are a number of general considerations in understanding the nature of leadership as an institution in Soviet-type societies. Perhaps the most significant of these is that the leader has a number of functions which are not paralleled in Western systems, because both the leader and the system as a whole lack popular legitimacy. What the leader has to achieve, therefore, is something short of legitimacy but which should provide stability. In the initial 'revolutionary' phase of Soviet-type systems, this was largely by coercion and, for a minority, belief in the official ideology. In the post-revolutionary 'administrative' phase, coercion on a mass scale has come to be regarded as inefficient in the achievement of goals and the ideology of Marxism–Leninism as officially propounded has largely lost whatever power of attraction it has ever had. Consequently, the system as a whole has had to find surrogates and it is in this context that leadership has come to play a pivotal role.

The argument put forward here, therefore, is that leadership in Soviet-type systems should be understood as one of the substitutes for legitimacy and is, in fact, capable of providing considerable stability, in certain circumstances. The Hungarian case illustrates many of these circumstances, which make it a particularly fruitful area of study. In Hungary, as in other Soviet-type systems, it is possible to identify four main actors in the context of leadership – the Soviet Union, the leader himself, the élite as a whole and society. Obviously, with the exception of the leader himself, these are not single, homogeneous actors and can be regarded as informal conglomerates; however, for present purposes they will be treated as capable of articulating a uniform set of pressures on the leader. Furthermore, there is some interaction among the four actors, so that this quadripartite model of political action does shift and change.

If the task of the leader is to create stability and he lacks the means to achieve this by legitimation proper, the alternatives that he has are concentrated in his person rather than the office he holds. In other words, the leader can substitute a mix of power (coercion) and authority for legitimacy, but whatever authority he may accumulate will very largely be personal to him and cannot be transmitted. This means that succession is an insurmountable source of weakness and that a new leader is especially vulnerable. In this case, the substitution of stability for legitimacy should be regarded as a continuous trade-off between the short term and the long term. It is evident that Soviet-type systems would benefit from the kind of long-term stability that is created by legitimation; but as long as this possibility is off the agenda, short-term expedients, like stabilisation through leadership (among others), have to be employed.

Another problem deriving from stabilisation is that the process tends to create its own set of expectations and codes of behaviour which are restricted to the pattern built by the leader. Thus when a new leader takes over, there is uncertainty and some resistence to change, reinforcing a general pattern of conservatism and antagonism to innovation in Soviet-type systems. All these propositions would generally tend to underpin the importance of leadership as an institution in Soviet-type systems and would also help to explain some of the major divergences which have arisen as between Soviet-type polities – again, there are other, political-cultural factors relevant here, and leadership is not being put forward as the sole factor in this respect.

The four-actor model of leadership demands analysis of how these actors affect the leader and what their interactions achieve. In the first place, there is the role of the Soviet Union. There is strong evidence that membership of Warsaw Pact Politburos is part of the informal *nomenklatura* of the Kremlin, Romania probably excepted. Thus no Warsaw Pact leader can hope to rise to the top without the approval of Moscow. It can even be argued that Moscow retains the veto over East European leaders and can remove them – the removal of Ulbricht in favour of Honecker in 1971 is a case in point. However, there is an equally strong counter-argument that longevity in office offers East European leaders a certain protection *vis-à-vis* Moscow, in that the Kremlin will be reluctant to sack a well-established East European leader for fear of provoking a succession crisis greater than the problem represented by the leader in question. Kádár in Hungary and Zhivkov in Bulgaria would certainly be in this category. Nevertheless, longevity is not in itself sufficient and every East European leader has to pay some heed to Soviet susceptibilities.

Secondly, the leader must avoid policies which would undermine his support in the élite as a whole. Whilst he has considerable power to change the personnel of the élite, he cannot afford to antagonise it in its entirety. The élite understands the task of the leader to be the satisfaction of the Soviet Union; the guarantee of the survival of the system (which ensures the privileges of the élite); and to prevent the eruption of such a degree of popular unrest as would threaten the system. Any major expression of popular discontent, particularly in the form of visible demonstrations of dissent like riots, threaten the Soviet Union's approval and the élite's confidence.

However, once the leader has gained the backing of the Kremlin and has consolidated his position internally, his power over the élite grows. He acquires control over the *nomenklatura* and will, to some extent, seek to promote his own clients, especially within the Party machine. Gierek's policies in the early 1970s, when he instituted a rapid turnover of local Party secretaries and later reshaped the pattern of Polish administration in order to prevent the emergence of strong local leaders, exemplifies this pattern. Ceauşescu in Romania has instituted a continuous replacement of cadres, moving them from one post to another with bewildering speed, with presumably the same objective. From the standpoint of the élite as a whole – as distinct from those demoted or removed – this consolidation of the leader's position is a mixed blessing. It stabilises the system but it also diminishes the power of the lower ranks of the élite. In particular, as the authority of the leader grows with longevity in office, he gradually begins to be regarded as 'indispensable', the system becomes his creation, the extension of his personal power, and he subtly reshapes the party machine through policies and appointments.

Nevertheless, in spite of all the creative reshaping undertaken by leaders, the élite will retain its separateness and will be conscious of its own distinct interests. When the behaviour of the leader threatens these separate interests, élite support for the leader will be withdrawn and transferred to someone else prepared to carry out what the élite regards as the leader's central task. Hence the relationship between the élite and the leader is not entirely one-sided – it does contain elements of reciprocity, albeit the élite's opportunity to validate its interests are few, usually occuring in the midst of a crisis, and the leader's position tends to be the stronger. There are several leadership changes which illustrate these propositions. The way in which the Polish élite was quick to rid itself of Gierek, whom it had backed with almost embarrassing devotion for a decade, at the moment when Gierek's incompetence permitted the interests of society to break through into politics and endanger the privileged position the élite had established for itself, was one example. Nor did it help Gierek that the élite had very largely been his personal creation, for he had largely dropped the officials he had inherited from Gomułka. This Polish instance illustrates the process of the élite delegitimation and the consequent collapse of the leader's authority very clearly.

The relationship between the élite and the leader has also played a key role in a rather different fashion in Czechoslovakia. By 1967 the outlines of an anti-Novotný coalition in the Czechoslovak elite could be clearly discerned. Novotný had alienated several of the client groups which had until then given him support – the technocrats, the Slovaks, the Party intelligentsia and eventually the core elements of the Party machine. Hence there existed an anti-Novotný coalition united on the issue of replacing him by late 1967; the removal of the Soviet ægis helped this process forward, as evidenced by the brief visit paid to Prague by Brezhnev in December 1967 to inform the Czechoslovak leadership of Soviet disinterest in Novotný's fate. Once agreement was reached on the person of a successor (Dubček) Novotný's demise was inevitable. But the fact that the coalition had come together for the rather limited objective of dumping Novotný helped to account for the hesitation in the unfolding of the reform programme and for the very different conceptions of reform that were propounded in the early months of 1968.

The third relationship is between leader and society. On the whole, the influence of social forces in Soviet-type systems is strictly limited and, as already argued, one of the tasks of the leader is to ensure that this does not change, for the aspirations of society are destructive of the system and of the privileged position of the élite, as well as of the power of the leader. None the less there are circumstances in which the leader can use the threat of social aspirations as an instrument to delimit the powers of the élite. The power of the leader over the élite is, as noted earlier, very considerable where individuals are concerned; the élite. as a collectivity is less amenable to being disciplined by, for example, *ad hoc* purges or scapegoats chosen to encourage the others. The threat of mass popular discontent, on the other hand, is too serious for the élite to ignore. Indeed, the argument can be made that one aspect of Gierek's failure as a leader was that he did not use the evidence of popular discontent in Poland in the late 1970s as a means of restricting élite overconsumption and mismanagement at a time when the economy was no longer expanding. A vivid example of a leadership that sought to use mass support for its own purposes, only to find that the aspirations of society were outrunning the limits set for it comes from Croatia in 1971. Here the Croatian Party leadership encouraged the intelligentsia and through the intelligentsia the population at large to raise demands against the centrists in the Croatian Party and the federation as a whole. By the end of 1971, social forces had begun to eat away at the leading role of the Party and the Tripalo leadership had no way of handling this; Tito chose to use the armed forces for resolving the crisis and to purge the Croatian Party.

The place of Hungary in the broad matrix of leadership as an institution is currently seen as being at the stable end of the spectrum. Kádár has been in office since 1956 and has established an unprecedented stability after the turbulence of the 1950s. This length of time has allowed the system to evolve, to adopt Kádárist colouring and to assume what might be regarded as its 'natural' contours. The Hungarian political community and system in the modern period have enjoyed two long periods of stability – between the wars and under Kádár. In both these periods they have assumed broadly similar contours, which might be defined as modified authoritarianism. This allows for a modicum of individual autonomy, but control over group activity; under Kádár, the control has been strict, whilst under Horthy it was rather more relaxed. The difference may be explained by the greater self-confidence and deeper roots of the élite before the war than since 1956. The Hungarian Party must count as one of the least stable in the history of Communist Parties. It was dissolved or fell apart in 1919, in 1936, in 1943 and in 1956, in different circumstances; it is the only ruling Party which has had to seize control of the country three times (in 1919, after 1948 and in 1956–7). And it is the only Party which has controlled the entire state, only to be ejected from that control (in 1919). With this record, the Kádárist stability begins to assume considerable distinction.

Kádár's own contribution to the system with which his name is associated and which had frequently been described in terms of envy by outside observers can be assessed both in positive terms – what Kádár has sought to achieve; and in negative terms – what he has tried to avoid. The negative factors are easier to delineate: Kádár, having been a victim of terror himself, has created a system in which repression is restricted to the goals set by the system and no more, what has been aptly described as the 'goal-rational' use of repression. Thus there is no mass terror, the secret police operate within rules, arbitrariness is checked, there is some attempt to maintain the distinction between political crime and political error and the instruments of coercion are by and large kept in the background. But this does not mean that Kádár accepts the autonomy of the law or the rule of law. The model from which Kádár has dissociated himself was the one imposed on Hungary under Rákosi, and which has been interpreted as the excessive concentration of power and the irrational use of coercion – both 'excessive' and 'irrational' being defined by the yardstick of the maintenance of the system in being with a measure of economic dynamism under conditions of mounting complexity.

Similarly Kádár has evidently sought to define his own position by contrasting it with the role played by Rákosi. Thus instead of the massive personality cult pursued by Rákosi, which elevated the Stalinist leader to superhuman proportions, Kádár has consciously projected himself as a human, approachable figure, whose role in the system is that of *primus inter pares*. This strategy, which might be called a 'negative personality cult', should again be understood as being a strictly goal-rational application of a particular technique of image building. Thus Kádár permits himself to be gently satirised in the cabaret, but this serves to enhance his authority as a human figure and, at the same time, to establish the officially permitted limits of criticism. It is preferable from the regime's point of view to encourage the appearance of open criticism than to live with the genuine article.

Kádár's conception of the goals and the strategy of socialism is fundamentally a rather conservative one. He obviously identifies socialism with a high degree of state power. The state is generally to be regarded as possessed of a higher degree of rationality than society and consequently the autonomy of the state from social control can be legitimised in the name of this rationality. The uses of the power of the state include a degree of commitment to welfare objectives, albeit the emergence of differentiation and inequality are accepted as normal. In this context too one can find a more or less conscious attempt to contrast the Kádárist pattern with that of the enforced equalisation of the Rákosi years, while the more relaxed approach of the former serves the objective of maintaining stability by satisfying some of the aspirations of the elite for preferential treatment.

In his relations with the Soviet Union, Kádár has almost invariably been loyal and supportive. The one, almost incredible exception is the outburst in the midst of the revolution (for which the evidence is imperfect), made on 1 November 1956, to the Soviet ambassador, Yury Andropov, when it had become clear that Soviet forces were not evacuating Hungary:

> It is not important what happens to me, but as a Hungarian, I shall fight if I have to. If your tanks force their way into Budapest, I shall take to the streets and fight you with my bare hands.

It is equally clear from Kádár's public statements at this time that he saw the future of Hungary as socialist and Hungarian, that Hungary would not follow the Soviet model but find its own road to socialism in its own way. Arguably, these statements were made under the impact of the highly liberal Soviet statement of 30 October 1956, which gave the green light to significant deviations from the Soviet model, but for all that, Kádár's views at this time were far less pro-Soviet than at any other. In his interview with the Italian paper *Il Giornale d'Italia*, Kádár declared, in answer to the question, 'What type of communism do you represent?':

> The new type, which emerged from the Revolution . . . It is Marxism–Leninism applied to the particular requirements of our country, to our difficulties and to our national problems. It is not inspired either by the USSR or by other types of communism.

How much significance is to be attributed to these statements is uncertain. What is clear is that at all other times, Kádár had consisttently given his backing to whatever the Soviet line happened to be and to whoever led the Soviet Union.

In the aftermath of the Revolution of 1956, Kádár would have had little choice. Only the power of the Soviet Union held the Soviet-type systems together and his own power base was narrow in the extreme. He obediently crushed the aspirations of Hungarian society in the process of re-establishing Soviet norms and presided over the judicial murder of Imre Nagy, to whom he had given his full support during the Revolution. Equally, as Khrushchev launched the second de-Stalinisation in 1961, Kádár responded to this initiative with enthusiasm and, with an unconscious irony mirroring Rákosi's devotion to Stalin, became Khrushchev's best disciple. Arguably, Khrushchevism as a programme of more flexible political management appealed to him personally. He weathered the removal of his mentor in 1964 skilfully, expressed his regrets cautiously and then cultivated the new rulers in the Kremlin with more than a measure of realism. He did not make the mistake committed by Novotný of criticising the Soviet leadership for having failed to consult with him over Khrushchev's removal; equally, he avoided the sycophantic silence adopted by Zhivkov in Bulgaria.

Four years later, Kádár sent units of the Hungarian army along with the forces of the other Warsaw Pact states (except Romania) into Czechoslovakia, but simultaneously signalled that he had done this with reluctance. During the Warsaw meeting of July 1968, he adopted a moderate position and sought to persuade the other Warsaw Pact leaders to do everything to avoid using force. On the eve of the invasion, he talked to Dubček and tried to warn him of the dangers of the collision course on which Czechoslovakia was moving. After the invasion, Kádár withdrew from public appearances until after the last Hungarian soldier had left Czechoslovak territory. This reluctance to be seen as a hawk did not, however, affect his relations with Brezhnev and these remained cordial until the latter's death. To some extent, it would seem, Kádár was regarded as a trustworthy figure, who had successfully transformed Hungary into an island of stability and prosperity without running the risk of political heresy. Kádár's relations with Andropov appeared to be equally good – the confrontation of 1956 had been forgotten – but the evidence was circumstantial. His relations with Chernenko were decidedly uncertain in the spring and summer of 1984, neither positively nor negatively. It is likewise noteworthy that even though Kádár's position in Hungary has been beyond challenge for many years, he has always been careful to demonstrate Soviet approval of his policies, more one suspects to disarm critics of Hungary in other Warsaw Pact states than at home.

Kádár's relations with the élite followed a more or less parallel course. In the early years, he was undoubtedly a prisoner of elements whom he neither liked nor trusted, the relics of the Rákosi's period whose support he needed, but whose views he distrusted. Over the years, he gradually distanced himself from the dogmatists, but equally cautiously he weeded out his opponents only when it was unavoidable. During this phase, Khrushchev's overt support against the Stalinists in the Hungarian Party was essential. Thus throughout 1957, the least discredited member of Hungary's Stalinist leadership,

József Révai, sought to define the ideology of the Party in the toughest terms possible; but by 1958 his activities ceased and, in any event, he died a year later. But other hardline forces remained on the offensive and at least some of the pressure to launch agricultural collectivisation must be attributable to them. The subsequent removal of Imre Dögei, the Minister of Agriculture and a dogmatic critic of Kádár's, marked another stage in the consolidation of the leader's power over the Party machine.

From this stage on, Kádár's ascendancy over the Hungarian Party was unchallenged. He was able to effect a major broadening of his base of support by his explicit abandonment of monolithism, symbolised in the reversal of Rákosi's slogan 'He who is not with us, is against us', to the more neutral 'He who is not against us, is with us'. As far as the élite was concerned, Kádár recognised that the Party, on its own, was incapable of building a strong economy, that the co-operation of the intelligentsia was required to achieve this aim, and that the most effective way of reaching this objective was to provide the intelligentsia with access to the outer periphery of power. Gradually by this means the great bulk of them gained a stake in the system and grew to accept it and the benefits it provided. In a word, Kádár recognised that co-optation was more efficient and goal-rational than coercion. The instruments by which the loyalty of this supporting cast is sustained include the relatively loose definition of ideological commitment. Whereas under Rákosi, repeated demonstrations of loyalty were obligatory, under Kádár the construction of socialism is flexibly defined to exclude ideological activism. Thereby loyalty is earned and the intelligentsia backs the system in the same kind of cautious, graduated fashion that has become the hallmark of the Kádár system. Loyalty is secured and Kádár is regarded as the personal guarantor of the system.

This bonding of the intelligentsia to the system has been a characteristic facet of the functioning of Kádár's leadership. Above all through his successful persuasion of the Party machine that the co-operation of non-Party technocrats was useful to the Party and that their access to the outer periphery of power did not in itself represent a serious dilution of the Party's position. This proposition does, however, contain an implicit warning to the Party that the political price to be paid for ruling without the intelligentsia is too high for the Party to pay. In the event, the Party has been generally content with the trade-off, both in terms of the actual (still rather uneven) distribution of power and with the flexibility which implies that from time to time and from place to place more Party functionaries would have to experience serious cutbacks on their powers.

Where Kádár has pursued a policy quite different from Gierek's is in his reluctance to bend the Party machine to his will by filling it with like-minded people. While Kádár obviously demands loyalty and respect for his authority, he does permit a measure of variation within the Party apparat, as long as this does not spill over into factionalism. In fact, the almost astonishing latitude allowed to former Stalinists at the middle level of the apparat (at county Party secretary level, for instance) has meant that some local parties have been markedly less conciliatory than others and have implemented Kádár's alliance policy less than enthusiastically. Overall, however, variations have been kept within limits regarded as tolerable by the Party as a whole and, it can be presumed, by Kádár himself. The outcome has been an organisation that maintains a certain level of cohesiveness and is conscious of the limits within which it has to operate, namely the limits of Kádár's toleration and that of society as a whole.

It has been convincingly argued that the Kádár system rests on a bipolar equilibrium between reformers and anti-reformers, neither group being allowed wholly to eliminate the other. In the main, the anti-reformers retain the upper hand, but not to the extent of rejecting all change. In effect, change is, like so much else in Kádár's Hungary, restrained and cautious and is subordinated to the overriding need to preserve the power of the Party over society. In this sense, the relationship between Kádár and the Hungarian élite remains reciprocal. On the leader's side, he lends his power and his authority to the maintenance of the system as it exists and ensures that the necessary minimum of change does take place. Without this, the system would begin to decay, as happened in Poland. The leader also imposes the style of rule by which the élite is expected to exercise power. Thus excess is discouraged, a modicum of discussion is regarded as fruitful and, perhaps most importantly, the élite is prevented from overconsumption by being allowed to indulge in massive corruption. The limits of self-discipline are set by the style of leadership.

The leader's role also includes the determination of broad strategy. This is an area extremely difficult to analyse in the absence of adequate documentation, but the assumption made here is that Kádár is not and has not been the prisoner of the élite, but on the contrary plays the role of the ultimate arbiter between different tendencies within the Party. Hence it was Kádár who was responsible for the tilt towards reform that produced the New Economic Mechanism of 1968; for the push in the opposite direction that resulted in recentralisation between 1972 and 1978; for the renewed reform debate after 1978–9; and for the ending of the discussion on political reform in 1983. In all these instances, the leader is assumed to have acted in the interests of the system as a whole and of all of the actors as well. Thus Kádár is regarded in this analysis as the political actor with the maximum power of initiative, whose function it is to integrate the various political pressures produced by the system and to guide it in new or old directions. Failure to choose the most rational and effective option could ultimately result in the decline of his authority over the élite and the loss of trust in him in Moscow as well. To date, Kádár has performed this steersman role with efficiency and thereby has continued to accumulate authority in the system.

The relationship between the leader and society is much more indirect, but it does exist and can affect other relationships. Kádár's actual succession to the highest office can in part be ascribed to the outbreak of the Revolution in 1956, which underlined the bankruptcy of the leadership of his predecessor, Ernő Gerő. Even more instructive and less well known were the events of 1976, because these illustrate the sensitivity with which Kádár responds to popular unrest and his readiness to apply rapid course correction. As part of the recentralisation introduced in the mid-1970s, restrictions were placed on the private plot with the aim of reducing the profitability of this semi-private sector. The restrictions were primarily the work of the anti-reform lobby, which resented the degree of autonomy enjoyed by this section of the peasantry and which used the mounting income differentials between the urban and rural population as the pretext for the anti-peasant measures. The result of these was to drive large numbers of private producers off the market, with disastrous consequences for urban consumption, which had come to rely on the private plot for the satisfaction of the demand for vegetables, fruit, pork, poultry and eggs. Once the consequences of the restrictions became clear, and the threat of serious urban discontent understood, the measures were quickly undone and the enrichment of the peasantry again became acceptable as the price for pre-empting urban dissatisfaction. Once again, there is no documentary evidence of the actual role played by Kádár in these events, but continuing the assumption made earlier, it can be argued that his function would have been to push the course in the flexible direction, in order to ensure the efficient functioning of the system, regardless of the short-term plans of the anti-reformers. In this sense, then, Kádár used the pressure of social forces to discipline a section of the élite with the ultimate objective of saving the system from its beneficiaries.

The role of the military in Hungary is uniquely insignificant. Hungary devotes only around 2 per cent of its budget to defence spending – one of the lowest figures in Europe – and the armed forces are kept out of politics in both real and symbolic terms. It is almost as if Hungary was signalling that its contribution to the Warsaw Pact is something other than the valour of its soldiers – perhaps a not altogether unwelcome message seeing that Hungary has been on the losing side in every war in which it has been involved since the fifteenth century. There are important, less remote historical reasons for the low profile accorded the armed forces. Reluctance to rearm characterised Hungarian attitudes after the Second World War and in 1956, the armed forces remained mostly on the sidelines. Only a few units actually fought against the Soviet Union; nevertheless, this was the only time that communist armed and trained units actually took up arms against the Soviet Army. Soviet attitudes were, therefore, influenced by the events of 1956, as well as earlier developments. Hungary was the only Axis ally not permitted by Stalin to change sides during the Second World War; Soviet trust in the Hungarian armed forces was low; and Soviet fears generated by 1956 have continued to be influential. In a sense, it can be argued that the insignificance of the armed forces in Hungary today is the price they are paying for their inability to do anything about the eruption of 1956. A political solution had to be imposed by the Soviet Army and the Hungarian armed forces have been downgraded as a result. On the other hand, it is also true that this arrangement suits Hungarians well, both the élite and society, for which military virtues have a low priority. Military careers have little prestige and the most important function of the military latterly has been to provide an avenue of upward mobility in a context of minimal overall mobility. Military education, conscription, attempts to militarise society all exist, but they tend to be regarded as something to be endured. There is, of course, no evidence whatever that Hungarian politics is remotely close to a Polish-style destabilisation, but should this occur and should existing patterns be maintained, it looks as if the armed forces of the Main Political Administration or generally the Party in uniform would find it hard to muster the resources to mount an effective takeover.

THE FUTURE

Kádár's longevity in office raises the question of the future. Born in 1912, he could well survive for at least a decade and thereby be his own successor. Arguably, as he grows older he will follow the example of Tito and withdraw from day-to-day political decision-making in favour of acting as the final court of judgement between the various contending forces in Hungary. There is, however, some evidence that Kádár's wish to diminish his day-to-day participation is real. In 1972, on his sixtieth birthday, he all but announced publicly that he would like to retire, but was obliged to stay on because of the pressures on him to do so. There is no clear and obvious heir apparent. One by one, his closest supporters have left the political scene and those who have formed the object of speculation as his successors – Béla Biszku, Károly Németh and others – have failed to stay the course. In any event, the succession in Hungary will also be determined by what is happening in the Soviet Union and the wishes of whoever is leader there at the time. This factor underlines Hungary's relative powerlessness in the matter of leadership as an institution. Although Kádár's own personal power is solid and recognised, no one else can inherit this from him. Whoever the new leader of Hungary is will again discover that the three constituencies that he (unlikely to be she) has to satisfy – the Kremlin, the Hungarian élite and Hungarian society – are not always easy to reconcile, especially not at first. Thus the succession is likely to see the emergence of hitherto invisible power brokers, factional disputes, political uncertainty and the nervousness of society.

THE PRESENT HUNGARIAN LEADERSHIP

Political Committee (Politburo)	Function
Kádár, János (1912)	First Secretary
Aczél, György (1917)	CC Secretary
Benke, Valéria (1920) (f)	
Gáspár, Sándor (1917)	Deputy President, Presidential Council
Havasi, Ferenc (1929)	CC Secretary, Chairman, Economic Policy

Korom, Mihály (1927)	CC Secretary, State Administration, Legal Affairs
Lázár, György (1924)	Prime Minister
Losonczi, Pál (1919)	President, Presidential Council
Maróthy, László (1942)	
Méhes, Lajos (1927)	
Németh, Károly (1922)	CC Secretary, Chairman, Youth Committee
Óvári, Miklós (1925)	CC Secretary, Chairman, Agitprop; Cultural Policy
Sarlós, István (1921)	Deputy Prime Minister

Secretariat

Kádár, János	First Secretary
Aczél, György	
Havasi, Ferenc	
Korom, Mihály	
Németh, Károly	
Óvári, Miklós	
Szűrős, Mátyás (1933)	

Head of State

Losonczi, Pál	President, Presidential Council

Council of Ministers

Lázár, György	Prime Minister
Maróthy, László (1942)	Deputy Prime Minister

Csehák, Judit (f)	Deputy Prime Minister
Czinege, Lajos (1924)	Deputy Prime Minister
Faluvégi, Lajos (1924)	Deputy Prime Minister, Chairman, National Planning Office
Marjai, József (1923)	Deputy Prime Minister
Sarlós, István (1921)	Deputy Prime Minister
Váncsa, Jenő (1928)	Minister of Agriculture and Food
Kőpeczi, Béla (1921)	Minister of Culture
Oláh, István (1926) Col.-General	Minister of Defence
Hetényi, István (1926)	Minister of Finance
Várkonyi, Péter (1931)	Minister of Foreign Affairs
Veress, Péter (1928)	Minister of Foreign Trade
Kapolyi, László (1932)	Minister of Industry
Horváth, István (1935)	Minister of Interior
Juhár, Zoltán (1930)	Minister of Internal Trade
Markója, Imre (1931)	Minister of Justice
Somogyi, László (1932)	Minister of Construction and Urban Development
Medve, László	Minister of Public Health
Urbán, Lajos (1934)	Minister of Transport and Communications
Szakali, József	Chairman, Central People's Control Commission

(f) = female

7 Romania

MICHAEL SHAFIR

'Only a fool', according to Romanian popular wisdom, 'rejoices in a change of kings' (*schimbarea domnilor-bucuria proştilor*). Proverbs, however, are not known for restraining the average political scientist's enthusiasm, and the warning is likely to be ignored. Political succession, whether of kings or others will continue to make us rejoice with professional (not to mention other, less spiritual) satisfaction. Yet, judging by precedent, we should know better. This applies equally to specialists in Communist affairs, who occasionally prove to be good analysts of leadership and succession in one or more political entities, but who seldom match such performance by developing generalisations capable of standing the test of time and space alike.

In 1976 and again in 1981, for example, Andrzej Korbonski was persuaded that the transition from individual to collective leadership in post-Stalinist Eastern Europe should be viewed as irreversible and as bound to become institutionalised (Korbonski, 1976; 1981, p. 325). Myron Rush, on the other hand, contended Korbonski's statement, indicating that the move from individual to collective rule was but temporary, being eventually replaced by a return to the previous pattern of leadership. Yet in his own pioneering volume, Rush viewed post-Stalinist successions as a form of '*limited* personal rule' (Rush, 1976, p. 25; 1974, p. 14. Emphasis mine). Neither of those generalisations is applicable to the Romanian case. The transition to 'collective leadership', which seemed to have occurred in the wake of Nicolae Ceauşescu's succession Gheorghe Gheorgiu-Dej in March 1965 proved to be not only *reversible* but also hardly fit to qualify for adjectives such as 'limited'.

In the Soviet Union, the general pattern of high politics in the post-Stalin era has moved from 'monocracy' to 'oligarchy' (Hodnett, 1975), to be more precise from one in which leadership cohesion was achieved through manipulation and maintained through cultivation of the leader's absolute power combined with his lieutenants' relative insecurity, to one in which each consecutive party leader has wielded less and less individual power than his predecessor over policy-making, but managed to increase power over his peers within the period of incumbency (Archie Brown, 1980, p. 136; Martin McCauley, 1983b, p. 13). One implication of this evolution has been the relative increase in 'authority building' patterns and the lesser prominence of 'power consolidation' techniques. The former refers to the process by which a ruler attempts to accompany his grip on power by demonstrating his competence and indispensability as a leader. The latter, on the other hand, purports to that leader's skills to protect and aggrandise his dominance via purges, patronage-allocation and manipulation of the main institutional pillars of the establishment (Breslauer, 1982, pp. 3–4). Once more, however, Romania does not fit into the pattern. On the contrary, an initial phase of 'building authority' has been replaced to an ever increasing extent by 'power consolidation'.

This is not to be taken as implying that Romania does not share common systemic traits with other countries of the Communist world, nor that leadership and succession are not affected by factors present elsewhere in Leninist systems. To begin with, the leading role of the Party, inscribed in Article 3 of the Constitution, places the Party leader in a more favourable position than that of his peers to become *national* leader, since he is the personal embodiment of the force supposed to guide society at large. Consequently, although lacking any provision for political succession, Romania fits into the Soviet pattern, according to which the man appointed to head the Party eventually becomes the country's indisputable leader (Martin McCauley, 1983b p.14; Bialer, 1983, p. 43). A second, albeit related, common trait rests in the necessity for a new leader to master absolute control over the professional Party apparatus, although in the initial phase of succession this might prove a necessary, though not a sufficient condition for the purpose of gaining political primacy. Control of the key political institutions, such as the Politburo (in one nominational variety or another), the Secretariat, the Presidium of the Council of Ministers, the army and the secret police, are as essential in Romania for the purpose of acquiring unchallenged leadership as elsewhere in the Communist world.

The list is by no means comprehensive. Additional parallels can – and will – be drawn between Romania and other 'fraternal socialist countries'. On the other hand, the idiosyncratic nature of the phenomenon of personal rule entrenched on family promotions, being unique in sheer quantity (if not in quality), warrants concentration on its evolutionary development in any discussion of contemporary Romanian affairs – even at the expense of other important data or details.

LEADERSHIP, POLITICAL INSTITUTIONS AND POLICY-MAKING

When Nicolae Ceauşescu inherited the position of First Secretary of the Romanian Workers' Party in 1965, many Romanians must have wondered 'Nicolae who?'. A few years later, the question became 'Nicolae why?'. A relatively unknown (though by no means unpowerful) Central Committee secretary, with no formal education and no experience in international affairs, at the outset of his leadership Ceauşescu seemed destined for political mediocrity. Yet in less than one decade, he managed to become an absolute ruler, hailed as a brilliant and original contributor to the treasury of Marxist–Leninist thought, and Eastern Europe's most travelled statesman. To trace this performance, it is necessary to distinguish between the period of succession and of consolidation of power, which roughly covers the time span between the Ninth (1965) and the Tenth (1969) Party Congresses, and the subsequent period, in which the powers of the Secretary General became unlimited. The first phase necessitated the adoption of tactics characterised by cautiousness, and by an effort to establish leadership on authority-building patterns, directed at other members of the political élite, as well as at society at large. The second phase began at the Tenth Congress, when Ceauşescu's personal merits were praised by speaker after speaker, and the Party leader began to be credited with all the achievements of his country. It saw a transtition from reconciliation to confrontational tactics, and the institution (as well as the institutionalisation) of one of the most ridiculous versions of the 'personality cult' ever registered by history (Fischer, 1981; 1982).

As he inherited Dej's Party position, Ceauşescu was faced with powerful political adversaries – above all the members of the 'old guard' who could claim both seniority and closer proximity to the deceased leader. The 'collective leadership' included Chivu Stoica,

who took over Dej's state functions and became Chairman of the
Council of State, Ion Gheorghe Maurer, who continued to function
as Prime Minister, and Gheorghe Apostol, who had 'filled in' Dej's
Party position during the short-lived implementation of the 'New
Course' (April–October 1955), as only First Deputy Premier. The
most immediate threat to Ceauşescu's position, however, came from
Alexandru Drăghici, a man who had joined the Politburo together
with him in 1954, and whom Dej had used to check on his power
aspirations by sporadically alternating the two adversaries to heir-
apparent position (Jowitt, 1971, pp. 151–2n; 193).

At the Ninth Congress, in July 1965, it was decided to set up a
commission to investigate and 'clarify the political situation of a
number of Party activists who were arrested and sentenced many
years ago'. Published in April 1968 and resulting, among others, in
the rehabilitation of Lucreţiu Pătrăşcanu, the 'national communist'
executed on Dej's orders in 1954, the investigation led to Drăghici's
downfall. At the same time, it neutralised all Dej's other associates,
who had acquiesced in the former leader's 'illegalities', for the April
Plenum stated that 'a heavy responsibility . . . falls on the then-
members of the Political Bureau' (*Plenara*, 1968, pp. 64, 70).

It is more than likely that initially the decision to bring about
Drăghici's dismissal was reached by a coalition in the leadership, the
main purpose of which rested in checking his ambitions. As Minister
of Interior and head of the secret police, he must have been perceived by Dej's other successors as a common personal threat, what
could be labelled the Beria-syndrome. The threat was not novel, for
(were one to take Ceauşescu's word), already in 1956 an attempt had
been made to convince Dej to remove Drăghici from the *securitate*
(Ceauşescu 1968–9, vol. 3, pp. 194–5). Novel was only the power to
remove it. From this angle, the Romanian succcession process fits
into both Meyer's (1983, pp. 163–5) notion of a struggle *against*
power (rather than one *for* power) and into Breslauer's concept of
building authority. It is safe to assume that demonstrating his 'indispensability' to the other members of the 'collective leadership' involved assurances from Ceauşescu that the commission's findings
would not bear on their political status. And indeed, apart from
Drăghici's removal, no major personnel changes affected the topmost
leadership for quite some time after succession. This places in doubt
Korbonski's statement (1976, p. 18) that political succession in Eastern Europe is accompanied by a fast turnover at the top of the Party

hierarchy, as well as Valery Bunce's thesis (1981) that leaders in both Communist and Western systems enjoy the greatest power and authority in the *early* period of their rule.

To achieve political primacy Ceauşescu had yet to reduce the institutional power of his colleagues. To this purpose, he introduced a number of 'innovations' in the structural build-up of the Party, while also pursuing some of the more classical patterns of 'power consolidation'. One of the earliest innovations was the creation of the Central Committee's Executive Committee (EC), an intermediary body created at the Ninth Congress between the Central Committee and the top Party leadership (*Congresul al IX-lea*, 1966, p. 739). The former Politburo was now replaced by a Standing Presidium of only seven members. It is important to remark that none of the faces on this body was new, while the Executive Committee included only three newcomers to national leadership. It was, however, among the ten candidate members of the EC that that one found the future resevoir of Ceauşescu's supporters. In retrospect, the purpose of the structural change introduced in 1965 appears to have been to provide a mechanism for the advancement of his protégés who could not yet make it to the topmost echelons (Shafir, 1981, p. 610). Displaying remarkable political skills, the new party leader built an alternative leadership in stand-by position, without having to adopt confrontational policies. With the exception of one change resulting from the death of Defence Minister L. Sălăjan in 1966, the Standing Presidium and the EC remained unaltered between July 1965 and December 1967. As Mary Ellen Fischer indicates, promotions (of his supporters) rather than demotions was the pattern of personal change at this early stage of the Ceauşescu leadership. Out of 27 new members elected between 1965 and 1967 to the leading Party organs, not one was demoted until April 1972 (Fischer, 1980, pp. 219–20).

The CC Secretariat, however, only partially fits into this pattern. For while it is true that this body also remained unchanged till 1967, it is not less important to remark that already at the Ninth Congress, half of its members (Manea Mănescu, Paul Niculescu-Mizil, Vasile Patiline and Virgil Trofin) were Ceauşescu clients. Control of the Party machine was obviously the highest priority on the new leaders scheme for consolidating power.

On closer scrutiny, the innovation introduced in the Party's structure in 1965 turns out to be strikingly consonant with the classical model of the 'circular flow of power'. Such 'flow' is based on the hierarchy of Party secretaries, who are nominally elected by provincial and local organisations, but who, in fact, are appointed by the Secretariat, and thereby ensure the reproduction of the 'patron's' dominance over selection to the Central Committee and Party Congresses (Daniels, 1971, p. 20). It should, however, be indicated that control and promotion of clients were not initiated in Romania *after* the takeover of Party leadership, but *preceded* it. As CC secretary in charge of organisation and cadres since April 1954, Ceauşescu built a clientele among regional First Secretaries, many of whom would eventually make it to the top, replacing the Dejist team. Out of the sixteen men who held the position of regional First Secretary, eleven had moved into leading positions in Party or state hierarchy by 1969 (Fischer, 1980, p. 222).

Successions, as Sewryn Bialer has remarked, are periods when the new leader as well as his opponents court the general public and 'engage in old fashioned election politics, with its exaggerated promises and programs' (Bialer, 1983, p. 45). Romania is no exception to this pattern. From 1965 to 1967 'the new leadership enunciated policies characterized by caution and ambiguity', which could appeal to both societal forces bent on change and to conservatives. Ceauşescu, however, would outbid all others in this game: he 'asserted that economic policy would continue to stress industry and central planning, but promised "big investments" in agriculture' and economic reforms (Fischer, 1982, p. 19). In the realm of the arts, 'socialist realism' was replaced by 'socialist humanism', the advantage of which, once more, consisted in diffuseness. Since nobody ever bothered to define the new doctrine, each side could interpret it as it wished (Shafir, 1983, p. 44). Authority building, in short, involved appealing to as many segments of the population as possible.

For the time being, however, the balance seemed to incline in the direction of reform. From this perspective, the succession process appears to have laid the foundations of Romania's peculiar version of 'simulated change' – the 'multilaterally developed socialist society' (A detailed discussion of this concept is to be found in Shafir 1985). The essence of such change rests in the adoption of the rhetoric of 'participation', while in reality the party and its leadership remain firmly in control of all aspects of the socio-political arena. This rhetoric was first discerned in the 1965–9 period, when the language of 'democratisation' served the personal purposes of Ceauşescu to establish 'legitimisation by dissociation' (see below). The pursuit of personal power aggrandisement under the mask of 'democratisation', it should be added, was considerably enhanced by the country's political traditions. As far back as 1894, the founding father of Romanian socialist thought, Constantin Dobrogeanu-Gherea, was pointing out that the *pays légal* was liberal in its constitutional provisions, whereas the *pays réel* was managed by a structure of neo-serfdom (the title of his famous book published in 1910), hiding a situation 'worse in some aspects than that of autocratic countries' (Dobrogeanu-Gherea, 1977, p. 183). As it turns out, the lip-service which continues to be paid to the loftiness of 'collective leadership' by Ceauşescu, at a time when the cult of personality has reached grotesque proportions (*Scînteia*, 5 August 1983) is not necessarily a new phenomenon on the banks of the river Dîmboviţa.

Having established complete domination over the Party apparatus, and having neutralised his colleagues in the leadership, Ceauşescu could proceed to do away with a statutory provision first introduced at the Ninth Congress, which required division of Party and state functions. In the name of enhancing efficiency and avoiding parallelism, in December 1967 the Party statutes were duly changed, and the Secretary General took over the Chairmanship of the Council of State as well. Ironically enough, it was Stoica, forced to tear himself away from the top state position, who was required to introduce the motion that Ceauşescu hold the two foremost positions in the hierarchy jointly. To add insult to injury, but typical of the essence of simulated change, the 'innovation' was formulated in terms suggesting that it implied Central Committee (that is, widely collective) control of social and state activity (Rush, 1974, pp. 125–6).

It should be remarked that Ceauşescu preceded Brezhnev, Husák and Honecker in restoring the title of Secretary General (instead of First Secretary) to the Party leader, thereby making it clear as early as July 1965 that the top Party position entailed qualitative, not merely quantitative, hierarchisation. The assumption of the post of head of state translated this hidden implication into open practice. It signified more than victory over political adversaries, for the institutionalisation of personal power meant an important stage in Ceauşescu's quest to transform his leadership of the RCP into national leadership. It also signified institutionalisation of an endeavour to unify personal and systemic legitimacy and entrench both on national history and tradition (see below). Such a quest would eventually be epitomised in 1974, with the creation of the office of President of the Republic, Ceauşescu's official portrait showing him decorated with the ribbons of office and holding a royal-like sceptre in his hand.

Unification of the topmost Party and state positions is partially required by a Party leader's perceived need to handle contacts with foreign chiefs of states from a position of formal equality (Archie Brown, 1980, pp. 142–3). Some East European Party leaders display a tendency to devote much attention to foreign affairs, and Ceauşescu is certainly one of them. In a country where historical experience teaches that only cultivation of wide international contacts may hinder some unfriendly neighbourly designs, international prestige becomes also a source of domestic support-recruitment. On the other hand, such conduct may negatively influence a leader's hold on power. It does not, however, in Ceauşescu's case. The explanation must be sought in the power consolidation techniques adopted by the Romanian leader.

By the time of the Tenth Congress only three members of the former Dej leadership (Ceauşescu, Maurer and Emil Bodnăraş) were members of the Standing Presidium and only two additional left-overs (Leonte Răutu and Ştefan Voitec) made it to the EC. The Party Secretariat (Ceauşescu, Mihai Gere, Niculescu-Mizil, Gheorghe Pană, Patilenţ, Dumitru Popescu and Trofin) was totally *Dej-rein* (*Congresul al X-lea*, 1969, pp. 757–8). By November 1974, at the Eleventh Party Congress, Maurer had retired from political life (he was replaced as Prime Minister in March the same year by Manea Mănescu) and Bodnăraş died in 1976. Răutu (a Jew) was forced to retire (*Scînteia*, 19 August 1981) following a request by members of his family to emigrate, thus bringing to an end the process of 'Roma-nianisation' of the leadership started in the 1960s. Consequently, at the time of this writing, only Voitec – largely a symbolical vestige of the 1948 merger with the Social Democratic Party – remains from the Dejist team. When he became Party leader in 1965, Ceauşescu was the youngest member of the Politbureau. By 1974, he was one of the oldest in the leadership (Fischer, 1980, p. 215).

The leading team had been changed, but the younger protégés promoted in the hierarchy were not to be allowed to build too strong a politcal base of their own. One further consequence of the 1967 amendment of the Party statutes was the strengthening of Party control over the state apparatus at all levels in the pyramidal power. This included the county level, where the Party secretaries were to function from now on as Chairmen of the people's councils (local government) as well. (In 1968, the former Soviet-inspired administra-tive division was replaced by a new system, based on the historical 'judeţe' (counties).) The measure heralded the most 'original' Romanian 'contribution' to institutional innovation in Eastern Europe, namely the 'blending' of Party and state bodies which, according to the Secretary General, is bound to become the main feature of the process of socialist development (Ceauşescu, 1970–83, vol. 7, p. 506). However, it also opened a new phase in the process of power consolidation, for since 1971, a 'rotation' principle requires high Party dignitaries to exchange positions in the central, state and Party apparatus. No precise set of rules for this principle was ever set up, but the only leaders not affected by it appear to be the Ceauşescus. This innovation has allowed a constant check on possible power contenders who could become too powerful in their acquired positions. Promotions were now replaced by 'rotations', with the county Party chairmanship serving as one possible location for 'enriching experience'. A related technique rests in the frequent interchange between the government and the Party Secretariat.

A similar purpose appears to have determined a further change in Party structure, introduced in 1974. In March that year the Standing Presidium, whose members were the most influential individuals in the Party, was replaced by a Permanent Bureau, which was to be appointed by the Political Executive Committee (PEC), as the former EC was to be named from now on. The Bureau should have consisted of five *ex-officio* members from Party and state structures, a change which might have been rational from the point of view of administrative efficiency, since a smaller forum may reach decisions more rapidly. By January 1977, however, four new members were added to the Bureau, increasing membership to nine, while at present the number of officials occupying positions on this body is thirteen. (In December 1984 the Permanent Bureau was again reduced to eight members, apparently a further manipulative move, the purpose of which remains unclear; see below.)

Neither the Bureau, nor the PEC, however, is the real *locus in quo* of power in Romania. The former body is under the complete domination of the Party leader's 'extended family' (see below) and clientele, and includes not only full but also some candidate members of the PEC. The latter is too large to provide a forum for decision-making. Although the PEC's meetings are regular, their formality is striking and – what is more – 'guests' representing state or joint Party-state bodies are often invited to 'participate' in its enlarged debates. Archie Brown's generalisation, according to which a 'good general guide to the degree to which the General Secretary's rule is a personal one is the frequency or infrequency of meetings of the collective bodies charged with policy-making responsibilities' (Archie Brown, 1980, p. 137) does not appear to be applicable to Romania under Ceauşescu.

By the mid-seventies, the country was practically ruled by Presidential decree. One 'hare-brained' solution followed the other, with blame for failure shifted on to subordinates. This explains in part the frequent changes in the government and in the upper Party hierarchy which became characteristic of the Romanian system and by the end of the decade. Furthermore, Ceauşescu's assumption of the office of President of the Republic opened the door to the introduction of a further 'innovation': the institution of the office of Presidential Counsellor, comparable only to Stalin's *pomoshchniki*. Initially an honorific title bestowed on those who enjoyed dangerously high prestige (such as former Foreign Minister Corneliu Mǎnescu), this office became the true decision-making *locus* of Romanian politics. It is manned by officials who happen to enjoy the President's ear, and who move from there to the Secretariat, the Council of Ministers or to county Party chairmanships.

The launching of the July 1971 'theses' (the so-called 'mini-cultural revolution') marked the departure from the former reconciliation tactics *vis-à-vis* society and the return to mobilisational and dominational patterns. Albeit the rhetoric of reform was maintained, policy-making clearly reflected the personal options of the Party leader. Investments in heavy industry took priority over raising standards of living, and strategies of extensive (rather than intensive) development were pursued despite contrary declarations of intentions. Central planning, under strict party supervision, continued to hinder decentralisation and initiative, although on paper workers' 'self-management' had been introduced in 1977. By the early 1980s, these strategies brought Romania to the verge of economic collapse, which partially stemmed from heavy borrowing in the West, based on non-realistic estimations of repayment abilities through exports. By 1983, the country's foreign debt was estimated at some US$9.5 billion. Ceauşescu's 'solutions' to these problems were sadly familiar: extracting more resources from the population and lowering living standards. Food shortages were widely reported by foreign observers and bread had to be rationed in October 1981. Yet Ceauşescu remains faithful to the rhetorics of simulated change: the Romanians, he warned, were too fat because they ate too much (Colas, 1982; Berindei and Colas, 1984).

PARTY 'FAMILIALISATION' AND THE CULT OF PERSONALITY

It was certainly not accidental that three of those promoted to the Permanent Bureau in January 1977 were relatives of Ceauşescu: his wife Elena, his brother-in-law Ilie Verdeţ and Corneliu Burtică, a nephew of the President. They joined on this body Manea Mănescu, Maurer's successor as premier. Resigning in March 1979 for health reasons, Mănescu was replaced at the helm of the Romanian government by Verdeţ, who held the position till 1982.

Mme Ceauşescu is nowadays the second highest Romanian official. In 1979 she became Chairwoman of the National Council for Science and Technology, a position with ministerial status. In 1980, the President's 'revolutionary companion' became one of the three First Deputy Prime Ministers. What appears to be by far more important, in January 1979 she became Chairwoman of the CC Commission for State and Party Cadres, a position from which she may oversee the security of what is commonly referred to in Romania as the 'Ceauşescu dynasty'. The rising star of the family, however, is Nicu Ceauşescu, one of the 'steering couple's' three children. Born in 1950, the young Ceauşescu was 'elected' First Secretary of the Union of Communist Youth in December 1983, a position which bestows on him ministerial status as well. Previously, at the National Party Conference of December 1982, he had been promoted to full membership of the Central Committee. At the Thirteenth Party Congress in November 1984 Nicu Ceauşescu was promoted to candidate membership of the PEC.

It is almost impossible to provide a complete list of the Ceauşescu kin promoted within the framework of family power consolidation. Among the more prominent figures are Gheorghe Petrescu, Elena's brother, who has been a Deputy Prime Minister since 1982; Nicolae A. Ceauşescu, a brother of the party leader, who since 1983 holds the title of Lieutenant General in the Ministry of Interior; Ilie Ceauşescu, yet another brother, appointed during the same year Deputy Minister of Defence and head of the Higher Political Council of the army; and Ioan Ceauşescu, also a brother, who is Vice-Chairman of the State Planning Commission.

However, the economic fiasco of the early 1980s, accompanied, as it was, by the endemic personal corruption of Party and state officialdom, affected even the President's family. Burtică was expelled from the CC and from the PEC. Verdeţ was replaced as Prime Minister by

Constantin Dăscălescu, but unlike Burtică, he did not suffer total political eclipse. First designated Vice-Chairman of the Council of State, he was later nominated secretary of the CC and Chairman of one of the many structures of simulated change, the Central Council of Workers' Control of Economic and Social Activity. Burtică's sacrifice and Verdeţ's partial demotion were, however, immediately balanced by Petresu's nomination to the First Deputyship in the government, as well as by the comeback of the other brother-in-law, Mănescu, who in October 1982 took over Verdeţ's Vice-Chairmanship of the Council of State and was eventually appointed anew to the CC and its PEC. At the Thirteenth Party Congress Mănescu returned to the PEC's Permanent Bureau.

The phenomenon of party 'familialisation', while not unknown in other Communist systems, has reached unique proportions in Romania. It appears to be connected with both a continuation of behavioural patterns typical of a scarcity-conditioned peasant society and with the regime's monopolist ethos. Kenneth Jowitt, who first coined the term 'party familialisation', indicates that in such societies the 'corporate family' becomes a basic self-defensive unit. His analysis is partially based on Foster's notion of the 'image of limited good'. Typical of peasant societies, this image perceives the 'goods' as existing in limited amounts, from which it follows that 'an individual or a family can improve a position only at the expense of others' (Foster, 1967, p. 305). Party familialisation could thus be viewed as the epitomy of patronage (in itself, according to Z. Bauman (1979), a way of life in peasant societies) induced by defensive postures, in societies where one's sense of security is enhanced through the distribution of 'goods' to people whom one knows and trusts, and who, at their turn, are expected to watch over the family's 'political courtyard'.

Nevertheless, both Bauman and Jowitt indicate that latent or actual peasant mentalities are reinforced by the Communist organisational matrix of social and political life. According to the latter author, Communist-type forms of 'familialisation' are related to both the routinisation of the party's charisma and to the rationalisation of society (Jowitt, 1978, pp. 69–71). Yet 'familialisation' may have less to do with routinisation of party charisma (Jowitt 1983) and more in common with an effort to bring about the 'charismatisation of routine'. Ever since the early 1970s, Romanian leadership cohesion seems to be anchored in a continuum, one end of which is Party preemption of the political arena, the other the preemption *of the*

Party by the Ceauşescus. Simulated change is employed to the same purpose, for numerous combined Party-state bodies (the backbone of 'political innovation' in the Ceauşescu 'era') are headed by members of the leader's 'extended family'. The Leninist representation of society's 'real interests' by the Party appears to have evolved into the embodiment of these interests by the 'family' – *via* the Party. Whether such gross infringements of the 'Party norm' are to be explained by Ceauşescu's own peasant origins must, however, remain an open question.

'Charismatisation of routine' refers to the attempt to transform the banalities of personalised power over a bureaucratic structure into superhuman qualities and popular support. Such manipulated charismatisation (a *contradictio in adjectio* if ever there was one) finds it blatant expresion in the 'cult of personality' which has been known to plague the Romanian public sphere ever since the Tenth Party Congress (1969). By the mid-seventies, the cult had reached paroxystic dimensions, as attested by the 'leviathanic' volume published on the occasion of the leader's fifty-fifth birthday, which might have taught even Stalin a lesson in public adulation (*Omagiu*, 1973).

The manipulated character of the cult notwithstanding, additional factors contribute, in all likeness, to its proportions. At the outset of his rule, Ceauşescu acted in what Korbonski terms as the manner of 'a traditional Balkan autocratic, yet benevolent ruler' (Korbonski, 1976, p. 13). Some five years after his nomination as Secretary General, his leadership style had obviously changed. He had become the 'leader, visionary, philosopher, apostle, father, saviour, synthesis of Latin genius, personification of Daco-Roman tradition, and superman of dizzying simplicity'. These titles and many more, are nowadays bestowed upon Ceauşescu. The sentence quoted, however, is not from one of the thousands of articles or odes glorifying him. It is a quotation from Eugen Weber's description of the introduction to a volume of speeches by Romania's wartime leader, Marshal Ion Antonescu (Weber, 1966, p. 567). Like Antonescu, Ceauşescu is his country's beloved *Conducător* (leader), not to mention a plethora of other official and non-official titles. Both men did more than merely reflect tradition-rooted authoritarianism when they allowed and encouraged adulation. In all likeness, they were driven by personal inclinations.

Ceauşescu might have started the process of self-canonisation as part and parcel of manipulation aimed at consolidation of power. He may have cynically consented to national support recruiting gimmicks, of which his official presidential portrait is just one example among many. He ended, however, by taking his 'imperial role' seriously. In other words, as Meyer reminds us (quoting Marx) he became 'the serious buffoon' who 'no longer takes world history for a comedy, but his comedy for world history' (*The 18th Brumaire of Louis Bonaparte*, as quoted in Meyer, 1970, p. 7). The 'cult' in its present form may consequently be said to have escaped the control of those whom it should cultivate. It may no longer be Ceauşescu who manipulates the symbols of power, but rather the other way around.

LEGITIMACY

Upon assuming office, the new leader of the RCP could obviously not opt for building legitimacy on the Stalin-like tactics of 'legitimacy by association', the endeavour of a new ruler to cast himself into the true and only faithful companion of his predecessor. His colleagues' seniority and long association with Dej precluded such an option. Consequently, the new leader had to pursue the opposite choice, which required an effort to repudiate the more compromising aspects of Dej's inheritance, that is, the Stalinist legacy. Hence the stress on reform, on the 'democratisation' of Party life and on 'participation'.

Personal legitimacy was therefore pursued between 1965 and 1969 by adopting the Khrushchev-like option of 'legitimacy by dissociation'. *Systemic* legitimacy, on the other hand, required both having the Party, which he headed, appear as the main instrument of reform, *and* the preservation of Dej's nationalist legacy of the last years of his rule. The latter was the outcome of the outbreak and development of the conflict with the Soviet Union, as a result of which the RCP had managed to secure some genuine popular support for the first time in its history. Ceauşescu's dilemma rested in preserving Dejism while rejecting Dej and his Politburo. Building legitimacy and the power consolidation tactics reviewed above were obviously interconnected.

Ceauşescu's speech at the forty-fifth anniversary of the foundation of the RCP (May 1966) castigated Moscow's position *vis-à-vis* the Romanian Party *and* state in the interwar period, and included opaque allusions to the justice of the boundaries established in 1918, that is, to Bessarabia (Ceauşescu, 1968–9, vol. 1, pp. 352–61). The position adopted by the RCP upon the invasion of Czechoslovakia by Warsaw Pact forces brought its leader to the heights of popularity.

On his part, Ceauşescu chose to emphasise such support by allowing almost unlimited growth in the number of Party members, and thereby ignore altogether the 'dilemma of Party growth' (Hammer, 1971). The RCP became proportionally the largest ruling Communist Party, with membership (Shafir, 1985) reaching some 14.4 per cent of the total population and 31.0 per cent of the active population in 1982 (over 3 300 000 in absolute figures for 1983) (*Scînteia*, 5 August 1983). Yet failure in the performance of the economy, accompanied by the ever more blatant aspects of simulated change brought about a gradual erosion in legitimacy (Fischer-Galati, 1981, p. 15; Linden, 1981; Fischer, 1981). By the late seventies, Ceauşescu appeared to be making an effort to salvage popularity by creating artificial 'crisis situations', such as the intensification of anti-Hungarian pronouncements pertaining to the historical dispute over Transylvania, or the over-dramatisation of the 1978 dispute with the Warsaw Pact over military budget increases.

These pronouncements should be regarded as part and parcel of the RCP's leader's quest to create a synthesis of ideological and national legitimacy in his own person. Within this framework, in 1966 and 1967 he staged 'personal encounters' with ancestral predecessors, such as the Roman centurion of Sibiu, the Moldavian prince Stephen the Great and the Wallach ruler Michael the Brave (impersonated by actors) in a veiled attempt to project the image of direct descendance from the high school manual of national history (*Tribuna*, No. 1, 1966; *Scînteia*, 19 June, 18 July 1967). The Dacian King Burebista – as anyone who visits the Museum of Party History in Bucharest can attest – became by implication the founding-father of the RCP, while Ceauşescu would gradually be transformed into his direct descendant. In retrospect, the decision adopted at the Ninth Congress to re-christen the Romanian Workers' Party as the Communist Party of Romania should be viewed as similarly motivated, for it stripped Dej of the founding-father mantle, placing the garment on 'worthier' shoulders. In Weberian terminology, the evolution marked a pronounced shift in the direction of grounding legitimacy on tradition.

However, it is not Weber's distinction between rational, traditional and charismatic legitimacy that best serves the purpose of surveying the evolution of legitimacy-building under Ceauşescu. Rather, it is Bauman's notion of 'pre-modern' legitimacy that appears to fit the Romanian situation. For there can hardly be any doubt that from the 1970s onwards, Romania became a society where 'the ruler is seen as repository and source of authority, and instead of needing confirmation of his rights from another social agent, he enjoys the unique capacity of confirming by his will the rights of all other agents to demand and to command' (Bauman, 1976, p. 81). In other words, the personality of the leader had become 'the fountainhead of authority for an entire political system'. This is precisely how Paltiel (1983, p. 50) defines the 'cult of personality', which involves 'the establishment of personal authority *as against* the institutionalised authority of the party' (emphasis in original). The final section of this study will address itself to this aspect, analysing it in the perspective of the future of Ceauşescu's rule.

THE MILITARY, PARTY COHESION AND LEADERSHIP SECURITY

In February 1983 there were rumours in the Western press concerning an alleged abortive military coup against Ceauşescu (*The Times* 7 February 1983). Although these could not be substantiated, the promotion of the Party leader's two brothers in the Ministry of Interior and in the Ministry of Defence (see above), and the demotion of a number of high officers which occurred soon thereafter, might be taken as an indication of the 'ruling family's' reaction to some threat emanating from the officer corps.

The military have clearly been courted as a group by Ceauşescu. Their representation in the CC rose from three to nearly 5 per cent of full members, and from 3 to five and a half per cent of candidate members between the eleventh (November 1974) and the Twelfth (November 1979) Congress (Bacon, 1978, p. 168; author's calculations. These figures include the security forces.). However, they have also been subjected to close scrutiny. As former head of the army's Main Political Administration (with the rank of General), Ceauşescu is undoubtedly keen on maintaining Party control over the military. The Main Political Administration was re-organised in 1964 and replaced by a Higher Political Council (Alexiev, 1979, p. 21), which appoints political officers to units down to subregimental bodies (Bacon, 1978, p. 173). The Higher Politic Council is under the direct control of a section of the CC's Secretariat. Institutional supervision is, however, combined with personal supervision for Ceauşescu is also Chairman of the National Defence Council and Supreme Commander of the armed forces. Instituted shortly after the Soviet invasion of Czechoslavakia, the Defence Council is composed of *ex-officio* political leaders, as well as of some of the country's top military. Local defence councils, staffed by a similar mixture of personnel, have been established down to county level, in an attempt to combine professionalism with political loyalty (Alexiev, 1981, p. 9; Bacon, 1978, p. 174).

Albeit enjoying support among the army, the autonomous foreign policy pursued by the regime, resulted in lagging modernisation due to Soviet reluctance to provide the Romanians with advanced military technology and equipment. Combined with the doctrine of the 'people's war', which is promoted by the leadership and which must result in the decline of professional prestige, as well as with the employment of the army in construction, mining or harvesting jobs, these policies might have produced a sense of injury among some generals (Moore, 1983). To such motivation for attempting to force Ceauşescu out of power, one should, perhaps, add more mundane reasons, for although Ceauşescu's courtship of the military brought about substantial rises in pay for officers and soldiers in the 1970s (Braun, 1978, pp. 157–8), salaries of the military are comparatively poor in comparison with those of the security forces (Volgyes, 1982, p. 53). The latter, who are entrusted with both domestic and foreign intelligence responsibilities (Bacon, 1981, p. 207), remain an important pillar in Ceauşescu's structure of power, although the July 1978 defection to the West of Lieutenant General Ion Pacepa demonstrates that their loyalty is not to be taken for granted either.

The attempted coup of January 1983 (if it ever occurred) was not the first instance in which the military in Communist Romania acted against the leadership. In 1972 General Ion Şerb, former commander of the Bucharest Garrison and a Deputy Minister of Internal Affairs, was executed after passing information on Sino–Romanian military contacts to the Soviet military attaché in Bucharest. Soon thereafter a great number of officers in the army and in the Ministry of Interior were removed (Bacon, 1978, pp. 170–1). However, there is a distinctive difference between the Şerb 'affair' and the 1983 events, for in the latter case there is no indication of Soviet involvement. The Romanian officer corps nowadays have little contact with Soviet and other Warsaw Pact allies. Indeed, not only do the Romanians only nominally participate in WTO general staff manœuvres and allow no entry of troops to their territory, but, unlike all other members of the Pact, Romania does not send its officers for training in Soviet military establishments, (Jones, 1981, pp. 206–10), thereby minimising the danger of Moscow-inspired military involvement in moves against the political leadership. (The last WTO exercises with troop participation on Romanian soil were held in 1962. Romanian troops have not participated in manœuvres abroad since 1967. In March 1984 general staff exercises were held in Romania too, but only Romanian officers participated in that part of the operation.) Yet if the alleged attempt of January 1983 had no strings leading to Moscow, it is unlikely that such a *coup* could (or would) be envisaged without at least some tacit support among other Party élites.

During the 1980s there were several indications that the establishment of personal authority as against that of the Party is not proceeding without resistance. The personal security of sub-national leaderships appears to be affected by measures such as the decision that during elections, Party bodies should ensure that not less than a third of cadres should be people freshly promoted (*Scînteia*, 30 July 1974). The measure is implied to be part and parcel of the drive for 'party democratisation'. The turnover in Central Committee membership in 1979 exceeded considerably this requirement, indicated that along the 'rotation' principle, the mechanism is at least partially employed for the purpose of either checking the power of suspected uncontrollable elements or for promotion of those who enjoy the confidence of the 'ruling family'.

In a speech delivered in Mangalia in August 1983, Ceauşescu, revealed that there was resistance among activists to the policy of 'rotation' and that even *leading* cadres dared 'argue whether or not to fulfil a task, whether or not to acquiesce in leaving a certain county'. Such an attitude, he stated, was tantamount to 'viewing the Party and state work as if these were some form of [private] property, as if they were a bailiwick with which one refuses to part' (*Scînteia*, 5 August 1983). During 1982, not less than 14 out of 41 county Party secretaries lost their position (Bacon, 1983, p. 327).

How far up the hierarchical ladder does such resistance go must remain a matter for speculation, but Virgil Trofin's case, which occurred in 1981, would seem to indicate that Ceauşescu's failures in 'building authority' no longer make him appear in the eyes of part of the élite as 'competent' or 'indispensable'. Moreover, he may come very close to being regarded as a personal threat, since cadres expect the blame for failures in policy to be shifted on to their shoulders. One of the more capable Party functionaries, Trofin was at one time head of the CC's cadre and organisation department. He was eventually subjected to the 'rotation' mechanism, occupying different positions, his last post being that of Minister of Mines, Oil and Geology.

Following repeated manifestations of unrest among miners, as well as the non-fulfilment of targets in energy which were accompanied by the common practice of reporting more coal than actually extracted (Ceauşescu 1970–83, vol. 23, pp. 53, 89), the Party leader attempted to shift the blame onto his deputies, 'reorganising' the ministry headed by Trofin. At a plenum of the CC held on 25–26 November 1981, however, Trofin apparently refused to comply with the practice and absolve Ceauşescu himself of responsibility (*Scînteia*, 27 November 1981). He was expelled from the CC and is reported (Bacon, 1983, p. 327) to have committed suicide.

Following the convening of the Thirteenth Party Congress in November 1984, it took more than two weeks for the PEC to announce the composition of its Permanent Bureau, which turned out to be considerably smaller. At the previous Congress the matter had been settled in only four days. This suggests possible resistance among the higher Party echelons to Nicu Ceauşescu's meteoric promotion (is he destined to take over foreign affairs, replacing Foreign Minister Stefan Andrei, who lost his position on the Permanent Bureau?), and to the dismissal of the last ethnic non-Romanian (Banc, an Hungarian) from that body. Other members of the former Permanent Bureau, (Virgil Cazacu, Nicolae Constantin, Petru Enache and Ion Pățan), whatever the reason for their demotion, may fear the future consequences of this ominous move, even though they still retain some power.

It is against this background that one should judge the reports (albeit unconfirmed) concerning the abortive military coup of early 1983. For the time being, and given the dominance of the instruments of power through 'familialisation', the possibility of a move in the Party against Ceauşescu appears very remote indeed. For precisely the same reasons, it would be unwise to pin-point any particular Party, state or military personality, as the one bound to succeed him. Yet, as observed, there are indications that the security of the 'ruling family' might be less immune to an upheaval than it seemed a few years ago. It should not be forgotten that Khrushchev, whose legitimation and power consolidation tactics bear a striking resemblance to those of Ceauşescu, finally lost his position due to failures in his 'harebrained' campaigns and, above all to the insecurity of the apparatus induced by measures such as the 'systematic renewal' of cadres (Hodnett, 1981, p. 88). Ceauşescu, who instituted a similar process, appears to be so much bewildered by his own 'imperial' status as to ignore, just as Khrushchev did, that political clientilism is a *two-way* relationship. And if Khrushchev was accused, following his fall, of having set up a cabinet of friends and relatives, one wonders what the resolution of the Romanian CC would read like. On the other hand, and if Soviet experience is to serve as a yardstick, Romania's way out of her present political stagnation can hardly consist of instituting a policy of 'trust in the cadres'. Besides, one should never forget that 'only a fool rejoices in a change of kings'.

THE PRESENT ROMANIAN LEADERSHIP

Permanent Bureau of the Political Executive Committee (Party)

Ceauşescu, Nicolae (1918)	Secretary General, President of Republic, President, State Council, Chairman, National Defence Council
Bobu, Emil	CC Secretary
Ceauşescu, Elena (1919) (f)	First Deputy Prime Minister
Dăscălescu, Constantin (1920)	Prime Minister
Mănescu, Manea (1916)	Deputy President, State Council
Oprea, Gheorghe (1926)	First Deputy Prime Minister
Rădulescu, Gheorghe (1914)	Deputy President, State Council
Verdeţ, Ilie (1925)	CC Secretary

Secretariat

Ceauşescu, Nicolae	Secretary General
Banc, Iosif	Head, Cadres
Bobu, Emil	Head, Organisation
Coman, Ion Lt. General	Head, Military Forces and Security
Curticeanu, Silviu	

Enache, Petru	Head, Propaganda and Media
Radu, Constantin	
Radu, Ion	Party Organisational Matters
Stoian, Ion	Head, Foreign Affairs
Verdeţ, Ilie	Head, Economy

State Council

Ceauşescu, Nicolae	President
Ciocan, Maria (f)	Deputy President
Enache, Petru	Deputy President
Mănescu, Manea	Deputy President
Rădulescu, Gheorghe	Deputy President
Voitec, Ştefan (1900)	Deputy President

Counsellors to the President of the Republic

Ancuţa, Dumitru
Bostina, Constantin
Cetăţeanu, Mihail Ionel
Nedelcu, Marin

Council of Ministers

Dăscălescu, Constantin	Prime Minister
Ceauşescu, Elena (f)	First Deputy Prime Minister
Dincă, Ion (1924)	First Deputy Prime Minister
Oprea, Gheorghe	First Deputy Prime Minister
Avram, Ion	Deputy Prime Minister

Constantin, Nicolae	Deputy Prime Minister
Enache, Marin	Deputy Prime Minister
Fezekas, Ludovic (1926)	Deputy Prime Minister
Găinuşe, Alexandrina (f)	Deputy Prime Minister
Ion, Nicolae	Deputy Prime Minister
Petrescu, Gheorghe	Deputy Prime Minister
Totu, Ion	Deputy Prime Minister

National Defence Council

Ceauşescu, Nicolae	Chairman, Supreme Commander of Armed Forces

Ex-officio Members

Dăscălescu, Constantin	Prime Minister
Andrei, Ştefan	Minister of Foreign Affairs
Homoştean, George	Minister of Interior
Bîrlea, Stefan	Chairman, State Planning Committee

(f) female

8 Bulgaria

J. F. BROWN

Todor Zhivkov has been First Secretary – later Secretary General – of the Bulgarian Communist Party (BCP) since March 1954. He is the dean of Warsaw Pact Party leaders.

Indeed, since the Second World War, the ruling Balkan Communist Parties have experienced a remarkable longevity in leadership. The apparently indestructible Tito finally succumbed in 1980; Hoxha, departed in April 1985 after heading the Albanian Party since 1941. Gheorghe Gheorghiu-Dej of Romania died in his bed in 1965 after twenty years of leadership; his successor, Nicolae Ceauşescu is approaching his twentieth year as leader – an anniversary likely to witness yet another outpouring of orchestrated adulation.

Not that the early leadership years of these men were without challenge or incident. In fact, only Tito was supreme from the start, and that was only after he had narrowly survived his rigorous vetting in Moscow in 1937 and 1938. Hoxha, for example, would have almost certainly lost his bitter struggle against the Yugoslav-backed Interior Minister Koce Xoxe had he not been able to exploit the Tito–Stalin break in 1948. For several years the power of Gheorghiu-Dej, a 'home communist', was checked and undermined by a 'Muscovite' group led by Ana Pauker which, mostly Jewish, might even have had him purged but for Stalin's paranoid anti-Semitism shortly before he died. (In the event it was Pauker and her associates who were themselves purged.) So it was with Zhivkov. In fact, his accession to power in 1954 reflected a real regime crisis in that not only did Party leader and Premier Vulko Chervenkov have to step down from one of those posts, thereby beginning his slow slide into political oblivion, but also in that there was considerable disunity over who should succeed him.

Zhivkov assumed a formidable responsibility when elected to succeed Chervenkov. The Bulgarian Communist Party was the oldest in the Balkans; among its leaders had been Blagoev, Rakovski, Dimitrov, Kolarov and Chervenkov; many had held senior positions in the Comintern; Dimitrov had earned world-wide fame at the Leipzig Trial in 1933 and had become Secretary General of the Comintern. This internationalist tradition, which really meant serving the Soviet Union, was very important for the BCP – and still may have a residual significance. It inculcated that habit of service to Moscow which has continued to this day, a habit passed on from Cominternists and 'Muscovites' to a younger generation of 'home' communists having no direct connection with either the men or the circumstances of a half-century earlier (Rotschild, 1959; Oren, 1971).

The BCP's record in Bulgaria itself was less dramatic and imposing than it had been abroad. In an overwhelmingly agrarian country it could not compete with the Agrarian Union for the loyalty of most of the peasants. But it picked up some support in the aftermath of the disasters of the First World War, which it then proceeded to dissipate in the early 1920s. It was outlawed after the Sveta Nedelya bomb outrage in 1925 which involved an unsuccessful attempt to kill Tsar Boris (128 others were killed) and it was then that many of its leaders left for Moscow and Soviet service in the USSR and abroad (Rotschild, 1959, pp. 259–64). In the 1930s, in Bulgaria itself, it operated in the guise of various front groups and, taking advantage of the growing economic and political dissatisfaction, was able to do quite well even in elections obviously rigged in favour of the governments in power. In the Second World War, with Bulgaria an ally of the Axis powers (though never declaring war on the Soviet Union) the BCP formed small, partisan detachments which, well though they fought, had nowhere near the same impact as the massive Partisan movement led by Tito in neighbouring Yugoslavia. Even before the Second World War began (certainly well before it ended) the Bulgarian communists were having to surrender their pride of place in the Balkans to their Yugoslav counterparts. This was to add yet another dimension to that rivalry and enmity between Sofia and Belgrade which the advent of communism has certainly done nothing to alleviate (Oren, 1971, pp. 200–20; Shoup, 1968, pp. 144–83).

After the invasion of Bulgaria by the victorious Red Army in September 1944 the stage was set for a classic communist take-over which was to last five years. It began with what seemed a relatively minor communist role in democratically dominated coalition governments. But the portfolio's held by communists, particularly that of the interior, turned out to be vital, while the gaining by communists of the countryside and small towns, often by brutally violent means, was allowed to proceed unchecked (Oren, 1971, pp. 221–58; Oren, 1973). Then came the achievement of communist dominance, guaranteed by the presence of Soviet troops, and settling of accounts with the main democratic leaders. It was mainly the Agrarian Union that had to be destroyed, and this was done by a combination of division, subversion and terror, culminating in the execution of Nikola Petkov, the most popular Agrarian leader. Once the Communist Party had established its ascendency it was the turn of the 'Muscovites' to round on the 'home' communists. Again, the struggle was one-sided from the very beginning and ended with the execution of Traicho Kostov. Had he somehow survived this phase, Kostov, with his courage, energy and nationalist tendencies, might have returned to power during the Khrushchevian period of 'rehabilitations' and the subsequent course of Bulgarian history would then have been different: while not necessarily seeking to follow a Yugoslav course, for which conditions in Bulgaria did not exist, Sofia might still have preceded and even outdone Romania in the autonomy it was willing and able to prize from a grudging Soviet Union. But in a Bulgaria dominated by Stalin's Janissaries, Kostov was doomed. His execution was the dramatic culmination of a terror that had affected many Bulgarians of all political persuasions. But repugnant though this terror was, it should be kept in historical perspective. It was by no means unfamiliar in the history of Bulgaria and every other Balkan country.

The death of Dimitrov (in mysterious circumstances in Moscow) at the end of 1949, followed almost immediately by that of Vassil Kolarov, cleared the path to power for Vulko Chervenkov, Bulgaria's 'little Stalin'. It was, indeed, the high noon of the cult of personality in Bulgaria. But Chervenkov's undivided and unchallenged mastery was brief, cut short by the death of Stalin himself in 1953. And it was in these circumstances that Zhivkov assumed the Party leadership in March 1954 (J.F. Brown, 1970, pp. 23–38).

He was obviously a compromise candidate. Following the post-Stalin pattern in Moscow, with its division of premiership and Party leadership, Chervenkov had to divest himself of one of these two posts. He kept the premiership – as, initially, did Gheorghiu-Dej in Romania – probably because Malenkov, apparently Stalin's successor, had taken that post. He fully intended to retain the substance of power and this presumably was one reason for the elevation of Zhivkov. Assuming that the post-Stalin emphasis in Moscow on the legitimisation of the East European regimes demanded that a 'home' communist be appointed, then there were at least two other leaders of such provenance whose claims seemed to be stronger than Zhivkov's: Georgi Chankov, Politburo member and Central Committee secretary, and Anton Yugov, Politburo member and former Minister of the Interior. Both were senior to Zhivkov in age, status and following; both were also considered superior in ability. Both, however, because of their experience and personalities, had enemies. Zhivkov had far fewer. Nor was he likely to disturb the balance and pattern of control in the Party as a whole. He seemed an ideal 'safe' figure in a situation fraught with uncertainty and apprehensiveness, where change was in the air but the direction it would take was unknown and where many, in Moscow and all the East European capitals, hoped the change would be minimal or temporary. None more so than Chervenkov himself. Like Stalin's other appointees in Eastern Europe he obviously hoped to negotiate the uncertainties in Moscow, and to him Zhivkov must have seemed to present no danger. But Chervenkov, like others, reckoned without first the rise and then the unpredictability of Khrushchev. He cannot have anticipated Khrushchev's *rapprochement* with Tito in 1955, one of the latter's conditions for which was apparently Chervenkov's own political demise.

Zhivkov was by no means without experience. Though not yet forty-three when he became First Party Secretary, he had been associated with the Party since 1928 and soon after began his long association with the Sofia district and then the city Party organisation. During the war he was active in the communist partisan movement and after the communist assumption of power rose steadily in the Party hierarchy. In 1945 he became a candidate member of the Central Committee and three years later a full member. In Sofia he simultaneously held for a time the key posts of head of the city Party central committee, president of the city branch of the Fatherland Front organisation (the communist-dominated 'unity' front) and president of the Sofia city people's council. Never since have these three posts been held simultaneously by one man – a mark both of Zhivkov's growing prominence before, and his political canniness after, 1954. In 1950 he became a candidate member of the Politburo and a secretary of the Central Committee. The next year he was promoted to full membership of the Politburo. In 1954 he assumed the leadership of the Party, which he has held ever since (J.F. Brown, 1966, pp. 257–8).

All this adds up to solid achievement, especially in a man so young.

He had undoubted assets facilitating his progress. The lack of controversy surrounding him has already been mentioned; it was ideally suited to the circumstances of 1954. But other, more positive, assets were:

(1) the Party following, especially among younger cadres, he had been able to build while connected with the Sofia organisation. (A close parallel exists here with the career of Antonín Novotný in Czechoslovakia who became head of the Prague Party organisation in 1945.);

(2) he was a 'home' communist at a time, immediately after the death of Stalin, when 'Muscovites' tended to be looked on with disfavour by the new leadership in the city whence they derived this appellation. They were now seen as obstacles to legitimisation. Zhivkov's partisan record was an added bonus in this regard;

(3) he was not *directly* associated with the crimes perpetrated after the Second World War and which were such an obstacle to legitimisation. Here his great rival, Anton Yugov, as Interior Minister from 1944 to 1949, was especially vulnerable and his activity during the period was one of the multiple charges leveled at him when he was finally disgraced in 1962 (J.F. Brown, 1970, pp. 135–7).

Zhivkov, therefore, enjoyed the rare advantage in 1954 of being acceptable to practically everybody (everybody, that is, save the Bulgarian people, whose views on the subject were not solicited). The new Moscow leadership, though it can hardly have known much about him, had nothing against him and he seemed to personify the new kind of satellite leader they were looking for. (At least, *some* of them: the Moscow leadership was in disarray and the 'Stalinists', though on the defensive, were still powerful). In Bulgaria he was preferable among the 'home' communists to other, more abrasive personalities. To Chervenkov, facing up to the 'objective' circumstances caused by Stalin's death, he appeared to present little threat to the continuation of his authority. But not only was Zhivkov considered acceptable, he was thought to be malleable. Quiet, amiable, modest, a poor speaker, an apparent mediocrity, he was acceptable because he could so lightly be dismissed. But therein lay the mistake of many. A calculating peasant shrewdness, in dealing with friends and enemies at home as well as patrons in Moscow; a first-rate organising ability; ruthlessness when necessary; a knowledge of his compatriots; an ability 'to grow into his job'; the knack of surviving and managing the vicissitudes of Kremlin and bloc politics; these have been some of the qualities that have helped Zhivkov first to survive, then predominate and then gain grudging acceptance as a leader with both profile and stature.

Having sketchily described the political situation from which Zhivkov emerged, the reasons for his initial elevation, as well as the man himself, there remains now to analyse the main features of his long rule, stretching so far over three decades. Some of these features are characteristic, in varying degrees, of other communist states; others are more exclusive to Bulgaria itself. Some reveal a historical continuity between the communist present and pre-communist past; others tend to be distinctive to the communist background against which they unfolded.

THE CONSOLIDATION OF POWER

Zhivkov prospered because Khurshchev prospered. In the beginning it was as simple as that. He became First Party Secretary in a period of great uncertainty. The death of Stalin obviously marked a turning-point in the history of communism, the Soviet Union and its very recently acquired East European dependencies. But more than that no one knew. More immediately, no one could predict the outcome of the power struggle obviously going on in Moscow. Its outcome redounded greatly to Zhivkov's benefit. It was not so much that he backed the right horse – as a canny Bulgarian peasant he would have hedged his bets – but that to the eventually victorious Khrushchev, Zhivkov, along with Kádár, Novotný and (after an inauspicious beginning) Gomułka, was the kind of leader who might combine loyalty to the Soviet Union with an ability to revitalise, and thus legitimise, communist rule in his country.

Zhivkov also benefited from a combination of Khrushchev's personal dislike for Chervenkov – which the latter apparently returned with contempt added – and, as already mentioned, from Tito's insistence, as part of the price of *rapprochement* with Moscow in 1955, on Chervenkov's removal. Then came the Twentieth CPSU Congress and Khrushchev's secret speech. Obviously Chervenkov's position as Premier was now untenable and at the BCP's Central Committee Plenum in April 1956 Chervenkov bore the brunt of the

ritualistic anti-Stalin criticism and immediately relinquished the premiership.

The repudiation of Chervenkov, however, like that of Stalin in the
Soviet Union, was still by no means total. He remained a Politburo
member, became a deputy Premier, and between 1957 and 1958 put
down a literary revolt by some dissident writers in his capacity as
Minister of Education and Culture. He is also believed to have been
behind much of the fascination with the Chinese-type 'great leap
forward' experiments in Bulgaria in 1957. But this was Chervenkov's
last show of power. He could not long survive destalinisation and his
descent accelerated after Khrushchev's final victory over his opponents in Moscow in 1957. He was to retain much respect among Party
cadres for several years to come, but politically his role had ended.

After the 1956 April Plenum, which is now constantly invoked as
the BCP's own turning-point and proof of its capacity for self-
regeneration, Zhivkov could turn his main attention to the enemies
'within his own ranks' – that is, amongst the 'home' communists. And
here there is no doubt that Chankov was his first principal target. The
purge of the 'anti-Party group' in Moscow in June 1957 gave him his
pretext and Chankov, along with two other prominent but less
menacing associates, were stripped of all their posts immediately
afterwards. On the *political* scene Zhivkov was without rival (J.F.
Brown, 1970, pp. 58–95).

MASTERY OVER THE SECURITY APPARATUS

So much for Zhivkov's political rivals. What Zhivkov now needed to
do was to subordinate the security apparatus to his will, to smash its
status of *imperium in imperio* which had become one of the hallmarks
of the Stalinist system.

Obviously in the Soviet Union it had been Stalin who, through
Beria and Abakumov, had controlled the security apparatus. The
pattern had been similar in some of the newly acquired satellites after
1945. Rákosi, for example, and Chervenkov himself, directed their
security apparatuses in the liquidation of enemies, real or perceived,
inside and outside the regime. The security apparatus helped destroy
the old system and lay the foundation of the new. But it was in the
uncertainty and often the sheer disarray that beset the Party in many
countries after Stalin's death, that the security apparatuses acquired
that independence which the new leaders needed to break if their

authority was to be secure. The Party and the security apparatus had been two distinct organisations, with the latter, especially at the middle and lower levels, often terrorising the former. To this the Party leader (or leaders) had no objection – in fact, they saw it as an essential buttress to their own power – as long as they could ultimately leash so dangerous an animal. After Stalin's death it was obvious that some could not, and for several years the most important power struggles in Eastern Europe were those where the new Party leaders sought to gain control over their own security apparatus.

These struggles are sometimes seen as battles for power between the heads of the Party, on one side, and of the national security apparatus, on the other. This personalisation does indeed dramatise the importance of the struggle but gives little idea of its complexity and comprehensiveness. Nor can it take into account, for example, the Soviet role in this, through the KGB, about which so little is known anyway.

Zhivkov was faced with a difficult task. His main rival among the 'home' communists, Anton Yugov, had been made Prime Minister after the demotion of Chervenkov in 1956 following the April plenum. An able, plausible man, Yugov not only had a strong following among many 'home' communists but had also been Minister of the Interior from 1944 to 1949 when he had acquired a reputation for ruthlessness that totally belied his amiability of manner. More relevant in this context was the fact that Yugov's experience in both Party and security apparatus had given him a following bound to be considered a threat by a new leader like Zhivkov. Nor was Yugov the only threat. The Minister of the Interior from 1952–61 was Georgi Tsankov, and it was he, the experienced incumbent at the interior ministry, who perhaps presented the most immediate danger.

With two powerful rivals like this Zhivkov had to bide his time. He had to wait several years, during which he was able to build up his own following in the Party and to cultivate ever better relations with the victorious Khrushchev in Moscow. His opportunity came with the second great bout of distalinisation that began in the Soviet Union with the Twenty-Second CPSU Congress in October 1961. Zhivkov used this, not only to purge Chervenkov comprehensively, but also to disgrace him. Chervenkov, after all, was not only the mightiest living symbol of Stalinism in Bulgaria (the dead Dimitrov could not be molested without removing the whole arch of the communist edifice) but also still carried considerable prestige among the older Party ranks.

This decision to grasp the nettle was followed by twelve months of strife in the run-up to the Eighth BCP Congress in November 1962. It was one of the most disturbed and unstable years in the history of the BCP in power. There were three reasons for this: one was the aftermath of Chervenkov's downfall – his fall elicited much sympathy in the Party; the second was widespread opposition to Khrushchev's new effort at *rapprochement* with Tito; the third was the obvious preparation for the settling of accounts with Yugov and Tsankov. It was evident that Zhivkov did not have the power to master the situation alone. Khrushchev had to visit Bulgaria in May 1962 and during a most colourful tour not only urged the necessity of (while professing to understand the objections to) a *rapprochement* with Yugoslavia, but also left no one in doubt about his total support for Zhivkov and his preference for him over Yugov. With the stage thus set, both Yugov and Tsankov were purged at the Eighth Congress amid a welter of charges, most of them so extendedly retroactive that many Bulgarians must have caustically wondered how either of them was ever allowed to assume office in the first place (J.F. Brown, 1970, pp. 96–142).

RELATIONS WITH THE ARMY

With the fall of Tsankov and Yugov, Zhivkov's leadership appeared unchallenged. But only two and a half years after this great political victory there occurred one of the most bizarre episodes in the whole of East European history since 1945: the army conspiracy of April 1965 (J.F. Brown, 1965; J.F. Brown, 1970; pp. 173–81; Lendvai, 1969, pp. 235–9). Obviously, military conspiracies, successful and unsuccessful, were nothing new in Bulgarian or Balkan history: they had been the staple of politics in the region since liberation from the Ottoman Empire, and army mutinies had been a basic feature of the Empire itself. Since 1945, despite the communist overlay – very transparent in patches – there have been many examples in all walks of public life of historical continuity. Was the 'April conspiracy' such an example in the military sphere, or should it be viewed more in a specifically communist context – symptomising unreliability to the system? Also, should the crushing of the conspiracy be seen as the final step in Zhivkov's consolidation of power or as an isolated episode aside from the mainstream of political life? Finally, what did the conspirators want?

It is difficult to see the conspiracy's leader, Ivan Todorov-Gorunya, or his associates, being motivated by any disloyalty to the system as such. Most had good Partisan records and were convinced communists, perhaps of a more nationalist school than that represented by Todor Zhivkov. As to the past, much as they might reject their historical legacy, they were nevertheless heirs to it – including the habit of armed conspiracy. To many communist Bulgarians, self-assertion through conspiracy still came more naturally as late as 1965 than through the 'proper channels', where the chances of a fair hearing cannot have been thought very strong. As to the conspiracy's bearing on Zhivkov's consolidation of power, the fact that it was exposed and crushed obviously strengthened him further, but it probably should be seen more as an isolated episode than as an integral part of the political process at that particular time. In other words, Todorov-Gorunya and his group were hardly representative of a meaningful military opposition to Zhivkov. Discontent there was in many sectors of both regime and society, but the army conspirators were symptomatic rather than representative of it.

What they wanted is also a question inviting many answers. How far were they politically motivated? The proceedings of their trial have been a strictly guarded secret so far. No satisfactory, single, answer can be given. Todor Zhivkov himself may have been partly right when he described them as victims of confused and sometimes conflicting motives, of which a vague pro-Chinese sympathy (present in the Party, too, almost 10 years earlier) may have been one (*Rabotnichesko Delo*, 9 May 1965). One motive that should certainly not be ignored was frustrated ambition. At a time when 'home' communists were coming into their own (considerably later in the military than in Party and state) many deserving Partisans may have felt their services were not being adequately rewarded. The top military positions had long been the preserve of Soviet-trained officers, many of whom had fought with the Red Army. This was an understandable Soviet precaution, particularly in a country which, bordering on two western allies, was so strategically important to them. But by the early 1960s, partly because many 'Muscovite' officers were getting older and partly because the 'home' communist regime of Zhivkov was considered 'safe', the complexion of the military began to change too. In 1962, for example, in the cabinet reshuffle following the Eighth Party Congress, General Ivan Mihailov, a 'Muscovite' of distinction, gave up the Defence Ministry (under no cloud, whatsoever; he remained in the Politburo for the next two decades) and was replaced by Dobri Dzhurov, a Partisan general close to Zhivkov, who has retained the post to this very day. At the same time the disgraced Tsankov was replaced as Interior Minister by Diko Dikov, another Partisan general. Similar changes were taking place lower down and it was obvious that in a process like this many would be disappointed. Among them may well have been some of the conspirators, who had waited for the hour that, for them, never struck. In the Balkan manner, therefore, they would strike instead.

THE ZHIVKOV ERA AND ITS CHARACTERISTICS

Whatever the circumstances of the 'April conspiracy', its revelation and failure meant that by 1965 Todor Zhivkov controlled the four main levers of power: the Party; the state apparatus (in 1962 following Khrushchev, he became Premier; in 1971, he became head of state); the security apparatus; and the military. What might accurately be described as the Zhivkov era has so far lasted, therefore, about twenty years. Its main characteristics have been:

(1)   loyalty to Moscow, regardless of who has been in power there;
(2)   a 'surrogate' nationalism, mainly evidenced in periodic confrontation with Yugoslavia over the still emotive Macedonian issue and 'equal-footed' relations with both Greece and Turkey;
(3)   economic progress and rising living standards;
(4)   a willingness to experiment in economic and administrative organisation;
(5)   strong central control over cultural and intellectual life;
(6)   political 'conservatism';
(7)   the emergence of a technical intelligentsia – created, nurtured, even pampered by the regime – acutely conscious of need for Western contacts in the modernisation of their country;
(8)   the rise and fall of several putative 'crown princes';
(9)   the phenomenon of Zhivkov's daughter, Lyudmila;
(10) the steady evolution of Zhivkov himself as a national leader.

A full discussion of all these points would, of course, involve a survey of twenty years of Bulgarian history hardly relevant to the subject of this volume. Only cursory treatment, therefore, need be given to some. The impressive figures for economic progress, for example, can be found in the Bulgarian press and the official statistical year-books, the reliability of the latter having apparently increased considerably over the last ten to fifteen years. The usual reservations about the significance of these figures, of course, should be kept in mind. The Bulgarian starting base was very low, probably lower than for any East European country except Albania. Large annual increases in heavy industry were only to be expected and, though these increases have been reduced considerably compared with the 1950s and 1960s, at about 4 per cent for the economy as a whole since the beginning of the 1980s they remain impressive. (See *Neue Zürcher Zeitung*. 9 November 1983, for a good survey of the economy.) A more serious reservation is that in adopting the classic Stalinist autarkical pattern of all-round industrial growth, the Bulgarian economy, like most other East European economies, has not deployed its resources to the best advantage. The great Stalinist metallurgical showpiece at Kremikovtsi, near Sofia, for example, has deservedly been the subject of much pejorative comment for many Bulgarians. More recently the disadvantages of 'bigness' have been realised by many Bulgarian officials (see *The Economist*, 4–11 November 1983) but, of course, once these huge complexes are there, the only course available is the thankless one of trying to rationalise the irrational.

In the meantime the standard of living, consumer supplies, the real purchasing power of most of the population, has increased perceptibly during the last decade. This has been due to more and better used investments in agriculture, more incentives to the peasants themselves, more investments in light industry, and a trading policy that has not led to export drives at the expense of the domestic consumer to anywhere near the same extent as those applied by neighbouring Romania and, more recently, by the Jaruzelski regime in Poland. Certainly, visitors to Sofia and other large Bulgarian cities without exception come away impressed by the look of prosperity contemporary Bulgaria presents. The contrast with Romania is often drawn. This is nothing new. But more recently Bulgaria has been contrasted favourably with even the most prosperous parts of southern Yugoslavia and with many parts of Greece. That *is* new and is a reflection of the improvement in Bulgaria's economic concepts, planning, resource allocation and management – and to Moscow's relative generosity.

The regime's 'conservatism' in politics has become a hallmark of Zhivkov's rule. The strictest insistence on democratic centralism has stifled not only dissent in the Party but also constructive discussion or criticism. Similarly with culture. After the brief flowering of intellectual and cultural dissent after the CPSU's Twentieth Congress and the BCP's April plenum – dissent with an obvious political impact – had been crushed (J.F. Brown, 1970, pp. 244–51), the Bulgarian cultural scene remained little more than a desert for some twenty years until Lydmila Zhivkov burst on the scene. Under her patronage and protection the arts briefly blossomed again, but they had become apolitical. True, they defied the ideological tenets of which Suslov in the Soviet Union and Todor Pavlov in Bulgaria were the high priests, just as, on a bigger scale and higher level, much of Polish drama, music and art had done throughout the Gomułka and Gierek periods. Socialist realism was largely ignored. But political connotations were still carefully watched. Literature, the art form most vulnerable to politics, felt little relaxation from the censor's grip.

Politically and culturally, therefore, Zhivkov's Bulgaria has deserved the obscurity into which the rest of the world has usually cast it. But in economic and administration reorganisation and reform it has deserved far more attention than it has received. From the 'great leap forward' experiments of 1957–60 which, in spite of denials, obviously had a Chinese flavour (J.F. Brown, 1970, pp. 83–95), to the most recent spate of economic reform first heralded in 1977 and still continuing, the Bulgarian regime has shown a receptive and innovative spirit that has quite belied the dull *Moskautreu*, political reputation it has acquired. In 1964 it announced an economic reform very similar to that elaborated by Ota Šik and his followers in Czechoslovakia (J.F. Brown, 1970, pp. 160–72). Parts of the reform began to be applied experimentally over the next four years but the entire programme was abrogated shortly *before* the Soviet invasion of Czechoslovakia. The Czechoslovak example had proved too dangerous politically. Šik's dictum that political reform must accompany economic had frightened too many cadres and threatened too many vested interests. It was almost certainly with relief, rather than regret, that Zhivkov announced the abrogation of the Bulgarian reform in July 1968.

After August 1968, except in Hungary, the term 'reform' acquired a pejorative, political connotation and dropped out of fashion in Eastern bloc terminology. 'Reorganisation' or 'new mechanism' became the more fashionable clichés or euphemisms. And here the Zhivkov regime came into its own. It came closer to any country in Comecon, for example, including the Soviet Union, to putting into reality the classic Bolshevik notion of *agrogorods*. This was through the nation-wide introduction of agro-industrial complexes in the early 1970s, for which the large-scale merger of collective farms at the end of the 1950s had laid the foundation. The introduction of the agro-industrial complexes necessitated a massive reorganisation of administrative districts, local government and Party administration generally. This was also carried out during the 1970s (R.N. 1977).

This bare outline gives no idea of the extent of change and dislocation involved. Certainly by the beginning of the 1980s Bulgaria was a very different place administratively, organisationally, and in some respects in sheer physical appearance than it had been fifteen years earlier. And yet industrial and agricultural production does not seem to have greatly suffered from these profound changes. Partially, of course, it may have been a case of '*plus ça change . . .*' But part of the explanation certainly lies in the sound preparation and implementation of the reorganisations and – probably even more important – the introduction of bonus and incentive schemes (particularly in agriculture but in parts of industry also) which closely followed the reorganisations and which stimulated both production and productivity. Further incentive schemes were introduced at the beginning of 1984.

These schemes were but the latest in a series of reforms of economic management and methods, the most important of which was the so-called New Economic Mechanism introduced in 1982 (*Rabotnichesko Delo*, 15 January 1982). The Bulgarian reform is, indeed, similar to the Hungarian not only in name but also in some basic points. It has been heartily welcomed by the Hungarians, though partly, one feels, because the Budapest leaders are anxious not to appear totally isolated in their reformist tendencies among their allies. Radio Budapest (2 May 1984) described the Bulgarian reforms principles as follows: the achievement of plan fulfilment through economic incentives and sanctions; the use of commodity and monetary relations; profit as the criterion of economic performance; the steady abolition of subsidies on consumer goods. There is some truth in Radio Budapest's description, but a loud note of caution must be sounded against seeing too close a similarity between the Bulgarian and Hungarian reforms. In essentials like the freedom of the price mechanism, degree of decentralisation, latitude for private entrepreneurship – to mention only three – the Bulgarian remains conservative; closer, in fact, to the East German model of reform than the Hungarian (Hudson, 1982; *Neue Zürcher Zeitung*, 3–4 June 1984).

But, still it remains impressive in its comprehensiveness. The question is whether it will be implemented with the required consistency by a leadership which remains *politically* conservative. Much could depend on the lead given by Moscow. If the new Soviet leaders demonstrate a pronounced distrust of domestic experiment it is quite likely that these promising Bulgarian beginnings of the 1980s will go the same way as those of the 1960s. Or, if the success of the economic reform begins to prompt demands for political change as is the case in Hungary, then the brakes will almost certainly be applied.

RELATIONS WITH MOSCOW

The reference to the lead from Moscow inevitably draws attention to the Bulgarian link with the Soviet Union – probably the most conspicuous aspect of Todor Zhivkov's rule to outside observers. The strength of the link is obvious. Zhivkov himself loses no opportunity to stress it, often in terms of more fulsome (or embarrassing) subservience than any other East European leader.

The question here is not about the link itself but about why the Bulgarian leaders have acquiesced in making it so strong and at times appear to have clamoured to make it even stronger. Has is been the BCP's internationalist tradition, personified best by Dimitrov both during and after his Comintern days? What is good for the Soviet Union is good for all communists! Has it been internal weakness on Zhivkov's part, compelling constant resort to the Soviet crutch? Or has there been a strong element of calculation in Bulgaria's loyalty – a calculation that has unquestionably brought 'most favoured nation' treatment in many aspects of economic relations? Like every other junior member of the Warsaw Pact alliance Bulgaria has had its own particular bargaining power with Moscow. As mentioned earlier, it is of great strategic importance, and since the early 1960s it has been the Soviet Union's ony dependable ally in the Balkans. These two factors alone represent real leverage.

It is possible that all three factors have played a part in strengthening the link with Moscow but that some are less relevant now than they were (J.F. Brown, 1970, pp. 263–9). The internationalist tradition still perhaps plays a role, but obviously a smaller one than a half century ago. In the 1950s and for several years during the 1960s Zhivkov was, indeed, far from secure and without Khrushchev's support he may not have survived. The 'weakness' theory, therefore, may have been plausible a generation ago. What remains stronger than ever now is the element of calculation. For the last twenty years this would seem to have been the strongest motive, and many Bulgarians, when they compare their lot with that of the Romanians (or many Yugoslavs for that matter) and see the meagre fruits that full or partial independence has brought, might not be dissatisfied with the results of the Soviet connection.

But few embrace it with that affectionate pro-Russian fervour which some fleeting travellers see as the main (in fact, the only) characteristic of the Bulgarian nation. The Bulgarian–Russian relationship is a complex one. Its most relevant aspect in this context is that, to a nation that believes itself cruelly wronged by history, Russia is seen as the country that has done it the least harm and, conceivably, might yet help it set right some of the wrongs it has suffered. The 'San Stefano' psychosis is still alive in Bulgaria the gains of the treaty (1878) were largely lost at the Congress of Berlin (1878) – not militantly so, but still flickeringly enough, even among the young, to make it a political factor of consequence.

And it is this psychosis that makes other aspects of Zhivkov's foreign policy so relatively popular. The most popular of all is the firmness on the Macedonian national issue that has antagonised the Yugoslavs for so long. Also popular are the firm, correct, 'equal-footing' relations with Greece and Turkey. These, after all, are the three nations (for Yugoslavs read Serbs) that have historically been Bulgaria's greatest enemies. What matters for most Bulgarians is the demeanour of their leaders towards *them*, not towards Russia. And here Zhivkov can hardly be faulted. He has adopted a form of 'surrogate' nationalism in relations with his neighbours which, to many, must more than compensate for the subservience to Moscow.

What of relations with the West? Again, the misconception has taken root that Sofia has no policy towards the West, that its Western relations are simply a reflex of Soviet policy. There is, indeed, much evidence to support the view: Bulgaria's prompt follow-my-leader withdrawal from the Los Angeles Olympics is a topical case in point. But, again, there are nuances too easily overlooked. Within a framework of loyal and ostentatious support for Moscow on all important foreign policy issues, the Bulgarians have on occasion quite clearly sought to secure their own national advantage. They were obviously receptive to West German pre-*Ostpolitik* overtures in the 1960s, for example, when the Soviet Union and the northern tier states were decidedly cool (J.F. Brown, 1970, pp. 284–5). During the periodic Soviet-inspired Balkan peace initiatives the willingness of Bulgaria to act as Moscow's proxy has been partly due to the opportunity for self-assertion which the situation presented. During the decade of *détente* in the 1970s Bulgaria pursued brisk economic relations with the West, particularly Western Europe, running up a sizeable debt while doing so – now steadily being reduced. It was during this period of *détente* that Bulgaria's growing economic and technical intelligentsia were first fully exposed to Western industry and technology. Obviously they were not converted to capitalism, but they recognised many aspects of Western superiority over the Soviet Union in science, technology and industrial method. And now they obviously wish that the hardening of East–West relations should not affect Bulgaria's economic relations with the West, particularly its access to Western technology. Equally important, they appear to have suffered no discouragement to their attitudes from the political leadership in Sofia. This reorientation of the economic and technical intelligentsia, in Bulgaria as well as in other East European countries, could be of lasting importance – one of the most significant results of the *détente* process.

THE TWILIGHT OF THE ZHIVKOV ERA

Born in 1911, Zhivkov is believed to be physically fit and (certainly by Soviet standards of longevity) if not still in his prime then still some distance from dotage. (He is also much younger than some previous members of the Bulgarian Politburo itself who remained rooted in office till into their eighties.) Like Kádár, Husák and Honecker he could continue for several years yet, assuming lighter duties and devolving the heavier responsibilities onto others and, most important, grooming his eventual successor.

Nowhere in Eastern Europe have the dangers of detecting an heir-presumptive been more apparent than in Bulgaria. This applies particularly to those men who have appeared to be filling that role. A handful of likely candidates have shone and then gone, beginning with Mitko Grigorov, who led the onslaught on Anton Yugov in 1962, flourished for a while and then found himself on the outer edge of the *nomenklatura* as ambassador to the Court of St James. (He is now back in Sofia as a vice-president of the State Council, nearer, but not closer, to the centre of power). He was followed by Luchezar Avramov at the end of the 1960s, an able official who apparently fell foul of Zhivkov for being too reformist too soon. The best prospect of all seemed to be Ivan Abadzhiev, a tough young *apparatchik*, former Komsomol head, who was sent to the Vratsa district, north of Sofia, towards the end of 1967 to clear out the strong remnants of support still existing for the army conspirators of April 1965, whose base had been in Vratsa. Abadzhiev cleared out this hornets' nest and was subsequently promoted to full membership of the Politburo and to the Central Committee Secretariat. But in July 1974 he was comprehensively purged, presumably because his reach for power exceeded his grasp. The meteoric rise of Lyudmila Zhivkov led many to assume that she would succeed her father, just as many in Romania assume (and fear) that Ceauşescu's son, the unspeakable 'Nicu', is being groomed to succeed in his own father (and mother). Even more recently the purge in 1983 of Politburo member and Central Committee secretary Alexander Lilov has removed yet another putative contender.

At present, then, predictions are scarce. The second man in the regime as a whole is clearly Premier Grisha Filipov – able, ruthless, disliked, with excellent Soviet connections. He seems to have evolved into an economic reformer, since there is no doubt that he is in charge of implementing the ambitious reform now in operation. But, in terms of an essentially political succession, Filipov's long experience as an economic official would appear to be a disadvantage. It has now become usual in the Soviet Union and Eastern Europe that economic experience is the avenue to the premiership, while Party cadre experience is essential for the Party leadership. This would obviously count against Filipov. But, though usual, the pattern is not universal, and in any uncertain situation after Zhivkov's demise Filipov's general experience, forceful personality and Soviet connections might stand him in good stead. He could move over to the Party, with the extremely able Andrei Lukanov, who personifies the new economic intelligentsia, assuming the premiership. On the other hand, Ognyan Doynov, Politburo and Secretariat member, as well as Minister for Machine Building is becoming increasingly prominent. Otherwise, a relative newcomer, Chudomir Alexandrov, is worth watching. The extensive personnel reshuffle in January 1984 took him out of the Central Committee Secretariat but made him a full Politburo member and First Deputy Prime Minister. Little is known of him. He still has time to distinguish or discredit himself. As number two in the government, he is also in potential conflict with Filipov. This may have been deliberately designed by Zhivkov both to test Alexandrov's mettle and to put a check on the burgeoning Filipov.

It would be typical of Zhivkov if it were. He has been thirty years at the top and became a master politician after a most difficult apprenticeship. He has handled Moscow and his own Party, each in its different way, with consummate skill and has brought his country into a state of relative contentment and prosperity. But what he has achieved is still brittle. The foundations of the edifice he has done so much to build are not yet solid. After him the Bulgarian Party could revert to the factionalism of the 1940s and 1950s. Economic and foreign policy could lose the sureness of touch it has recently acquired. The final verdict on Todor Zhivkov must be reserved until it is seen what arrangement he has made to secure what has been achieved. Any effort he does make may, of course, come to nothing. But he has yet to show he is prepared to make it.

THE PRESENT BULGARIAN LEADERSHIP

Politburo	Function
Zhivkov, Todor (1911)	Secretary General, President
Alexandrov, Chudomir (1936)	First Deputy Prime Minister
Balev, Milko (1920)	CC Secretary, international relations
Bozhinov, Todor (1931)	Deputy Prime Minister; Minister of Energy and Raw Material Resources
Dzhurov, Dobri General (1916)	Minister of National Defence
Filipov, Grisha (1919)	Prime Minister
Kubadinski, Pencho (1918)	Chairman, Fatherland Front; social issues
Mladenov, Petar (1936)	Minister of Foreign Affairs
Todorov, Stanko (1920)	Chairman, National Assembly
Yotov, Yordan (1920)	Editor in Chief, *Rabotnichesko Delo*; also in charge of BCP history and contacts with non-ruling Western CPs

Candidate Members

Atanasov, Georgi (1933)	CC Secretary, party and youth organisations
Bonev, Stanish (1931)	Deputy Prime Minister: Chief, planning
Dyulgerov, Petar (1929)	Chairman, trade unions
Lukanov, Andrei (1938)	Deputy Prime Minister; foreign economic relations
Stoichkov, Grigor (1926)	Deputy Prime Minister; territorial, administrative planning
Stoyanov, Dimitar (1928)	Minister of the Interior
Yordanov, Georgi (1934)	Deputy Prime Minister; culture

Secretariat

Zhivkov, Todor	Secretary General
Atanásov, Georgi	Head, party and youth organisations
Balev, Milko	Head, international relations
Doynov, Ognyan (1935)	Head, economy
Hristov, Emil (1924)	Head, economic and social affairs
Mihailov, Stoyan (1930)	Head, ideology
Stanishev, Dimitar (1924)	Head, foreign relations
Tsanov, Vasil (1922)	Head, agriculture
Zarev, Kiril (1926)	Head, planning

Council of Ministers

Filipov, Grisha	Prime Minister

Alexandrov, Chudomir	First Deputy Prime Minister
Bonev, Stanish	Deputy Prime Minister
Bozhinov, Todor	Deputy Prime Minister
Karamanev, Georgi (1931)	Deputy Prime Minister
Lukanov, Andrei	Deputy Prime Minister
Stoichkov, Grigor	Deputy Prime Minister
Yordanov, Georgi	Deputy Prime Minister
Zarev, Kiril	Deputy Prime Minister

Council of State

Zhivkov, Todor	Chairman (President)

National Defence Committee

Zhivkov, Todor	Chairman

Notes

1. Between 1948–9 and 1971 the National Defence Committee was called the Main Military Council and it is not known under whose jurisdiction it had been placed. Since 1971 it has been attached to the Council of State; no other details are available.
2. Angel Tsanev, former Minister of the Interior (July 1971–April 1973) and Candidate Member of the Politburo (November 1966–July 1973), was mentioned as having been deputy Chairman of the National Defence Committee between April and July 1973. Since Tsanev lost his candidate membership of the Politburo and his membership of the Central Committee in July 1973, no replacement has been made publicly known.

9 Albania*

PATRICK ARTISIEN

The introductory section of this paper addresses itself to the salient manifestations of Albania's isolation, as it is the author's belief that centuries of foreign occupation combined with geographical isolation from the outside world have influenced significantly the domestic and foreign policies of the post-war administration. Derived from the above is the proposition that Ramiz Alia will be unwilling to break away from the siege mentality of the Hoxha leadership. Ramiz Alia and the younger generation of leaders who were trained in almost complete isolation from the outside world have been carefully selected for their endorsement of a strict authoritarian system, and thus will have little incentive to innovate in the fields of ideology and policy.

The roots of Albania's isolation are essentially to be found in its geography and past history. The mountainous terrain, poor communications and transport links to the outside world have strengthened an acute nationalism and mistrust of outsiders fostered by long periods of foreign occupation and the covetous policies of neighbouring states. Every schoolchild in Albania is taught the significance of the League of Prizren (1878), a benchmark in Albania's national awakening and independence movement, and a symbol of the Albanians' opposition to the partition of the country by the Great Powers at the San Stefano and Berlin Conferences (1878). The Albanian school curriculum also stresses that, within months of the declaration of independence at Vlorë in 1912, the London conference of Ambassadors (representing Great Britain, Germany, France, Italy, Austro-Hungary and Russia) recognised in principle the sovereignty of the Albanian state, but guaranteed Serbia's commercial access to the Adriatic, which resulted in the much disputed annexation to Serbia of

*The author would like to thank Louis Zanga and Peter R. Prifti for their comments on an earlier draft.

Kosovo. The appointment in 1914 of a German Prince, Wilhelm von Wied, as Regent of Albania did little to stabilise the country; his unpopular reign lasted a mere seven months and left a power vacuum on the eve of the First World War. A secret treaty signed in London in 1915 partitioned Albania once again, this time among Italy, Serbia, Montenegro and Greece. Until the end of the Second World War (during which it was occupied by Italy and Germany, and an ethnic Albanian state was proclaimed) Albania remained at the mercy of larger and more powerful neighbours.

Foreign occupation and partition of the country have left an unmistakable imprint on the post-war socialist administration: Albania has been a protégé of Yugoslavia, the Soviet Union and China, but has jealously guarded its independence from the strategic ambitions of its protectors. Since its ideological break with Moscow in 1960–1, the Party of Labour of Albania has used its close adherence to Stalinist ideology to implement a policy of self-reliance and isolation. Central to Albania's siege mentality is the argument that the country is subjected to a relentless ideological, economic and political blockade by 'the agents of capitalism, revisionism and imperialism'. The concept of encirclement has been abundantly illustrated by historical publications, colloquia and propaganda to illustrate the 'historical grounds' for the administration's mistrust of neighbours and superpowers. Strengthening the above, is the 'ideological justification': Albania is presented as 'the last bastion of socialism, the defender of the purity of Marxism–Leninism and the forebearer of the class struggle against the heresy of Soviet and Yugoslav revisionism'. These historical and ideological underpinnings form the basis of the Party of Labour's two-pronged policy: the imposition of a strict authoritarian social system combined with the cultural isolation of the population from external influences. The fact that Tirana no longer refers to geographical encirclement without mentioning the ideological, political and economic blockade of the superpowers shows that Albania's isolation has intensified (Tönnes, 1983). Official claims that the extension of diplomatic relations with over 90 countries bears witness to Albania's 'open-door policy' belie the reality of its absence from international fora: with the exception of its representation at the United Nations Albania has boycotted most international summits and conferences.

LEADERSHIP

Martin McCauley (1983b, p. 12) writes, with reference to the Soviet Union, that there are four ways in which the country can change its leader: the death of the incumbent; his incapacitation through illness; his resignation; finally, his enforced removal. During the four decades of its existence, the People's Republic of Albania has had two leaders, Enver Hoxha, who held the post of First Secretary since the formation of the Communist Party of Albania, till his death on 11 April 1985, and Ramiz Alia, his successor. Hoxha staved off potential coups and challenges to his authority until his death by skillfully outmanoeuvering and silencing his opponents. A recollection of sackings and demotions of rivals illustrated an ability to survive. During the 'Yugoslav period' (1945–48) founding members of the Party Koçi Xoxe, Sejfulla Malëshova and Nako Spiru were purged. During the 'Soviet period' (1948–60) personnel reshuffles culminated in the liquidation of Liri Belishova, a Politburo member and Party secretary, and Koço Tashko, the Chairman of the Party's Central Auditing Committee. Pano (1977) writes that, at the time of the Third Congress of the party in 1956, Hoxha remained the only member of the original Central Committee established in 1941 who continued to serve on that body; furthermore, 13 of the 31 members and candidate members elected at the First Congress of 1948 had already been purged. Hoxha faced one of the most serious challenges to his leadership at the city Party conference in Tirana in 1956: military officers openly questioned his style of leadership, and demanded the rehabilitation of previous purge victims and the re-examination of Albania's relations with Yugoslavia (Griffith, 1963). Hoxha resisted the officers' challenge successfully and immediately put the armed forces under the control of the Party. Thereafter the mildest deviations from the Party line or associations with disgraced politicians would result in automatic dismissals. The 'Chinese period' (from 1961 to the mid-1970s) witnessed the most sweeping purges: among the intelligentsia, Fadil Paçrami, a leading playwright, and Todi Lubonja, the former President of the Youth Union – both Central Committee members — were purged for 'counter-revolutionary aims' and 'liberal-opportunist tastes' respectively. Among the military, the major victims included, in 1974, Defence Minister Beqir Balluku and Chief of Staff of the armed forces Petrit Dume, for their alleged involvement in a foreign plot to overthrow Hoxha. The following year, the dismissals spread to other ministries:

amongst the most prominent figures to disappear were Koço Theo-
dhosi, the Minister of Industry and Mining and full member of the
Politburo, Abdyl Kellezi, Deputy Premier and Chairman of the State
Planning Commission, and Kiço Ngjela, Minister of Foreign Trade
and Central Committee member. By sacking the aforementioned
ministers when they were actively involved in raising loans from East
European countries to meet construction deadlines for oil refineries
and the Elbasan metallurgical complex, Hoxha had little difficulty in
blaming their 'revisionist management by association' for the economy's shortcomings. In 1976 Pirro Dodbiba, the Agriculture Minister, suffered the same fate for 'professional misconduct'. Thus, by
1977 Hoxha had succeeded in increasing his hold over the military,
economic and cultural sectors. Finally, came the most spectacular
dismissal to date: Mehmet Shehu, Hoxha's closest ally and
comrade-in-arms for almost forty years, Prime Minister and former
Defence Minister, was 'exposed' in 1982 as the agent of the American, Soviet and Yugoslav secret services. *Zëri i Popullit* (27 February
1985) confirmed that Shehu was 'liquidated as a secret agent' rebut-
ting an earlier version that he had committed suicide in a moment of
deep depression.

From the survey of dismissals two major trends emerge: first, the
endemic nature of the purges suggests that they have been a *sine qua
non* for the strengthening of the position of the First Secretary. It is in
this respect that the similarities between Hoxha's and Stalin's styles
of leadership were most evident: the not infrequent imposition of
capital punishment for ideological and economic deviance suggests
that Hoxha exercised paramount control of the instruments of power.
Secondly, the unity of the Albanian Party has been strengthened
whenever consensus among the leadership has been required on
foreign policy issues: the 1960s, during which the energy of the Party
was channelled into the ideological dispute with the Soviet Union,
witnessed relatively few dismissals. During this period, the need to
maintain a united front at home took precedence over inner-party
feuds, and reflected the seriousness of the Comecon blockade for
Albania's economic survival.

THE PARTY AND THE ARMY

In Albania, as in other East European states, it has been essential for
the Party leader to cultivate the support of the military, which

together with the security police, form the major instruments of coercion upon which he has called successfully to anticipate and defeat challenges to his authority. The bond which was forged between the Party and the army in the wartime partisan struggle explains to a large extent why the army has remained loyal to the First Secretary. The working relationship between Party and army was the outcome of a historical accident: the Party found its support among the dispossessed and disillusioned peasantry, which itself made up the backbone of the partisan movement. Hoxha cleverly exploited the similarity of interests between the Party and the army by reminding the population of the interdependence of the two institutions. In 1961 when relations were severed with Moscow, the army gave its full support to Hoxha and Shehu: Defence Minister Balluku defended Hoxha against the attacks of Khrushchev in two major ways: first, he supported the 'two worlds' theory in foreign policy, namely that Albania must fight with equal vigour both 'US imperialism and Soviet revisionism'; secondly, Balluku endorsed the theory of 'people's war' by acknowledging that the Party had ultimate authority over the military.

The Party–army relationship in Albania deserves due emphasis as there are similarities between the purges of Balluku and Shehu who held the Defence portfolio for a combined period of 27 years (21 and 6 years respectively). The demise of both men came as a surprise to observers as there was no public record of major differences between them and Hoxha. Yet their challenge must have worried Hoxha sufficiently to justify the removal of other senior army figures: in the case of Shehu, his power base (including his nephew and Interior Minister Feçor Shehu, his brother-in-law Kadri Hazbiu who briefly succeeded Mehmet as Defence Minister in 1980, and his wife Fiqrete). Both domestic factors and foreign policy differences have been put forward as reasons for the military shake-ups; in the case of Balluku, the evidence points first to foreign policy divergences between him and Hoxha. According to Prifti (1978) Hoxha's view that Albania was surrounded by a 'capitalist-revisionist encirclement' was contested in the early 1970s by Balluku, who hinted that the country should gradually come out of its isolation. An arctile in *Rruga e Partisë* stressing that 'only the Party could understand the complex connections between domestic and foreign policy' suggested that Balluku's alternative view of Albania's place in the world community was interpreted by Hoxha as a threat to the party's monopoly of decision-making. It seems likely that Balluku's visits to China made him question the wisdom of the siege policy, and argue that the constant barrage of hostile propaganda directed at the superpowers and their allies might eventually provoke Albania's enemies into action and pose a threat to national security. Hoxha could not tolerate a Politburo member, least of all the Defence Minister, who did not heed his warnings against the superpowers.

Albania's burgeoning split with China in the early 1970s also played a part in Balluku's dismissal: a benchmark in Albanian–Chinese relations was President Nixon's visit to China in February 1972. The temporary 'ideological accommodation' which Balluku arranged during his visit to Peking that year was later used by Hoxha to discredit the Defence Minister. When it became clear in Tirana that the 'reformists' and supporters of the 'Three Worlds' Theory' were defeating the 'Gang of Four', Hoxha used Balluku as a convenient scapegoat to discredit China's foreign policy (Kaser 1979).

A third contributory factor to Balluku's downfall was the issue of defence. According to Prifti (1977), 'lengthy commentaries on military matters in the national press left the impression that top army commanders had argued in favour of a defence policy based on a professional army, well-trained and relying heavily on modern weapons'. This clearly alarmed Hoxha who declared that 'there was no stronger army that an armed and militarily trained nation'.

The dismissal of Balluku has taken on renewed significance since the death of Shehu, as several parallels can be drawn between the two incidents. In both cases, there were no obvious indications of the ministers' imminent departures. Moreover, both men's relatives in power were promptly relieved of official status and their power bases dismantled. Finally, after long periods in office, Balluku and Shehu were accused of treason for their 'services to foreign powers'. The last accusation against Shehu remains unsubstantiated and prompts two questions: first, why did it take the Party and the security apparatus a full thirty years to uncover Shehu's 'treacherous activities'? Hoxha's version of events is that successive Interior Ministers (namely Xoxe, Mehmet Shehu, Hazbiu and Feçor Shehu) were 'uncovered throught the strength and vigilance of the Party and its leadership, and not by the state security' (Hoxha 1982, p. 629). If this is the case, Hoxha's argument is significant in that it highlights at best a breakdown of communications, and at worst a serious ideological rift between the Party and the Ministry of Interior. Secondly, if Shehu's ultimate goal was to overthrow Hoxha, why did he not carry out his plan from a position of authority in the Ministry of Defence? Shehu's unceremonious departure does shed some light, however, on the 1980 ministerial reshuffles: first, the transfer of the Defence portfolio to Hazbiu did not form part of the ongoing 'rejuvenation scheme' within the Albanian leadership, but signalled that Shehu was losing favour with Hoxha. Secondly, Shehu's two-stage demotion has a precedent in Albania: the tactics employed are reminiscent of the dismissal by Hoxha in 1948 of Interior Minister Xoxe, who was initially moved to the Ministry of Industry and replaced by a close ally, Nesti Kerenexhi, in preparation for their combined dismissals. By the time of the Eighth Party Congress in November 1981, Shehu had become a threat to Hoxha; the latter, aware of Shehu's strong power base, support in the army and parts of the country, was eager to avoid a direct confrontation. Instead, he demoted Shehu with a view to his final dismissal. Contributing factors to Shehu's downfall could have included the deteriorating situation in neighbouring Kosovo, Hoxha's continued support for economic isolation calling upon further sacrifices from the population, as well as Shehu's lack of enthusiasm for the new generation of leaders.

The enlargement of the Politburo from twelve to thirteen members at the Eighth Congress (barely six weeks before Shehu's death) reinforces the view that Hoxha encountered opposition within the Party. The retirements of veteran members Toska and Koleka and the death in office of Kapo left four seats vacant which were filled by candidate members Lenka Çuko and Simon Stefani, Central Committee member Hajredin Çeliku, who all enjoyed Hoxha's backing, and the little-known Muho Asllani. The subsequent purges of Shehu and Hazbiu and the death of Hoxha have since reduced the Politburo membership to ten. It is now likely that Alia will use the interim period before the next Party Congress, planned for November 1986, to study the future size and composition of the Politburo.

The appointment to the post of Defence Minister of Prokop Murra, former Vice-Chairman of the State Planning Commission and Minister of Industry and Mining, an economist by training without any military background, was clearly intended to strengthen the Party's control of the military. The underlying assumption must be that a liaison mechanism is now in operation between the Party and the army to frustrate any future dissenting elements in the military from posing a threat to the First Secretary.

LEGITIMACY

The Albanian political system has built its legitimacy around the charismatic figure of the Party's First Secretary, who was portrayed as the country's natural leader: Hoxha was presented as the founding father of the Party and as the leader of a partisan army which defeated the Italian and German invaders in the Second World War as well as the nationalist forces of Balli Kombëtar, and established a new social order without the assistance of foreign troops. Hoxha was one of eleven members and five candidate members of the Politburo, which represents the seat of power in the Party hierarchy. An examination of the Politburo membership since the First Party Congress in 1948 shows that Hoxha was the only survivor. The others (except for Kapo and Nushi who died in office, and Koleka, who recently retired) were purged, thus giving Hoxha the 'best record' of political longevity among East European leaders. Hoxha's leadership was strengthened by a concentration of power at the centre, an all-embracing bureaucracy and a ruthlessly efficient security apparatus. Until Shehu's death, Hoxha's strength as a political leader was cushioned by the military experience of his Prime Minister. Power was concentrated in their dual leadership on the basis of complementarity rather than subordination or competition. Hoxha, the statesman who had gained political experience abroad, pronounced on ideology, domestic and foreign policy, whilst Shehu, the military leader with credentials second to none after his spell of fighting in the Spanish Civil War, ran the security apparatus. In spite of Hoxha's statements to the contrary, there can be little doubt that he vested unquestioned trust in Shehu for almost four decades. The latter became Interior Minister in 1948 and took over the Premiership from Hoxha in 1954, a post he held until his death. Shehu strengthened his authority when in the wake of the military reshuffles in 1974, he was entrusted with the Defence portfolio. Moreover, both he and Hoxha consolidated their power by appointing members of their families to the Politburo and the Central Committee Secretariat as well as to some of the ministries. Already in 1962 over half of the 53 members of the Central Committee were related.

The Hoxha–Shehu leadership was complemented by another wartime veteran, Hysni Kapo, Politburo member and Secretary to the Central Committee, who died in office in September 1979. With the benefit of hindsight, it appears that Kapo (third ranking next to Hoxha and Shehu, and respected by both) may have acted as mediator when Hoxha and Shehu failed to agree on major points of policy, and that Kapo's death prompted Hoxha to prepare Shehu's downfall for fear of being overthrown by him. This line of argument would explain why barely six months elapsed between Kapo's death and the 1980 ministerial reshuffles.

A major element in Hoxha's personality cult was the Albanian leader's ability to pronounce on ideology: he is the author of no fewer than 39 volumes of 'Works', of which a second edition was recently 'commissioned by popular demand' (*Zëri i Popullit*, 16 September 1983). The revised edition, which obliterates all positive references to purged politicians, is a vivid illustration of how reporting has been distorted to further the teachings of the Party and ultimately to enhance the charisma of the Party leader.

As there was scarcely an area of policy left where Hoxha has failed to have an impact, a campaign to legitimatise his place in Albanian history got underway shortly before his death. Alia, speaking on the occasion of Hoxha's seventy-fifth birthday, described the First Secretary as 'a distinguished figure in the long history of the Albanian people' (Zanga, 1984), whilst Agolli, the Chairman of the Writers' Union, spoke of the Albanian leader's 'humane personality' in an effort to promote Hoxha's fatherly figure. Michael Shafir's reference in this book to 'the quest to create a synthesis of ideological and national legitimacy in the person of Ceauşescu' is applicable to Hoxha. Both leaders grafted legitimacy on to tradition. The difference, however, between Hoxha and Ceauşescu lies in the depth of grassroot support which the former enjoyed amongst cadres and the population at large who viewed him as the founding father of modern Albania.

POLICY-MAKING

The first Albanian leader concentrated on three areas to demonstrate his policy success: ideology, domestic and foreign policy. As noted in the introduction to this chapter, Hoxha has systematically argued that there were no inconsistencies between the teachings of Marx, Lenin and Stalin, and the implementation of Albania's policies both at home and abroad. Albania's economic development strategy, based essentially on self-help, is in the main consistent with its policy of isolation. Central to the concept of self-reliance is the 1976 Constitution which forbids the acceptance of loans and capital from 'capitalist and revisionist' countries. As, according to Albanian definitions, there are no other revolutionary countries left, this seems to exclude any further external assistance. When Hoxha quarrelled with Khrushchev in 1960, he launched the slogan 'We shall survive, even if we have to feed ourselves on grass'. Since then, a strategy has been adopted which concentrates on the development of heavy industry. In the period of aid from the USSR, foreign assistance (defined as the difference between imports and exports) paid for more than half of imports, whilst during the association with China, one-third of Albania's imports was paid for by foreign assistance. Since the break with China, enforced self-reliance has heightened the urgency to complete the industrial complex 'Steel of the party' which will create 10 000 jobs by the mid-1980s, and was coined by Hoxha as 'Albania's second revolution'. Exports of oil, copper, chrome, electricity, fruit and vegetables have increased and now seem to cover the import bill, which represents a major achievement for a country which was previously so dependent on foreign aid. It should be added, however, that the Albanian leadership appreciates the limits of its industrial strategy: self-sufficiency in the production of steel does not imply that Albania could enter the world market as a strong competitor. For this reason, agriculture remains an important part of the economic base: the sustained modernisation of agriculture has resulted in a surplus throughout the 1970s. Thus, the general picture is one of internal accumulation from agriculture, light industry and mineral processing. Another area of domestic policy where some success has been recorded includes social services and education: the stock of qualified people has grown significantly; educational opportunities (especially for women) have increased, and priority been accorded to the training of a skilled labour force. Improvements in the health service, the eradication of malaria, and the increase in life expectancy also form part of the repertoire of Party members and government officials.

Since the Second World War the main thrust of Albania's foreign policy has been directed at the Soviet Union, Yugoslavia and China. Both Brezhnev and Andropov hinted at a willingness to reopen a dialogue with Tirana, but were rebuked. Gorbachev has been treated in the same way. Recent declarations from Tirana, including the new leadership's decision to send back Moscow's condolences at Hoxha's death rule out any form of reconciliation with the Soviet Union for the foreseeable future. Relations with China are less tense today than at any time since the exchange of diplomatic notes in July 1978 which formalised the termination of an eighteen year association (Kaser, 1979). Although China is not expected to resume its role of ideological mentor, the visit to Tirana in 1983 of a Chinese trade delegation – the first official Chinese visit since 1978 - illustrates a degree of pragmatism on both sides. Tirana's criticism of Peking has been noticeably milder than that *vis-à-vis* Moscow or Belgrade, whilst the Chinese, unlike the Soviets at the height of their feud with Tirana, have ignored rather than fuelled the Albanian invective: by maintaining diplomatic relations at ambassadorial level, the Chinese government has left options open for a future normalisation of economic relations.

Arguably, the most important aspect of Albania's foreign policy is its relationship with Yugoslavia. First, there is the geographical proximity of Albanian and Slav communities which share historical claims to disputed territories. Secondly, there are economic considerations: Yugoslavia is Albania's largest trading partner. In view of its isolation, Albania has in Yugoslavia a vital corridor to the markets it services in Central Europe. It is significant that, although the intensity of the anti-Yugoslav (and anti-Serb) propaganda has often been a sound indicator of internal developments within the Albanian leadership, the most sweeping purges amidst the latter have not unduly affected trade with Yugoslavia. Thirdly, the presence in Southern Yugoslavia of a large Albanian nationality has been a dominant factor in Albanian–Yugoslav relations since Yugoslavia's break with the Cominform, and has provided the leadership in Tirana with a platform from which to revive the 'unsettled' Kosovo question. The relationship between the two countries is further complicated by the depth of mistrust which a country of the size of Albania has generated in its larger and more powerful neighbour. The sources of Belgrade's obsessive concern with Albania are twofold: the strength and penetration of Albania's ideology in Kosovo are seen in Yugoslavia as the cause of the Kosovo riots of 1981; and the Serbian lobby, which perceives the Kosovo Albanians as a threat to the stability of the Federation, continues to advocate stern measures to counteract Albanian 'irredentism', thus prompting the predictable reaction from Tirana that the Albanians in Yugoslavia are persecuted and exploited by the Serbs. At present there is no indication that Alia intends to alter Albania's foreign policy towards Yugoslavia; as neither country would benefit from too severe a deterioration of relations, the mutual quest for a *modus vivendi* has resulted in the acceptance of two-tier relations: normal at state level, but totally opposed politically and ideologically/(Artisien and Howells, 1981; Artisien, 1984). The conflicting ideology of the Western world has so far hampered the normalisation of relations with Great Britain and West Germany. Little progress was made in Hoxha's lifetime in re-opening diplomatic relations with Britain which were severed in 1948 when Albania declined to pay compensation for the loss, two years earlier, of two destroyers in the Corfu channel. Britain retaliated by refusing to return two and a half tons of Albanian gold seized in Italy by the Allied forces during the Second World War. Michael Kaser (1983) has suggested that, as the International Court's evidence against Albania was largely circumstantial, the deadlock could be broken by a request by both parties, simultaneously with the resumption of diplomatic relations, to the International Court to re-examine the evidence. Within weeks of assuming power, Britain and Albania were reported to be holding secret talks in Paris in an attempt to break the 40-yearold diplomatic impasse.

Albania's steadily increasing trade with West Germany since the late seventies has prompted both sides to reappraise the feasibility of a resumption of diplomatic relations. Although Albania's demand for war reparations is unlikely to be met in full in the foreseeable future, there are indications that German companies (possibly with financial backing from the Federal Government) are contemplating channelling investments into industrial projects in Albania.

Of all the Western countries, Italy and France have the most 'normal' relationship with Albania: diplomatic relations and cultural exchanges have recently been strengthened by proposals of increased commercial cooperation.

Albania's relations with Greece are complicated by the disputed size of the Greek minority in Southern Albania, estimated at 40 000 by the Albanians and 400 000 by the Greeks. In February 1984 the Greek Prime Minister, Papandreou, renounced his country's longstanding claim to Southern Albania as a prelude to the opening of negotiations with Tirana. According to one source, Greece would be prepared to put an end to the state of war which has existed since 1945 in return for guarantees for the human rights of the Greek minority in Albania (*Sunday Times*, 14 August 1983).

SUCCESSION

Hoxha has been succeeded by Ramiz Alia who has emerged from the late leader's careful selection of a new generation of ideologists and technocrats who favour the same course of self-reliance and mistrust of the outside world. The fact that at the time of writing (July 1985) only three of the eighteen Cabinet members still occupy the positions they held in the Shehu administration illustrates the point that Hoxha had elected to rejuvenate the power structure in anticipation of his own departure.

Born in 1925 in the northern town of Shkodër, Alia joined the Party Secretariat in 1960, became a full member of the Politburo the following year, and was elected Chairman of the Presidium of the People's Assembly in November 1982. His pronouncements on ideology, economic and military matters, and foreign policy have received much exposure in the Albanian press. He delivered the opening speech on the occasion of the Centenary of the League of Prizren in 1982 and at the 1983 Conference on Marxist–Leninist thought, which served to underline two of his main strengths. First, that he possesses the correct background as Party ideologist. Whilst gaining experience in the 1960s in the Office of Propaganda and the Ministry of Education, he devoted himself to the Cultural Revolution and gained respect on questions of ideology. Secondly, Alia's pronouncements have increased his stature in the eyes of the population as a natural successor to Hoxha. Another indication that Alia was being groomed for the post of First Secretary was found in Hoxha's frequent references to him as Secretary of the Central Committee rather than as President of the Presidium, the latter carrying less political power.

Alia's much quoted weakness in the West (that his power base is in the north, traditionally under-represented in the leadership) did not prevent his promotion. In fact, Alia's origins may even play in his favour: his parents fled from the Slav repression in Kosovo in the inter-war years. For the future of Albanian–Yugoslav relations, Alia could play his own family card either to bring the two countries closer or to add to the propaganda exchange (Artesian, 1985).

In recent speeches Alia has reiterated Hoxha's position on the United States and the Soviet Union and has contrasted Albania's 'economic successes with the failures of the reformers in the Soviet Union and Eastern Europe'. He has laid the blame for the economy's shortcomings (especially in the energy sector) at the door of Mehmet Shehu, and has advocated a degree of rationalisation in new investments, implying that wastage and production costs are unjustifiably high.

Another Hoxha protégé whose position has been in the ascendancy is Adil Çarçani, who succeeded Shehu as Prime Minister in January 1982. Çarçani's promotion from the post of First Deputy

Prime Minister, to which he was appointed in the wake of the 1974 ministerial reshuffles, indicates that he enjoyed the confidence of Hoxha. An economist by training with his power base in northern Albania, Çarçani became a Central Committee member in 1961. In his inaugural speech as Prime Minister, he commended Hoxha for his support of isolation and economic self-reliance and for rejecting a dialogue with the superpowers.

Although Alia is the new leader, other politicians may play a significant role in the post-Hoxha era. Among these are Hekuran Isai who served as Party secretary in the district of Elbasan in the 1960s and was elevated to full membership of the Politburo in 1975. His appointment as Minister of Internal Affairs in Çarçani's government is one of two significant ministerial changes. Isai's interests are in the economic and social sectors. The other ministerial change is the appointment of a southern Albanian, Qirjako Mihali, to the post of Deputy Prime Minister; like Isai, he belongs to the new generation of Party officials who came to prominence in the the early 1970s when relations with China became strained. Both ministers are strictly of Party background, and their appointments have strengthened the Party's hold on the government.

The most unexpected new Cabinet appointment is that of Prokop Murra as Defence Minister. The choice of a non-military man for this post created a precedent in post-war Albania, and is significant for the following reasons: first, as in the cases of Isai and Mihali, Murra's political credentials have taken precedence over experience in the field where the appointment is made. Secondly, all of Murra's predecessors have met a violent death: thus, although Murra is in a potentially very strong position, combining the Defence portfolio with a candidate membership of the Politburo, the sensitive nature of his ministerial responsibilities makes him particularly vulnerable to future Cabinet reshuffles.

It is still premature to judge the full significance of the aforementioned appointments. Other newcomers to the Politburo, who will need to be watched closely over the next five years, include Stefani, Asllani, Çuko and Çeliku. The Albanian leadership listed in the appendix shows that most Politburo members and government ministers belong to the post-Hoxha generation. The remaining Party veterans include Myftiu and Marko, who are unlikely to exercise much authority in the post-Hoxha era.

THE PRESENT ALBANIAN LEADERSHIP

Politburo	Function
Alia, Ramiz (1925)	First Secretary
Asllani, Muho	
Çarçani, Adil (1922)	Prime Minister
Çeliku, Hajredin	Minister of Industry and Mining
Çuko, Lenka (f)	CC Secretary
Isai, Hekuran	CC Secretary; Minister of Internal Affairs
Marko, Rita (1920)	Deputy Chairman, State Presidium
Miska, Pali	
Myftiu, Manush (1919)	Deputy Prime Minister
Stefani, Simon	CC Secretary

Candidate Members

Bekteshi, Besnik	Deputy Prime Minister
Çami, Foto	
Gegprifti, Llambi	
Mihali, Qirjako	Deputy Prime Minister
Murra, Prokop	Minister of Defence

Secretariat

Alia, Ramiz	First Secretary
Çuko, Lenka (f)	

Isai, Hekuran

Stefani, Simon

Çerava, Vangjel

State Presidium of the People's Assembly

Alia, Ramiz	Chairman
Marko, Rita	Deputy Chairman
Spahiu, Xhafer	Deputy Chairman
Guri, Emine	Deputy Chairman
Tozaj, Sihat	Secretary

Council of Ministers

Çarçani, Adil	Prime Minister
Myftiu, Manush	Deputy Prime Minister
Bekteshi, Besnik	Deputy Prime Minister
Mihali, Qirjako	Deputy Prime Minister
Thomai, Themie (f)	Minister of Agriculture
Arapi, Kudret	Minister of Communal Economy
Babameto, Luan	Minister of Communications
Hoxha, Farudin	Minister of Construction
Çami, Tefta	Minister of Education and Culture
Hametaj, Lavdosh	Minister of Energy
Gjyzari, Niko	Minister of Finance
Malile, Reiz	Minister of Foreign Affairs
Korbeci, Shane	Minister of Foreign Trade
Çeliku, Hajredin	Minister of Industry and Mining

Isai, Hekuran	Minister of Internal Affairs
Murati, Osman	Minister of Internal Trade
Kapo, Vito (f)	Minister of Light and Food Industry
Murra, Prokop	Minister of Defence
Alushani, Ajli	Minister of Public Health

(f) female

10 Yugoslavia

DENNISON RUSINOW

Although, but also because, it was devoid of drama and surprises, the nearly total reconstruction of Yugoslavia's nine-member State Presidency on 15 May 1984 was a significant event. The state leadership that the country 'inherited' (because it was already in place, ready and waiting) when Josip Broz Tito died on 4 May 1980 was being changed for the first time and in an orderly fashion prescribed by the 1974 Constitution. The cumbersome system of collective state and Party leaderships designed for the post-Tito era thereby continued to defy numerous predictions that it would not last even this long – but that is not all. Like the smoothness of the initial transition from Tito to his successors precisely four years earlier, the orderliness of this top-level transfer of power also defied an older and more general tradition in Communist-ruled countries. This is 'that historical practice', as Tito's chief ideologist Edvard Kardelj once described it,

> 'under which every political change imposed by the course of events in a socialist state, be it a change of government or practical policies, is always attended by political disturbances which are reminiscent of a *coup d'état*'. (Kardelj, 1966, p. 8)

All Communist-ruled countries are different, but some are more different than others, and the Socialist Federal Republic of Yugoslavia is most different of all. The Yugoslav differences which are of significance for the comparison of leadership and succession in these countries are not limited to orderly transitions from Tito to successive sets of successors since 1980 and to the so far genuinely collective leaderships, each with a strictly temporary and largely symbolic *primus inter pares* as its presiding officer. Power is also diffuse in many ways that are unique or at least exceptional under Communist rule. Yugoslavia is in effect a confederation, not a unitary state or a pseudo-federation, and this is almost as true of the Party (the League of Communists of Yugoslavia, hereafter the LCY) as it is of governmental organs. State leaderships at all levels are potentially, and often in practice, as powerful and therefore important as corresponding Party ones. Even the military and the political police are partly decentralised, although the extent and effectiveness of residual central control in these two cases, while disputable, is probably greater than in other parts of the system. There is no state property or 'command' planning and less central (but not necessarily less regional or communal) control or even influence over economic activities than in other 'socialist' or even most 'capitalist' societies. The answer to the question 'Who's in charge?' – currently being asked by the LCY itself as well as by anxious Western and international bankers – frequently seems to be 'Nobody', which is a fine state of affairs for a Communist regime and for a country with serious economic problems at least partly attributable to that condition.

LEADERSHIP

In the last years of his long reign Tito's extraordinary (but not unlimited) power was based, apart from his personality and status as a 'living legend', on a combination of two top offices, both in later years held 'without limitation of mandate'. He was head of state as President of the SFR Yugoslavia, which also made him permanent President of the collective State Presidency created in 1971 and Commander-in-Chief of the armed forces, and at the same time head of the Party as President of the LCY, which empowered him to convene and preside over the 165-member Party Central Committee and its 23-member Presidency and to serve *ex officio* as the ninth member of the State Presidency.

One reason for the smoothness of the initial transition from Tito to his 'faceless' collective successors in May 1980 was that these two offices were deliberately designed to 'self-destruct' when Tito departed the scene. The 1974 Constitution specified that the office of the President of the Republic existed for Tito alone ('In view of the historic role of Josip Broz Tito . . .') and explicitly provided for its disappearance whenever he should cease to occupy it (Articles 333–45). The powers of that office were then to devolve to the collective State Presidency (Article 328), which would now be headed by an annually rotating President of the Presidency (*not*

President of the Republic) chosen according to a specified order of the eight Republics and Provinces represented, by one person each, on that body. The office of President of the LCY was simply 'vacated' (the term used by the Belgrade news magazine *NIN* at the time) under a 'provisional solution' pending the first post-Tito Party Congress, in June 1982, when it was formally deleted from the Party Statutes and ceased to exist. Here too the post-Tito presiding officer, called President of the Presidency of the Central Committee (*not* President of the LCY), rotates annually by Republic and Province, which means that the ninth *ex-officio* member of the State Presidency also changes annually. The roles of both Presidency presidents have been largely reduced to chairmanship and representational functions.

These complex arrangements meant that a potentially contentious choice of one or two people to fill Tito's official shoes – doubly contentious because, unlike Tito, each candidate would be identified with a particular one of Yugoslavia's nationalities – was thereby avoided. But programming Tito's two power-concentrating offices to self-destruct also implicitly recognised that they if not Tito himself, although untouchable as long as he lived, had become an anachronism in the political system and its legitimating ideology as they had evolved over time (Denitch, 1978; Johnson, 1980; Rusinow, 1980a).

By the 1970s years of lip-service to 'socialist democracy' based on 'self-management' and what Kardelj in his last exegesis of the system called 'a pluralism of self-management socialist interests' had bred a corresponding infrastructure of autonomous and semi-autonomous institutions, expectations, constitutional checks and balances, and decision-making procedures. These together had already genuinely 'pluralised' decision-making in public affairs and (of equal importance) public appointments in all sectors and at all levels except the very top, which was Tito himself. The powers of the federal state and Party apparatuses, with the former constitutionally limited in scope, depended on inter-regional consensus about their use, and officials assigned to them depended on the approval of the regional or local authorities who were now in charge of a decentralised *nomenklatura* – except when Tito chose to intervene in any of these matters, and except for foreign policy, to the end his jealously guarded private sphere. Public policy at all levels was now usually the product of tortuous and sometimes stormy public or private negotiations within and among economic enterprises and sectors, institutionalised interest groups, state organs, and a variety of other 'socio-political organisations' – always including but not always dominated by the chief of these last, the appropriate Party organisation.

It is in this system of diffused power and pluralistic decision-making, legitimised by an elaborate ideology, that Tito's offices and their powers gradually became anachronistic and were functionally as well as formally 'deletable' without changes elsewhere in the system and discontinuity or crisis at the moment of transition. Only his chief actual and personal rather than official function in his later years, as authoritative final arbiter when pluralism of national and other interests produced deadlock or incipient crisis, was still compatible with the logic and possibly essential to the stability of the system, and may be sorely missed. Whether it can and will be performed by the collective State Presidency, which has been constitutionally assigned this role since 1974, has not yet been seriously tested.

The principle of collective leaderships with rapidly rotating tops, extended to other parts of the political system at Tito's 'suggestion' shortly before his death, is now generally pervasive except for executive and administrative posts where longer experience and continuity were deemed more important. It was explicitly designed both to defuse the mutual jealousies and suspicions of Yugoslavia's traditionally quarrelsome nations, which can be equally or proportionately represented in collective leaderships and have their turn at chairing them, and to preclude concentrations of power in one or several sets of hands at any level. But it is also part of a larger design, a systematic emphasis on institutional permanence, stability, and primacy over individual leadership roles that is considered the only way – other than reversion to centralised dictatorship, again probably dominated by Serbs as the most numerous and widespread nation – of coping effectively with 'the ethno-regional complexities and internal tensions that define Yugoslavia' (Zaninovich, 1981, p. 186, in making the same point). A Yugoslav fond of Weberian terminology described the intent more broadly, in a 1980 conversation, as a system based on 'routinised bureaucratic rather than charismatic leadership'.

Whether the Yugoslavs are ready for such a system, with or without intransigent problems or a crisis to stimulate nostalgia for 'charismatic leadership', and whether current institutional arrangements are appropriate or even in the longer run workable are important but separate questions. (The answer to the first is probably 'no', as it is in many supposedly more 'modern' societies, but the answer to the second may be closer to a qualified 'yes' than many Yugoslav and foreign commentators currently think.) What matters for present purposes is that 'faceless leadership', which worries so many Yugoslavs and outside observers, is therefore also the intent as well as the result of the country's currently complex political arrangements.

In these circumstances participants as well as observers of leadership and succession in post-Tito Yugoslavia – where 'leaderism' (*liderstvo!*) has been declared a cardinal sin, which is awkward: sins must usually be committed in private to avoid public condemnation and sanctions, but this one is by its nature a public act – will often find it more profitable to focus on institutions rather than individual functions and those who are only momentarily performing them. This is also the underlying reason why political struggles, whether for power or over policy, usually assume the form of a debate about institutions and their reorganisation. 'The central question is not "who will rule?" but rather "what form will that rule take?"' (Ramet, 1984, p. 290).

LEGITIMACY

Acceptance of a claim to rule or to lead as somehow 'rightful', which is for present purposes an adequate definition of legitimacy, can be won in many ways and exist in varying degrees of intensity and universality. In societies where it is claimed as a result of victory in a contested election, conducted according to regular procedures sanctioned by custom or a constitution, even those who voted for another candidate usually if grudgingly accept the legitimacy of the victor's rule, however much they may dislike it and hope to end it at the next election. No Communist ruler has so far enjoyed this particular form of acceptance, which is generally the hardest to challenge wherever the idea of popular sovereignty has become part of the political culture.

Tito's legitimacy, which shed its light on personally anointed subordinates, was that of a *pater patriæ* twice over, as founder of his reborn country and for his defiance of Stalin, which made that country genuinely sovereign. It was unquestioned and to the end almost undiminished within the governing élite and for all but the most die-hard anti-Communists and ethnic nationalists among his countrymen. In addition, he exuded authority and behaved appropriately (that is, like a monarch) which also helps.

When he died, the only fellow-founders in whom a paler shadow of this kind of legitimacy might have been generally acknowledged were already dead or irretrievably disgraced. His collective successors could not and so far have not really tried to build up personal legitimacy in this sense. As a symbol of their reluctance to try, his portrait is still the one on display in official and public places, not theirs. In any case, the name of the game is now the de-personalised institutionalisation of leadership and the Revolution. It is therefore offices, whose usually collective holders are subject to frequent obligatory rotation, that must struggle and perchance compete for similarly depersonalised legitimacy. This kind of transfer is notoriously difficult whenever a Monarchy becomes a Republic that attempts to foreswear 'charismatic leadership', but Tito's successors have other problems as well.

On-the-job performance can often provide an effective substitute for 'charisma', genuine election, and other fonts of legitimacy, but theirs has not. This is partly bad luck and unfair. The grave economic crisis that has so far spoiled their tenure is largely the belated harvest of mistakes committed in Tito's reign and brought to fruit by primarily exogenous factors, but its onset happened to coincide with Tito's death. The comparison this timing invites, between misery under the new regime and 'the good old days' when Tito was alive and standards were rising as giddily as they have since been falling, inevitably encumbers the legitimation of his successors. But they have themselves contributed by wasting the valuable and possibly crucial months of their 'honeymoon period', in which 'everyone was willing and in fact desperately eager to grant them automatic legitimacy' (the words of a young non-Party Yugoslav), but had to wait for two years, after a promising start in the first weeks after Tito's death, for further decisive but still fatally compromised measures to combat the deepening economic crisis (Rusinow, 1983). Legitimation that was originally there for the taking (on this view) became something that had to be won anew and in increasingly difficult circumstances.

In this situation the tenuous residual acceptance of Tito's successors as somehow rightful and hence legitimate leaders derives almost exclusively from the broader legitimacy of the regime they purport to represent, which is in turn based on the integrity of its two founding myths and its record in two areas: maintaining non-alignment (particularly from the Soviet bloc) and some success in managing inter-nationality relations and conflicts (Denitch, 1976 passim.; Burg, 1983, p. 82).

The first of the founding myths is the legendary National Liberation Struggle of 1941–5 that created the regime and the new Yugoslavia together, with the young regime's equally legendary defiance of Stalin from 1948 to 1953 as its epilogue and ratifier. The second is 'self-management', in its manifold aspects, as their distinguishing feature and claim to fame. The hyper-sensitivity of post-Tito leaders to anything construable as an attack on either of these myths, displayed in speeches and resolutions from Party and state forums and in successful or failed attempts at censorship and sanctions against offending authors, publishers, and producers, suggests that they are fully aware of how dependent they are and how naked they would be without them.

In the nature of such things, both myths have meanwhile been weakened by time as well as more public exposure and reluctant high-level confession of their respective weaknesses: the first not quite as uncompromising and devoid of errors and atrocities as its legend, the second gravely marred by inefficiency, corruption, and unfulfilled promises. They never the less appear to retain enough strength, in large part derived from the genuine heroism and accomplishments of the first and lack of desirable and at the same time realistic alternatives to the second, to sustain the regime and its institutions (but not necessarily individual leaders) as long as the second historic pillar of regime legitimacy, its commitment to non-alignment and to 'brotherhood and unity' minimally guaranteed by scrupulously multinational élites, is also regarded as intact.

The legitimation of regional leadership in the eight federal units, which is a distinct and also important matter in a *de facto* confederation, has a partly different base and means of generation. The principal difference, which offers regional leaders a separate but slippery road to legitimacy, is the joint product of three distinguishing characteristics of Yugoslav federalism: the national base and nationalist rationale of most of the federal units, the regionalisation of the *nomenklatura* described above, and the autonomy enjoyed by regional economies and regional economic policy-making. The first of these also pertains, at least formally, to other Communist ruled federations (the USSR and Czechoslovakia); the others do not.

Five of the six Yugoslav republics – Slovenia, Croatia, Serbia, Macedonia, and Montenegro – are explicitly and constitutionally identified with particular Yugoslav nations as their own nation-states within the federation. Two of the other three federal units, which are formally multi-national, have come to be similarly regarded by 'nationally conscious' members of their numerous nations. These are the South Slav Muslim plurality in Bosnia-Herzegovina, now officially a separate nation, and the Albanian majority in Kosovo, although the latter are collectively uncertain whether they want their Auton-omous Province to become a second Albanian state within Yugo-slavia or part of the sovereign one that already exists next door (Rusi-now, 1980b; 1982a). In each federal unit the decentralising reforms of the 1960s have left regional leaderships more dependent on re-gional than on central political élites for their appointment and survival. And in all cases crucial elements of economic power, no longer wielded by the federal centre, are still highly politicised at regional and local levels, creating a situation officialy but vainly condemned as 'eight closed and autarkic republic and provincial economies'.

The combined result of these three characteristics is a symbiosis of regional political leaderships and regional economic interests perhaps best described as classic mercantilism aggravated by modern national-ism. Regional leaders are primarily the protectors and promoters of their regional economies. They are supported and obeyed – and recognised as *national* leaders of their respective nations – in accord-ance with how well they are seen to do it. The national element in this formula is particularly important. In an age of nationalism and in the Yugoslav historical context it offers regional leaders a singularly potent and therefore tempting additional font and kind of legitimacy that is not available to federal leaders on a country-wide (Yugoslav) basis.

Succumbing to the temptation and seeking recognition as national leaders can also, however, prove dangerous for the stability of the multi-national country, for federal units that are in fact, if not formally, also multi-national, and for individual leaders who attempt it. All these dangers were amply demonstrated during the political crisis of 1971–2, the most serious the regime has so far endured, when Tito was there to condemn offending regional leaders as nationalists and force them into resignation and disgrace in order to restore stability on his terms. With Tito no longer there, the outcome of a future and similar crisis is far harder to predict.

INSTRUMENTS OF POWER

General acceptance of the legitimacy of a regime and its leaders will normally reduce if never totally eliminate their need for instruments of power and coercion; in such cases fewer citizens will usually have to be pressured or forced to do what is wanted by authorities they regard as rightful. Stated the other way around, regimes and leaders can often live with a low level of acceptance as rightful if they are well endowed with such instruments and ready to use them, the degree of necessary ruthlessness and ubiquity varying in inverse ratio to that level of acceptance. Communist regimes are generally well endowed in this sense, although those with particularly low legitimacy quotients (along with other weaknesses) have sometimes needed outside help, in the form of additional instruments of coercion provided by 'fraternal' countries, to maintain themselves.

The principal instruments of power that are specific to Communist-ruled countries normally include the following: state control of the economy through monopolistic state ownership and centralised command planning; Party control of the state through the *nomenklatura* and a one-party system; top leadership control of the Party through the heirarchical rules of democratic centralism; Party 'co-optation' of the political police and the military; and a judiciary accustomed to holding political directives in greater awe than the law. When it works as intended, all other 'sub-systems' are subsumed under and controlled by the hierarchically organised Party in a global socio-political monolith sometimes described as totalitarianism.

Almost nothing in this list applies fully or without significant qualification to Yugoslavia. The first item (monopolistic state ownership, and so on) simply does not pertain; 'politicisation' of the economy, although extensive at regional and local levels (as noted), assumes other forms that are more usually associated with the 'capitalist' West than with the Communist world, where state monopoly brings total and direct rather than partial and mediated politicisation. The *nomenklatura* and democratic centralism have been so thoroughly decentralised that Yugoslavs joke about having a competitive eight-party rather than a monopolistic one-party system. The judiciary is usually, but under pressure not entirely and always, autonomous and respectful of the law. And decision-making has generally become so diffuse, with so many participants, that the role and power of the Party at any and all levels is often unclear, even and perhaps especially to perplexed Party members who are constantly told that they are responsible for 'correct socialist' choices but must not command or interfere, as Party organs, in decisions constitutionally assigned to state and 'self-management' ones. Only in Party 'co-optation' of the police and the military does Yugoslavia conform as fully as most, but there are other significant differences, described below, in this sector as well.

The situation created by these total or partial Yugoslav deviations from the standard version or ideal type of a Communist regime can be summarised as follows. The Party's monopoly of permissible organised political activity, the *nomenklatura*, and democratic centralism are still basically intact as instruments of power and the glue of Party discipline. However, the first of these is qualified by the Party's own quasi-'federalisation' into eight Leagues of Communists representing diverse and frequently competing national and regional interests. The other two are consequently effective only at the regional level and below. The effectiveness of all these instruments is further and importantly qualified by a complex decision-making system which is basically pluralistic, highly susceptible to atomised domination by 'informal groups' in which representatives of the Party *per se* are frequently at most *primus inter pares*, and characterised by diminished or vanished accountability (because anonymous power is by nature irresponsible power). If pluralism is good and non-accountability is bad, 'Nobody' as the answer to 'Who's in charge?' is both a virtue and a vice.

INSTRUMENTS OF COERCION

In terms of the list of model characteristics of Communist regimes suggested above, the principal exception to the rule that Yugoslavia is different concerns Party 'co-optation' of the police and the military, which seems to be as thorough and effective as anywhere else in the Communist world. However, two other features distinguish Yugoslavia in this sector as well. The first is partly decentralised (that is, 'federalised') control over these ultimate instruments of coercion, which is arguable in the case of the political police (the state security service, still known as UDBa, where the evidence is largely circumstantial) but clear and demonstrable in the organisation of the army and territorial militias (Johnson, 1971, 1978; Dean, 1976; Roberts, 1976). The second is a tradition of greater restraint, which is contingent and unreliable, in using the police as instruments of political coercion.

At least since the state security service was purged and humbled after its mentor, Aleksandar Ranković, was disgraced in 1966, preference for other means of persuasion and even acceptance of failure to persuade have generally been more common than is usual under Communist rule. However, spasmodic outbreaks of political arrests and harassment and the massive repression suffered by Albanian 'irredentists' in Kosovo since 1981 have been particularly vivid and deliberate reminders that UDBa is still there and will be used to suppress dissent and undesirable ideas when 'somebody' considers it necessary. It is nevertheless frequently unclear who that 'somebody' is. In several recent instances the circumstances surrounding police actions of this kind have been more conducive to speculation than to clear determination of the source and hence the level of the orders they are following (is it local, republican, or federal?). The extent of effective central control is therefore also hard to ascertain.

Meanwhile, the periodic display of blatant political coercion functions as a limiting factor, inhibiting and perhaps circumscribing the further development of pluralism (however defined) and deliberate attempts to change the system. It performs this function in two ways: with immediate effect on the target of the moment and as a general reminder that such coercion is still possible, potent, and subject to arbitrary and potentially ubiquitous use. Such reminders also and inevitably revive old speculations concerning the putative availability of the military and the police as instruments for a *coup d'état* 'to preserve socialism' (again however defined) or to restore centralised autocracy. This possibility, although often exaggerated, cannot be excluded.

KEY POLITICAL INSTITUTIONS

Key political institutions in the Yugoslav system are by its nature more numerous than in Communist-ruled states further east, and include more than Party and central organs. Which institutions are 'key' can also vary over time and by locale, often depending on the strength of their respective clienteles and shifting coalitions with other forces represented in Kardelj's 'pluralism of [institutionalised] interests'. The importance of 'informal groups', often more powerful than formal institutions, has already been mentioned; while by no means a uniquely Yugoslav phenomenon, they probably play a greater role than in theoretically similar systems. Organs that are formally part of the economic system – for example management organs of large enterprises at the local or republican level and economic chambers at the republican or all-Yugoslav level – may sometimes also be more 'key' than corresponding political ones in making political as well as economic policy. Even institutions that are traditionally mere 'transmission belts' for Party policy under Communist rule, such as the trade unions, occasionally assert themselves as important and autonomous actors (Rusinow, 1977, pp. 114–9, 159–62; Carter, 1982, pp. 159–64).

In the functioning of the Party itself, the eight regional Leagues of Communists and their umbrella organisation, the LCY, are still sufficiently hierarchical for their Presidencies to be generally more powerful than their Central Committees, and the latter more powerful than the Party Congresses and 'Party base' to which all are supposedly answerable. At least, this has usually been the case to date, although the political culture as well as the LCY statutes in principle permit the kind of by-pass operation performed by Nikita Khrushchev in 1957, when he out-manoeuvred the 'anti-Party' majority (that is, his opponents) in the Soviet Politburo by appealing to the full Central Committee, where he was confident of support. Periodic appeals by Yugoslav politicians for a more active Central Committee and genuine adherence to the statutory principle that a Presidency is a Central Committee's executive organ, not its boss, at least sometimes appear to be similarly motivated. However, this observer can recall only one important (but still partly obscure) instance in which a Central Committee seriously attempted to assert its statutory authority in this way. This was the Serbian Central Committee of 1972, which tried and failed to resist Tito's insistence that its President and Secretary must resign (Burg, 1983, pp. 167–78; Rusinow, 1977, pp. 318–26).

Yugoslavia is more clearly distinguished from other Communist-ruled countries by the relatively far greater weight enjoyed by state organs *vis-à-vis* corresponding Party ones at all levels. This is at times (particularly in the later 1960s) and partly a matter of principles: a theoretical Yugoslav Communist separation of powers in which the Party is supposed to be responsible for ideology and guiding principles and the government for governing; the influence exerted by individual Communists, as members and electors of state organs, is the only permissible link between the two. At other times a contrary thesis has prevailed: in order to fulfil its special ideological and programmatic mission, the Party has a right and duty to direct participation, as an institution, in the governing process. The second thesis was in fashion, providing the rationale for making the head of the LCY an *ex-officio* member of the *State* Presidency, when the current constitution was adopted in 1974. In the same spirit the new Constitution established a new parliamentary system, in which Party units and other 'socio-political organisations' constitute a third kind of electoral body, in addition to citizens aggregated in territorial units and again in 'working organisations' (enterprises, and so on), sending delegates of their own to separate or joint chambers in local, regional, and Federal assemblies. These measures have not had as much effect as intended. The principle of separate Party and governmental competencies would be more easily and frequently violated, and the anachronism of direct Party participation in state organs would be more effective, if appropriate Party organs were not so regularly distracted by obsessive contemplation of their own organisational forms and failures (a complaint frequently heard at and between all Party congresses) and by the drafting of principles and policy proposals that are usually so compromised into generalities and platitudes that contradictory interpretations are possible and duly ensue.

The resulting tendency, especially since Tito's death, is for governments – the Federal Executive Council (since May 1982 under a woman president, Milka Planinc of Croatia) and eight Republican or Provincial Executive Councils – to get on with their own business, which is not unimportant, with greater autonomy than is foreseen by the Constitution and the tutorial and formal role it assigns to the League of Communists. At the top of the pyramid of state institutions the nine-member State Presidency also frequently seems to be more active and more authoritative than the 23-member Party Presidency.

A third set of potentially and formerly key state institution, the Federal and regional parliaments (in Yugoslavia called Assemblies), has not lately merited the title. From 1963 to the end of that decade the curious and corporativistic five-chamber parliaments created by the 1963 Constitution, although cumbersome and open to other criticisms, played an active, critical, and in large measure autonomous role in governing the country and genuinely represented a broad range of clearly articulated sectoral and regional interests (Rusinow, 1977, chs 5–7, passim; Cohen, 1977, pp. 122–53). This is no longer the case. The powers of the Federal Assembly were emasculated in the early 1970s by three developments, the first two of which also affected the regional assemblies. These were a new system of intentionally or incidentally ineffective chambers and representation by indirectly-elected 'delegates and delegations' introduced with the 1974 Constitution; a retreat from the contested elections (quite often lost by the Party's preferred candidate) that had become fashionable in the late 1960s; and the earlier rise of inter-republican committees and other sometimes extra-constitutional devices for achieving a delicate pre-parliamentary consensus on draft legislation that the Federal Assembly cannot challenge or amend without grave risk to inter-regional relations. As a result, the performance of Yugoslavia's assemblies now more closely resembles that of the 'rubber-stamp' parliaments of the Soviet bloc – except that the Yugoslav ones take much longer to do the job and perform some useful work in committee stages along the way.

One other political institution also merits negative mention: the Socialist Alliance of the Working People of Yugoslavia (SAWPY), an eight-million-member mass organisation originally designed as a Party 'transmission belt' and umbrella for other pre-emptive mass organisations. Since as early as 1950–2 leading political figures and ideologists, including Kardelj, have periodically argued that SAWPY should play a more important and autonomous role. In extreme versions, which surface whenever the question of a multi-party system is gingerly re-opened, it has even been suggested that it might be turned into a kind of second political party, a 'socialist' and mass alternative (or permanent loyal opposition?) to the communist and supposedly 'cadre' LCY. None of this has ever happened (Carter, 1982, pp. 100–4). Instead, the LCY itself, with over 2 000 000 members by 1984 (from a total population of 23.5 million), hovers indecisively between 'mass' and 'cadre' status, eternally unable to decide which it should be – or indeed whether it is a political party at all, which its name, programme, and statutes deny.

Membership is all of the institutions listed above has meanwhile changed over time in four generalisable ways. Representatives of the long dominant 'Club of '41' (participants in the wartime Partisan movement from its beginning, including survivors of the small pre-war Communist Party) have inevitably declined in number and therefore in influence with the passing years. The proportion of members with any and later higher formal education has increased dramatically. The number who are of peasant origin, in the beginning an overwhelming majority, has declined far more rapidly, the earlier, than the farming population as a whole; the country's largely private, unorganised, but economically and socially still important peasantry is thereby virtually unrepresented in any political élites. And 'republican-provincial and national keys', meaning equal or proportionate representation for all federal regions and all numerically significant nations and nationalities, have been applied to 'cadre policy' (personnel selection and promotion) in more and more institutions, at least at higher levels and with partial exceptions like the Army. These 'keys' have provided smaller republics and nations with additional guarantees that their identities and concerns will not be ignored, but their application has also complicated staffing and often negatively affected the quality and qualification structure of personnel. Nor is it a system that is likely to encourage sentiments of brotherhood and unity in individuals shunted aside or left cooling their heels in an ante-room because it is some other nation's turn to claim a desirable and otherwise merited office.

Membership in *federal* institutions has meanwhile changed in one further way. As their importance has declined with progressive decentralisation and as the risk of losing or alienating one's local political base by going to Belgrade has increased, it has become increasingly difficult to recruit first-class people for federal organs.

POLITICAL SUCCESSION

From the re-founding of Yugoslavia under Communist rule until 1980 succession at the authoritative state and Party summit, which was Tito, was a matter of anticipation, speculation, and latterly assiduous preparation – all of it for many years unpredictably premature. At this level, it has actually happened only twice for each of these previously united summits. The first time for both was in May 1980, when Tito died and was untraumatically succeeded by already-in-place and well-rehearsed collective State and Party Presidencies. For the Party the second succession, as required by its Statute, was at first post-Tito Congress in June 1982, when no significant changes in leadership or policy occurred (Rusinow, 1982a). For the state it was in May 1984, when seven out of eight Republican-Provincial representatives on the nine-member State Presidency were changed, five of them because their constitutionally permissible two five-year terms had expired. (The ninth and *ex-officio* member, the current President of the Party Presidency, rotates annually in September, as previously noted.)

Apart from noting the orderly and undramatic character of these successions, despite trying circumstances in each case (doing without Tito in the first and deepening economic crisis in the others), no valid generalisations can be made on the basis of such a short and particular record. It is possible, however, to wonder whether these same characteristics are not beginning to smell less like healthy stability and more like sterility and petrifying fear that real changes in leadership and institutions, however desirable to make them more responsive and efficient, would not be so orderly and undramatic.

At immediately subordinate and middle-rank levels the record is longer and the sample is larger. Most successions at these levels have also been ordinary and orderly, occurring when and as required by Constitutions or Party statutes, but have tended to resemble a game of musical chairs: same people in different seats, with an occasional drop-out or addition, whenever the music stops. However, meaningful successions here – that is, those that have brought genuine and significant changes of personnel and policies – have occurred more dramatically, at irregular times between Party Congresses and other fixed dates for successions, and in connection with serious crises. This was the case after the break with Stalin in 1948 and in connection with the 'Djilas crisis' in the winter of 1953–4, the 'Ranković crisis' in 1966, and the 'Croatian crisis' and its aftermaths elsewhere in 1971–2 – each significantly associated with an 'historic plenum' of the LCY Central Committee. In these four instances the way it began and the number and nature of subsequent dismissals, resignations, and sanctions imposed at various levels, from federal or regional leaderships down to local organisations, conformed to 'that historical practice' ascribed to Communist regimes by Kardelj. In the words of his dictum, pronounced with reference to the Ranković affair and quoted at the beginning of this chapter, all were indeed 'reminiscent of a *coup d'état*'.

Only one other generalisation, albeit a singularly important one, emerges from a comparison of these four critical successions: all were also carried out at Tito's instigation and unlikely, probably even impossible, without it. The severity of sanctions meted out to erring comrades varied, including death only in the first instance and 'merely' dismissal and disgrace, without trials and prison terms, for leading offenders (some lower-rank and non-Party ones went to prison) in the last two. The nature and consequences of changes in personnel and policies were also various and sometimes contradictory. The first and third led to liberalisation of the regime and pluralisation of the system. The second and fourth led to temporary re-assertion of centralist and 'Leninist' principles and Party dictatorship. The third also led to a rejuvenation of leadership, as senior 'veterans of the Revolution' were largely replaced by junior ones and people who had come to maturity and into the Party only after the war. The fourth, eliminating many of the brightest and best of the junior veterans, produced a mix of resuscitated seniors and post-Revolution recruits. These last, frequently but not always regarded as careerists and/or sycophants, included many educated and competent administrators and technicians and have displayed (or hidden) such a mixture of authoritarian and democratic or pluralistic preferences that the balance of forces between the two is a matter of guesswork.

As the remaining senior veterans fade from the scene one by one, it is primarily these last who rule Yugoslavia today. If anyone does.

THE PRESENT YUGOSLAV LEADERSHIP

Presidents of the Presidency (Heads of State)

5.80　　　Koliševski, Lazar (1914) (Macedonia)[1]

5.80–5.81　Mijatović, Cvijectin (1913) (Bosnia–Herzegovina)

5.81–5.82　Krajger (Kraigher), Sergej (1914) (Slovenia)

5.82–5.83　Stambolić, Petar (1912) (Serbia)

5.83–5.84　Špiljak, Mika (1916) (Croatia)

As elected to a five-year term on 15 May 1984

Name	Republic or Autonomous Province represented	Should serve as President from May-May
Djuranović, Veselin (1927)	Montenegro	1984–5

Notes

1. Served only ten days after Tito's death (4 May 1980), completing his one year term as Deputy President (procedure specified in article 328 of SFRY Constitution)

Vlajković, Radovan (1922)	Vojvodina	1985–6
Hasani, Sinan (1922)	Kosovo	1986–7
Mojsov, Lazar (1920)	Macedonia	1987–8
Mikulič, Branko (1928)	Bosnia–Herzegovina	1988–9
Dolanc, Stane (1925)	Slovenia	
Ljubičić, Nikola (1916)	Serbia	
Vrhovec, Josip (1926)	Croatia	
ex officio: Šukrija (Shukri), Ali (1919) 6.84–6.85	President of CC, LCY Presidency (rotates annually, currently in June)	not eligible

Presidents of the Presidency of the Central Committee, LCY (Heads of Party)

5–9.80	Doronjski, Stevan (1919) Vojvodina[1]
9.80–9.81	Mojsov, Lazar (1920) (Macedonia)
9.81–6.82[2]	Dragosavac, Dušan (1919) (Croatia)
6.82–6.83	Ribičič, Mitja (1919) (Slovenia)
6.83–6.84	Marković, Draža (Dragoslav) (1920) (Serbia)
6.84–6.85	Šukrija (Shukri), Ali (1919) (Kosovo)

Notes

1. Completed one year term to which elected as 'Presiding Officer' (with little now changed to 'President') of LCY Presidency ('Provisional Solution' of 12.6.80)
2. 'Rotation' date changed from September to June at Twelfth LCY Congress in June 1982

Presidency of the Central Committee, LCY (June 1984)

Members elected at Twelfth LCY Congress, June 1982 (except Pozderac, who replaced Franjo Herljević on 12 June 1984 and Žarković who replaced Ali Šukrija on 25 June 1985)

Name	From	Nationality
Belovski, Dimče (1923)	Macedonia	Macedonian
Bilić, Jure (1922)	Croatia	Croat
Dragosavac, Dušan (1919)	Croatia	Serb
Hadži-Vasilev, Kiro (1921)	Macedonia	Macedonian
Kučan, Milan (1941)	Slovenia	Slovene
Marković, Dragoslav (1920)	Serbia	Serb
Matić, Petar (1920)	Vojvodina	Serb
Milatović, Veljko (1921)	Montenegro	Montenegrin
Pozderac, Hamdija (1923)	Bosnia–Herzegovina	Muslim
Radović, Miljan (1933)	Montenegro	Montenegrin
Ribičič, Mitja (1919)	Slovenia	Slovene
Stojanović, Nikola (1933)	Bosnia–Herzegovina	Serb
Vidić, Dobrivoje (1918)	Serbia	Serb
Žarković, Vidoje	Montenegro	Montenegrin

Federal Executive Council

Planinc, Milka (1924)   Croat (f)   President (Prime Minister)

(f)   female

11　China

PETER FERDINAND

This chapter will concentrate on the problems of succession in the People's Republic of China (PRC) since the death of Mao. This is not to say that there were no problems of succession during the earlier years of the regime, but the period between the Cultural Revolution beginning in 1966 and Mao's death ten years later still casts such a shadow over the Chinese political scene both in terms of issues and personalities that it will continue for years to be the major determining influence over succession.

THE POLITICAL SYSTEM IN 1976 AND THE SUCCESSION OF HUA GUOFENG

One of Mao's goals in launching the Cultural Revolution in 1966 was to resolve problems of political succession in the PRC, and on two levels in particular. On the level of society as a whole, Mao hoped to recreate the same toughening experience of struggle and self-sacrifice that his generation had undergone during the Chinese revolution, so that younger generations would become hardened and determined to continue the revolution. At the same time, he also wanted to remove those leaders of the Chinese Communist Party (CCP) whom he believed to have taken the 'capitalist road'. His most prominent target was his own designated successor and head of state, Liu Shaoqi. The latter was humiliated and vilified in front of huge crowds of Red Guards, imprisoned, taken away from Peking in such secrecy that even his guards were not told who he was, and when he died in 1969, it was ordered that his ashes were to be scattered so that no trace of him should be left.

In the turmoil of the factional disputes and street fighting of the Cultural Revolution, the CCP was reduced to a shell of its former self. Almost all of its top leaders were humiliated and disgraced. Almost all of the bureaucratic procedures which it had evolved over the preceding seventeen years were smashed, and many of its internal institutions were disbanded. The security organs and the Red Guards, encouraged by Mao, claimed the right to investigate any Party member like any other citizen, and the scale of such 'investigations' can be seen from the fact that in 1983 it was announced that unjust or erroneous decisions involving some three million cadres from the period 1966–76 had been redressed, that wrong judgements against 120 000 Party members had been reversed, and that over 470 000 Party members had been reinstated, many posthumously. The state apparatus, too, did not escape the upheavals, and in most provinces of China it was the People's Liberation Army (PLA) which became the *de facto* dominant political institution. Already, even before the Cultural Revolution, the PLA had been presented as a model Maoist institution, and its leadership under Lin Biao grew accustomed to thinking of itself as a key guardian of Maoist ideology. And now, in addition to its responsibilities for national defence, it also assumed charge of all armed internal security work.

From 1969 onwards, and especially from 1973 when Deng Xiaoping, the former Party Secretary General, was recalled to be Vice-Premier, political life was to a limited extent revived and stabilised. Nevertheless, the Cultural Revolution left an indelible mark. One crucial legacy was the personalisation of politics. This had two aspects. First, it meant that Mao personally dominated everything. He was the sun whose radiant beams touched everyone, and who could do whatever he wished. A striking example of this came at the Ninth CCP Congress in 1969, where Mao claimed the right to name his own successor, Lin Biao, without even the pretence of consultation with the Party Congress, Central Committee or Politburo. Every Party member, every citizen, owed loyalty primarily to Mao, rather than to any institution – indeed, the obligation previously placed upon all Party members to uphold Party discipline was removed from the Party rules approved in 1969. Even in the PLA discipline became lax, with commanders on occasion refusing to accept postings or orders for manoeuvres (Deng, 1983, p. 17). The second aspect of 'personalisation' concerned the way organisations operated. Though many organisational boundaries and hierarchies survived, they were frequently ignored. Thus political power and the authority to make decisions were extremely blurred. Individuals rather than institutions held power.

Decision-making came to be beset by 'factions' (that is, groups pursuing their own self-interest), rivalries, intrigues, petty jealousies, though they often were presented in 'ideological' terms which may or may not have been genuine. Also, the Cultural Revolution had led to major cuts in administrative organs. In the Party, for example, the Central Committee Secretariat had been abolished, leaving only its constituent departments in place at the centre, and the head of Mao's security, Wang Dongxing, had been put for a while in charge of the most important, the General Office. Effectively, Mao alone constituted the 'centre' of Chinese politics, but as he grew older, feebler and less coherent, the central co-ordination of day-to-day policy was gravely weakened. So at moments of crisis there was often no clear line flowing from the centre throughout the country. Indeed, it sometimes seemed as though the Party line was determined by whichever group happened to be in control of the telegraph office that day – always assuming the telegraph was working.

Apart from this, one other characteristic of the political system needs to be stressed, for it was of crucial importance in determining the succession. This was the continuing dominance at the top of the Party of the survivors of the Long March. Even though the Cultural Revolution represented an assault of the young on the old, and even though particular representatives of the same Long March generation had been disgraced, nevertheless 80 per cent of the Central Committee elected in 1969, and 63 per cent in 1973, had joined the Party before 1936 (Domes, 1980, p. 159). The fact of having accompanied Mao on the Long March still conferred great prestige on those whom he trusted. Equally importantly, however, this group itself, including those disgraced, appear to have believed themselves superior to all other Party members. There seems to have been a widely felt instinct that no survivor of the Long March deserved the treatment which had been meted out to some of them, and that even though they might ultimately have to put up with disgrace from Mao, they would never be reconciled to it.

When Mao died in September 1976, these features of the personalisation and fluidity of politics, and of the continuing prestige of the Long March generation, were to prove crucial in determining his ultimate succession. This time Mao had not designated his successor, but initially the Politburo appeared united that one of its youngest members, Hua Guofeng, should assume the leading role. To ease the transition, great play was made of an undated note which Mao was reported to have given Hua during 1976: 'With you in charge, I am at ease.' Reference was also made to another, though slightly less flattering, comment by Mao about Hua: that he had wide provincial experience and had not done badly as Minister of Public Security, that he was loyal and conscientious, and that he was not stupid. Whether or not Mao had actually intended Hua to succeed him, it is no doubt the case that Mao had sponsored promotions for Hua, for example, the move from being Party Secretary in Mao's own province of Hunan to various posts in Peking from 1971 onwards, and he possibly headed the sensitive investigation into the attempt by Lin Biao to assassinate Mao in 1971. From 1975 he was Minister of Public Security and Vice-Premier.

Nevertheless, no better indication of the fluidity of political arrangements can be found than the downfall of the Gang of Four one month later. Here were four members of the Politburo being arrested by other members of the Politburo, whilst yet other Politburo members were only apparently informed after the event. These arrests were later justified on the grounds that the Gang themselves had been planning a *coup*, and that immediately after Mao's death they had instructed provincial Party organisations to route all reports to them rather than to other leaders. Nevertheless, the immediate task of their overthrow proved relatively painless. Only in Shanghai did supporters put up armed resistance, and this was crushed after a little over a week.

Hua himself played a leading part in the arrests – as indeed the Minister of Public Security would have had to do. His initiative obviously united behind him, for the time being, those groups and individuals who wanted the downfall of the Gang. In addition, however, Hua set about enlisting the support of a broader coalition of various groups, none of which had taken the side of the Gang of Four, but whose attitude towards many of the Maoist policies pursued in the 1970s had often been positive (Fontana, 1982). The most important of these was the PLA. There seems no doubt that the bulk of the High Command approved of the removals, and there are even reports that some of the arrests took place at the house of Marshal Ye Jianying, who was Minister of Defence and a Vice-Chairman of the Party. It seems no coincidence that afterwards Hua was often seen in public wearing military uniform. A second group apparently supporting Hua at that time was the so-called 'oil faction', headed by Politburo member Li Xiannian. This group reportedly wanted high priority to be devoted to the development of China's heavy industry, and in particular the oil industry, which could lead to rapid industrial development of the country. A third group which obviously supported Hua were later nicknamed 'the whateverists', that is, they believed that, as Hua himself claimed in February 1977, 'whatever policies Chairman Mao laid down should be resolutely upheld, and whatever instructions Chairman Mao gave should be unswervingly respected'. Their leaders were all Politburo members based in Peking: Wang Dongxing, the commander of the praetorian guard 8341 Unit, who had organised the arrest of the Gang; Ji Dengkui, First Political Commissar of the Peking Military Region and a Deputy Premier; Chen Xilian, Commander of the Peking Military Region; and Wu De, Mayor of Peking. Overall, these were disparate groups of supporters, not necessarily linked by any organisational affiliation, but their leaders had one crucial advantage over Hua: they were all older in terms both of age and revolutionary seniority. Therefore provided he remained true to the tacit operating principle of respect for the Long March generation (and he himself did just belong to it), to none of them did he represent a threat.

Apart from seeking support from these top national figures, though, Hua sought to broaden the appeal of both himself and the regime. To the population at large he offered assurances that the methods of the Cultural Revolution would not return, and that there would be an easing of restrictions on the economic activity of the peasants. And lavish promises were made to middle-level elite groups. For example, increased aid was promised to under-developed regions, such as the province of Yunnan, which was granted so much aid between 1977 and 1979 that it represented 38 per cent of the total amount delivered in the whole period 1952–79 (He Shiyuan, 1981, p. 166).

In the short run, Hua's strategy was clearly successful. There does seem to have been an upsurge of genuine enthusiasm for the new leadership, and he quickly came to hold a collection of posts that exceeded even those of Mao: Head of State, Chairman of the CCP, Premier, and Chairman of the Party Military Commission. He also began laying the foundations of a reputation as a theoretician by making himself editor of the fifth volume of Mao's *Selected Works*, and a mini-cult of him developed.

THE RETURN OF DENG XIAOPING, AND THE RISE OF HU YAOBANG AND ZHAO ZIYANG

Despite Hua's apparent success in consolidating his position, there remained a number of serious problems to be resolved, and two in particular were of crucial importance. The first can be summed up in the words: Deng Xiaoping. Deng had been brought back to power in 1973 to take over day-to-day running of the Party and state bureaucracies, but he had again been dismissed following the April 1976 Tiananmen incident, when an enormous crowd had to be forcibly dispersed after gathering in the main square of Peking to honour the memory of Zhou Enlai, who had died in January. Clearly Mao had approved this dismissal. Yet it also seems clear that many senior leaders disapproved of it – there were even reports of Politburo members, like imperial ministers of old, leaving their offices in protest (Teiwes, 1984, p. 75). Deng was spared public humiliation and, again according to reports in Hongkong, he was sheltered in the Southern province of Guangdong by the local military commander, Xu Shiyou, and the First Party Secretary, Wei Guoqing.

After Mao died, there seems little doubt that many of the most senior Party members and leaders felt that Deng, as the most prominent Party figure still living, simply could not be ignored, especially in view of the many injustices he had endured. Yet those who had risen to power as a result of the Cultural Revolution attempted to prevent, or at least delay, his return. The issue began to come to a head in February–March 1977. Articles started appearing in the Party press, with Hua's approval, proclaiming the need to carry out 'whatever' Mao had laid down. Not merely did this represent a pious wish to remain faithful to Mao's legacy, it also had an organisational connotation. Since Mao was known to have approved Deng's dismissal, it followed that all loyal Maoists should keep Deng out of office. In fact, at this time, there was probably a majority in the Politburo opposed to Deng's return. Certainly it seems highly likely that those members of the 'Whateverist' faction mentioned above were strongly opposed to it, for it was they who had suppressed the Tiananmen demonstration which had led to his removal.

Nevertheless, the mood of the time and the mood of the Party was not one which favoured automatic acceptance of Politburo wishes. For one thing there was the disorientation and uncertainty left by the passing of a charismatic leader, compounded by the shock of the arrest of the Gang of Four. For another, there was the continuing fluidity of political hierarchies and institutional boundaries left by the Cultural Revolution. There was the continuing lax Party discipline. And too there was the sense that the most senior generation of Party leaders as a whole ought to determine the Party line, whether or not they were members of the Politburo. Thus regular sessions of the

Politburo or Central Committee might be less important than other, less 'formal' meetings. One particularly key meeting was a Central Committee 'work conference' in March 1977. There Hua attempted to defend the principle of the 'Two Whatevers', but ran into strong opposition from people who wanted Deng's return, and two of Deng's strongest supporters are reported as having been Chen Yun (then Deputy Chairman of the Standing Commission of the National People's Congress) and Wang Zhen (then Deputy Premier), neither of whom at that time was in the Politburo (*Zhongguo gongchandang lishi jiangyi*, 1981, p. 168). This meeting must have done a great deal to swing opinion behind Deng, and the following month he wrote a conciliatory letter to the Central Committee in which he declared his complete support for Mao thought directing the work the Party, army and masses, with the proviso that it should be 'accurately and correctly used'. At the July CC Plenum Deng was restored to the posts of Deputy Chairman of the CCP, membership of the Politburo Standing Committee, Deputy Chairman of the CCP Military Commission, Deputy Premier, and Chief of Staff of the PLA.

Once back, he energetically set about bending official policies in the direction he wished to see them go, and particular stress must be placed on the word 'energetically'. Deng wrested the initiative from his formally higher-ranking rivals by his vigour and his advocacy of the need for reform. In fact, his strategy can in many ways be seen as an application of Maoist principles of guerrilla warfare. Though 'Xiaoping' means 'small peace', and he is small in height, the one thing he was not was peaceful. He was constantly on the move and tireless in his pursuit of every opportunity. He harried opponents unceasingly, making flanking movements wherever possible and concessions wherever necessary, then looking for alternative ways of achieving the same objectives. Initially, rather than attack Party rivals head-on, he sought to enlist the support of the state bureaucracy. He took the mantle of Zhou Enlai's successor, resurrected the economic and military reform programme he had advocated in 1975, and used his position as Deputy Premier to try to win over the intelligentsia by emphasising the regime's desperate need for expertise. To reassure them that there would be no repetition of the ill-treatment of intellectuals, he, much more than Hua, became associated with the revival of Mao's 1957 slogan: 'Let a hundred flowers bloom, let a hundred schools contend.' And although the Hundred Flowers campaign of 1957 had rapidly led to punishments for 'rightist' critics of the regime, many of those punishments were now rescinded.

Also, Deng initially used newspapers and journals not immediately responsible to the Central Committee to spread his ideas, such as the PLA newspaper, *Liberation Daily*. And it was not *The People's Daily* but the newspaper for the intelligentsia, *Guangming Ribao*, that in May 1978 carried the first article to outline his own interpretation of the essence of Maoism' that is, the fact that 'practice is the sole criterion of truth' and that what was needed was 'to seek truth from facts' (a phrase which Mao himself had urged upon the Party school in Yanan).

Deng was also aided by successful early reforms in particular provinces, especially Sichuan, where the Party Secretary, Zhao Ziyang, took advantage of the centre's weak control to introduce his own agricultural reforms far different from those advocated by Hua.

Nevertheless, although Deng could begin his campaign by concentrating on groups outside the Party hierarchy, his ultimate goal was to capture the Party, for he wanted to restore to it the role it had played in society before the Cultural Revolution. And although he emphasised the need for responsibility for technical issues to be transferred to the state apparatus, he also wanted the boundaries between the Party and other organs, and the differentiation of respective roles, to be made much clearer, so that the Party could exercise more effective general leaderhip of society.

The issue which he used to win control was that of the rehabilitation of disgraced former Party and state leaders, and the person who took the lead for him was Hu Yaobang. Before the Cultural Revolution, Hu had been prominently engaged in youth work, and from 1957 until 1965 he was First Secretary of the Communist Youth League. More importantly, he had become closely associated with Deng Xiaoping, then Secretary General of the Party, and in the period 1966–76 his career followed the same pattern of ups and downs. Deng's reinstatement in the Party leadership, however, led to Hu's insertion into the Party apparatus, and in July 1977 he was appointed Deputy Director of the CC General Office. By October he was also Deputy Director of the CC Party School, and it was in the same month that, to commemorate the first anniversary of the downfall of the Gang of Four, an investigation group at the school published an article in *The People's Daily* which called for the speeding up of the rehabilitation of cadres wrongfully 'dragged down' by the Gang of Four. Clearly this was an issue about which Hua Guofeng and other beneficiaries of the Cultural Revolution would have serious misgivings. Yet others in the leadership felt equally strongly about the need for rehabilitation. The article in *The People's Daily* brought the issue more into the open, and in December Hu was appointed Director of the CC Organisational Department. Immediately, he set the whole department on the task of reversing false verdicts, and the process of rehabilitation rapidly gathered momentum (*Zhonggongdang lishi zhuyao shijian jianjie*, 1982, pp. 237–8).

Clearly Hu's appointment represented a victory for Deng, and the process of rehabilitation had the effect not merely of undermining Hua's position, since he had previously semed to be dragging his feet over the issue, but also of bringing back into political life venerable Party leaders, most of whom might be assumed to support Deng, or at least be sufficiently grateful to him to support his reforms.

Immediately, Deng launched another series of attacks. During January and February 1978, a number of articles appeared in *The People's Daily* attacking, sometimes by name, various groups of his opponents. (Wang, 1982, p. 808) May saw the launching of the slogan 'Seek truth from facts', already mentioned above, which led to a sharpening of the ideological dispute, and later in the year, Hu achieved a reversal of the verdict on the Tiananmen incident – it was now declared to be a truly revolutionary demonstration.

Finally, in December came the historic Third Plenum of the Central Committee, which marked the ascendancy of Deng and his followers and established the basic path of reform which the Party would follow over the next few years. In view of the strong disagreements which existed within the leadership, the Central Committee again called a 'work conference'. This met for thirty-six days prior to the Plenum and made 'full preparations' for it – conceivably including personnel changes, for the Plenum itself was only attended by 169 out of 201 members (*Zhongguo gongchandang lishi jiangyi*, 1981, p. 174), and at its close over thirty of Hua's supporters were replaced. Hu was elected the Party's Chief Secretary (*mishuzhang*), Third Secretary of the Party's Central Commission for Discipline Inspection (which he actually ran), a member of the Politburo, and (until February 1980) Director of the CC Propaganda Department. His position in the Party was now much more assured. In February 1980 the Fifth Plenum of the Central Committee either dismissed or accepted the resignation from the Politburo of the 'Whatever' faction (Wang Dongxing, etc.), and reconstituted the CC Secretariat. Hu was promoted to the Politburo Standing Commission and appointed Party Secretary General (*zongshuji*).

So far what has been outlined has been Deng's 'guerrilla' strategy for taking control of the Party leadership. Yet his success cannot simply be explained in terms of his own actions. Attention also needs to be paid to the mistakes and miscalculations of his opponents. Hua Guofeng, by contrast, adopted much more of a static strategy, based upon the belief that if he could hold together the 'strong-points' of the central organs of Party and state, he could control China (Fontana, 1982, p. 246). His problem, however, was that in the volatile climate of post-Mao China this was far from easy. Despite his mini-cult, he did not have the authority among the senior ranks of the Party to impose his leadership where necessary. He allowed himself to be dominated by powerful élite groups and he even accepted the reverses imposed upon him by Deng. In one way this was a good thing, for he was much more difficult to dislodge than more outright opponents since, like a disciplined Party member, he was prepared to implement in the name of greater Party democracy the compromises forced upon him. Yet he ultimately was defeated because his style of leadership was too weak and led to major policy failures. The reason for this was that he had to contend not merely with Deng Xiaoping but also with China's poverty.

In February 1978 the Fifth National People's Congress met, and Hua Guofeng presented the report on the work of the government. In it he called, among other things, for work on 120 new major heavy industrial projects, for instance, ten large steel plants, nine large non-ferrous metallurgical bases, ten new oil fields. All this was in addition to increases in military spending, improvements in the standard of living of workers and peasants, and increased grants for education and science. This highly optimistic programme for the realisation of the Four Modernisations clearly represented the most ambitious goals of each of the responsible agencies, but it soon became obvious that it far exceeded China's means. Nevertheless, in the course of the next two years individual agencies set about realising their part of the programme without always coordinating their actions with the centre, and indeed ordered equipment abroad without always checking that foreign currency would be available to pay for it. Thus during 1978 overall state spending increased by 51 per cent, and 1979–80 saw by far the largest budget deficits in the PRC's history, with spending exceeding receipts by 15.4 per cent in 1979 and by 11.7 per cent in 1980 (*Zhongguo tongji nianjian 1983*, pp. 445, 448). This was despite the fact that already in April 1979 the CC had launched a programme of retrenchment to restore balance to the economy. The responsibility for these errors was clearly not all Hua's, since many other institutions and individual leaders had contributed to them. Yet ultimately it could be said that he had failed to provide sufficient leadership to prevent them. And, too, there was further sniping from Deng's group, criticising the cult of Hua and spreading whispers that there was something suspicious about Mao's note 'With you in charge, I am at ease'. So during 1980 Hua lost most of his posts. He was replaced as Premier by Zhao Ziyang, as Chairman of the Party's Military Commission by Deng Xiaoping, and, after a CC special work conference in December 1980, as Chairman of the Party by Hu Yaobang, although the latter post seems first to have been offered to Deng who turned it down (*Inside China Mainland*, December 1981).

Thus from the middle of 1981 China had a triumvirate of top leaders, and in many respects the relation between them resembled that at the top of the CPSU after the dismissal of Khrushchev in October 1964. First, there was an overt attempt to divide the chief leading posts, especially those of Party and state, among several people as a way of preventing excessive concentration of power in the hands of one man (Khrushchev in the USSR and, allegedly, Hua Guofeng). Secondly, at the moment of their accession, the new Party leaders were not the dominant figures in their respective Politburos (Brezhnev, Hu Yaobang). Thirdly, there was a 'kingmaker' in each Politburo (Suslov, Deng Xiaoping). Fourthly, in the immediate ensuing period, it was the head of the state apparatus who played a more assertive role. In the case of the USSR, Kosygin took the lead at home by introducing experimental market reforms in the economy, whilst in foreign affairs he was prominent as a mediator in the Vietnam War and the Indo–Pakistani conflict of 1966. In the case of China, it is Zhao Ziyang who has had a much higher profile both at home and abroad. At home he has been associated with the introduction of market reforms of agriculture and industry. Abroad he has travelled to all continents since becoming Premier, and he has become much more self-confident – it was he who publicly warned President Reagan of the dangers of US policy in Central America. By contrast, Hu has largely confined himself to Party re-building, his only forays abroad being either to 'fraternal' countries such as Romania and Yugoslavia, or to Japan. Zhao has even taken the lead sartorially, so to speak – it was he who began wearing in China as well as abroad Western suits at official functions attended by foreign guests, which prompted a number of letters to Chinese newspapers enquiring whether the wearing of Western suits was still a sign of ideological corruption.

Clearly the higher profile of Zhao was closely connected with the higher current salience of issues which are particularly the preserve of the state apparatus, that is, economic reform. Yet it may also not be unimportant that Zhao has had much greater experience in the Party apparatus than Hu, having served with apparent success in the provinces of Guangdong, Inner Mongolia and Sichuan. He has been much less indebted to Deng Xiaoping for his career, and he has shown an ability to get on with various groups in the Party, ranging from Zhou Enlai to moderate supporters of Cultural Revolution-type policies. He does not seem at present a rival of Hu's, but he is three years younger and under certain circumstances he might be a replacement.

CURRENT PROBLEMS AND PROSPECTS FOR THE FUTURE

So far what has been charted has been the emergence of the triumvirate who currently dominate the Chinese political scene. There are, however, a number of unresolved difficulties which are likely to affect future successions.

Many of them are to be found in economic policies, and friction over these may increase as 1986 approaches, the year in which comprehensive reform is supposed to begin. And in the sphere of ideology, many cadres in both the Party and the PLA have been disturbed by manifestations of materialism and decadence, especially among young people. In late 1983 Deng Xiaoping responded by declaring the need to combat 'spiritual pollution'. Propaganda work has intensified, incidentally raising the profile of the Party relative to other institutions in an area for which it claims sole responsibility – ideology. Nevertheless, to the extent that critics attribute these unhealthy signs to the economic reforms so far attempted and to the opening of China to the outside world, it may be presumed that the core of support for radical reforms is neither as great nor as whole-hearted as it was.

In terms of institutions, there are difficulties with both the Party and the PLA. What the new Party leadership has attempted to do is turn the PLA into a much more professional institution and confine it to a more purely 'military' role. Pre-1958 ranks and uniforms have been restored. Officers are now required to attend military academies. Military doctrine has been updated. Some new equipment has been provided, and the current Defence Minister, Zhang Aiping, has long been associated with the development of Chinese military technology. And the tasks of armed internal security have now been transferred to a reconstituted armed police force, with an estimated strength of 700 000 men (*CHINA aktuell*, March 1984, p. 148).

Many of these changes will no doubt appeal to some officers. Nevertheless, there is still discontent from two sides. On the one hand, more 'professionally-minded' officers may remain dissatisfied with their still predominantly backward military equipment, although the Party leadership has consistently maintained that military modernisation must take place within the limits of what the country can afford. On the other hand, officers harbouring sympathy for the policies and the PLA role of the post-Cultural Revolution period may be less than wholly enthusiastic about the current reform strategy. Some features of the latter may in any case lead to undesirable military repercussions, for example peasants are reportedly now much less eager to send sons to serve in the PLA when they could earn large sums of money under the new responsibility system. Moreover, the Party leadership has indicated that the PLA as a whole should be reduced and the average age of its officers lowered. Even though some of the cuts may be quite painless – for example the PLA Railway Corps was transferred to the Ministry of Railways, and no doubt many former PLA men will join the new armed police force – the Secretary General of the Party Military Commission, Yang Shangkun, recently reminded the military that its command structure was 'enormously overstaffed' (*Hongqi*, 1984(15), p. 4).

Given these problems, it is not surprising that tensions between the army and the party leaderships should remain, and that complaints about the remnants of 'leftist' ideology should regularly appear in the Party press and even in the speeches of top military commanders. It is doubtless no coincidence that the first article in Deng Xiaoping's *Selected Works* begins with the statement: 'We in the army have a good tradition . . . The Party commands the gun, the gun does not command the Party.' Nevertheless, the coalition which initially supported him has cracked in places, and one indication of this has been the fate of the two who 'protected' him in Guangdong in 1976: Xu Shiyou was dismissed in February 1980, (one report suggested it was because Deng refused to make him Chief of Staff), and Wei Guoqing, who was promoted head of the General Political Department of the PLA, was dismissed in 1982 over the publication of a 'leftist' article in the PLA newspaper *Liberation Daily*, although he has retained his membership of the Politburo. If these difficulties are combined with the reports in Hongkong of the refusal of the High Command to accept Hu Yaobang as Chairman of the Party's Military Commission in 1980, relations between Party and army leaders after Deng's death will remain problematic.

A second cause for concern is the Party itself. The leadership has done a great deal to restore Party institutions and the principles of Party life and Party discipline which existed prior to 1966. Yet the attitudes of many of the rank-and-file, especially the eighteen million who joined between 1966 and 1976, still disquiet them, and in the latter part of 1983 the Party launched a three-year rectification campaign. Nor is discipline only a problem for the rank-and-file. The ability of the Party centre to control the actions of provincial Party authorities seems less than perfect, even though all the First Secretaries of provincial-level Party organisations have been appointed since February 1977, and twenty-five out of twenty-nine provincial governors have been appointed since the beginning of 1983. 'Leftist mistakes' continue to be made and admitted in Hunan and Guangxi, for example, yet the centre seems unable to remove the Leading (First) Secretaries, who were both appointed before Deng Xiaoping's return.

The problem of fluctuating currents of opinion within the Party apparatus is complicated by the high priority accorded by Deng Xiaoping in particular to the promotion of younger cadres into leading positions. Despite various blandishments, including the establishment of Advisory Commissions at all levels of the Party to assure retired cadres an honoured position, elderly officials often will not make way. In the Politburo, for example, the seventy-nine year old Li Xiannian was elected head of state for the first time in 1983, whilst the eighty-seven year old Marshal Ye Jianying continues in office despite requiring attendants to read aloud on his behalf even short public statements. 'Younger' senior cadres have been retired, however, particularly those with a history of more open opposition to Deng Xiaoping. So there is no doubt some resentment over this partisan use of the weapon of retirement.

There is no doubt resentment, too, over the choice of replacements. Individual cadres have had spectacular rises, and the one with the most meteoric owes his advancement to Deng. This is Wang Zhaoguo, who was 'discovered' by Deng during an inspection tour in 1980, when he was the forty-year old Deputy Director of the No. 2 Car Factory in Hubei. He was elected to the Central Committee at the Twelfth Congress, in November 1982 became First Secretary of the Youth League, and then in spring 1984 he was appointed Director of the CC Secretariat General Office. Clearly he may have a bright future. As yet, however, Hu has not, or has not been able, to implant many people with close ties to him in the past into the Central Committee. Out of the 210 CC members elected in 1982, probably less than ten had an association with the central Youth League apparatus before 1966. For the moment opponents and those threatened with removal are still in position to hold him back. Thus far the most significant turnover has taken place at the provincial level, as outlined above. Yet even though this turnover might suggest an opportunity for Hu to appoint officials sympathetic to his views, it is also usually the case that those appointed have had a lengthy career in the provinces, and therefore the extent to which they should be regarded as 'clients' of the centre is open to question. Only two of the new provincial Leading (First) Party secretaries for example, Li Ligong in Shanxi and Xiang Nan in Fujian, were leading members of the central Youth League apparatus before the Cultural Revolution. Only in the CC Secretariat do there seem to be no strong opponents of the strategy of reforms.

There are always tensions in the succession of one political generation by another, but in China the problem is made particularly acute by the need to complete the process in such a short period of time. Deng is an old man in a hurry, but his haste risks uniting opponents over various separate issues, ranging from ideological to personal, into a recalcitrant coalition, which Hu Yaobang may not have the personal authority, or the personal following, to overcome on his own.

So far what has been discussed has been the relationship between future succession and domestic policy problems. What, though, about foreign affairs? Would fundamental changes in Chinese foreign policy be associated with a possible change in leadership? The answer is probably no. There have been various shifts in PRC foreign policy since 1976, but these seem to have been accomplished without serious top-level disagreements, certainly nothing to compare with the disagreements over the original contacts with the United States in the early 1970s. After Mao's death, Chinese policy first veered towards a heady honeymoon with the West and Japan, but in the 1980s has become more level-headed. For one thing the limits of China's purchasing power became apparent, and a large number of contracts with Western and Japanese firms had to be cancelled. For another there arose the concern over the dangers of subversive foreign ideas. And there was also the dissatisfaction of the PRC over continued United States restrictions on the export of certain types of military equipment, coupled with US willingness to maintain some military supplies to Taiwan. To a limited extent, the PRC has developed more conciliatory policies towards the Eastern bloc. Her leadership no longer asserts the inevitability of war with the Soviet Union, and 1983 saw a number of gestures intended to improve relations with Eastern Europe. The latter can provide alternative, and possibly cheaper and more appropriate technology for industrial development. It can provide experience of reforming the Soviet-type economy – and contacts with Hungary have noticeably increased. And it may be seen as a less likely source of 'corrupting' foreign ideas than the West. Yet as long as the Soviet Union continues to maintain large numbers of troops on the Chinese border, persists in her invasion of Afghanistan, and supports the Vietnamese invasion of Kampuchea, there is no likelihood of significant improvement in Sino–Soviet relations. And even if they did improve, it seems unlikely that they would ever reach the degree of closeness of the 1950s, for above everything else the current Chinese leadership is concerned with preserving national independence. As a recent commentator put it:

The Chinese people . . . have realised from history that not to ally with large countries furthers the policy of maintaining complete freedom to oppose hegemonism, because an alliance with a large country would hinder our resistance and opposition to impermissible behaviour by the other side, and might lead to us being used against another country. (*Hongqi*, 1984 (14), p. 28)

Instead, China has turned in the 1980s to the Third World, (for example the Palestinians and the Latin Americans) asserting open solidarity with their struggles for development and independence, even if that meant displeasing the USA. In his speech to the Twelfth Party Congress Hu Yaobang described the emergence of the Third World on the international scene as a historic event which had severely restricted the ability of the superpowers to manipulate the world to their advantage.

CONCLUSION

The main argument underlying this chapter has been that the emergence of first Hua Guofeng and then Hu Yaobang as leaders of the
CCP was determined by three groups of factors. The first was the
continuing legacy of the Cultural Revolution, and the need to pass
from a charismatic leadership to a more 'routinised' one. The second
was the continuing pre-eminence of the Long March generation of
Party cadres. The third was the exploitation of particular issues by
individual leaders. What does not seem to have been so important
(with the exception of the PLA certainly not consistently so) was a
pattern of interaction between established institutions acting as homogeneous blocs in the political structure. The reason for this was
partly the Cultural Revolution itself, when institutions became particularly permeable, and partly the breadth of experience of senior
Party leaders. A great number of the latter had served as military
commanders, commissars, administrators, educators and propagan-
dists both before 1949 and after. Thus they all had acquired a broader
perspective which no doubt attenuated the extent to which they
identified exclusively with the specific goals and procedures of the
particular institution in which they happened to be working at a given
time. No subsequent generation of leaders is likely to have this same
breadth of perspective. So it is difficult to derive generalisations
from, or base predictions about future successions upon, the paths by
which Hua Guofeng or the current leadership triumvirate came to the
top of the Chinese political system. With the specialisation and
division of labour which developed in Chinese institutions between
1949 and the Cultural Revolution, and which is being gradually
restored, leading cadres in future are likely to have had narrower
professional experience. They probably will identify more with 'their'
respective institutions, and also, as time passes, institutions will
reacquire a life of their own. Institutional bargaining may become as
important in future successions, as it seems to be in the Soviet Union.
    As for possible future leaders, Hu Yaobang gave an interview in
1983 in which he divided Party leadership at the centre into three
'echelons'. The first echelon, which decided all major issues, he
identified as consisting of the first ten ranking Politburo members,
with the exception of himself and Zhao Ziyang. It was the second
echelon – Hu Yaobang, Zhao Ziyang and Vice-Premier Wan Li –
whom he said were in charge of day-to-day policies. The third
echelon, including Hu Qili, the executive secretary of the CC Secre-

tariat, was in charge of administering those policies (Chang, 1983, pp. 69–70). Hu added that the members of the second echelon could continue to work for seven to ten years. By then Hu Yaobang would have been Party leader for ten years or more, and no doubt would be in a position to have a large say as to his successor. If so, it could well be that he has in mind Hu Qili, the present executive secretary of the Secretariat, a man fourteen years younger and a close associate of his in the Youth League apparatus up to 1965. Possibly after him would come Wang Zhaoguo. Certainly at present there is in the Politburo only one member from the younger generation who might be a rival, and that is Ni Zhifu, the Chairman of the Trades Union Federation. Yet ten years is an eternity in politics, and the fate of previously designated successors in China does not encourage prediction. As for the short term, Hu Yaobang's power and authority, even though there is no obvious alternative to him, still seem to depend greatly upon the heartbeat of Deng Xiaoping.

THE PRESENT CHINESE LEADERSHIP

Politburo[1]	Function
Hu Yaobang (1915)	Secretary General
Ye Jianying (1897)	Deputy Chairman of the CCP, Marshal
Deng Xiaoping (1904)	Chairman, CCP Military Commission; Chairman, CCP Central Advisory Commission
Zhao Ziyang (1918)	Prime Minister

Note

1. The first six members of the Politburo comprise its Standing Commission, and the first thirteen are listed in the ranking recorded in the list of condolences for PB member Liao Chengzhi (*CHINA aktuell*, June 1983). The rest are in Western alphabetical sequence.

Li Xiannian (1905)	Head of State
Chen Yun (1905)	Chairman, Central Discipline Inspection Commission
Peng Zhen (1902)	Chairman, National People's Congress
Deng Yingchao (1904) (f)	ex-Second Secretary, Central Discipline Inspection Commission
Xu Xiangqian (1902)	Deputy Chairman, CCP Military Commission; Marshal
Nie Rongzhen (1899)	Deputy Chairman, CCP Military Commission; Marshal
Ulanhu (1904)	Deputy President of the PRC
Wang Zhen (1908)	Party School President
Yang Shangkun (1904)	Permanent Deputy Chairman and Secretary-General, CCP Military Commission
Fang Yi (1916)	State Councillor; Chairman, State Commission for Science and Technology
Hu Qiaomu (1912)	Honorary President, Academy of Social Sciences
Li Desheng (1916)	Commander, Shenyang Military Region
Ni Zhifu (1932)	Chairman, Trades Union Federation
Song Renqiong (1909)	ex-Director, Organisation Dept., CC Secretariat
Wan Li (1916)	Deputy Prime Minister
Wang Zhen (1908)	President, CCP School
Wei Guoqing (1906)	Deputy Chairman, National People's Congress

Xi Zhongxun (1908)	Member, CC Secretariat
Yang Dezhi (1910)	Chief of PLA General Staff
Yu Qiuli (1914)	Director, PLA General Political Department; Member, CC Secretariat
Zhang Tingfa	Air Force C-in-C

Candidate Members

Chen Muhua (f)	State Councillor; Minister for Foreign Economic Relations and Trade
Qin Jiwei (1910)	Commander, Peking Military Region
Yao Yilin (1917)	Deputy Prime Minister; Member, CC Secretariat

Secretariat	**Function**
Hu Yaobang (1915)	as above
Chen Pixian (1916)	Secretary, CC Commission for Politics and Law (with possible de facto control of police)
Deng Liqun (1915)	Director, Propaganda Dept
Gu Mu (1914)	State Councillor
Hu Qili (1929)	Executive Secretary of Secretariat
Wan Li (1916)	Deputy Prime Minister
Xi Zhongxun (1908)	as above
Yao Yilin (1917)	as above
Yu Qiuli (1914)	as above

Candidate Members

Hao Jianxiu (1935) (f)

Qiao Shi (1924)   Director, Organisation Dept

CCP Military Commission

Deng Xiaoping (1904)	Chairman
Yang Shangkun (1904)	Permanent Deputy Chairman and Secretary General
Nie Rongzhen (1899)	Deputy Chairman
Xu Xiangqian (1902)	Deputy Chairman
Ye Jianying (1897)	Deputy Chairman
Hong Xuezhi (1911)	Deputy Secretary General and Director PLA Logistics Dept
Yang Dezhi (1910)	Deputy Secretary General and PLA Chief of Staff
Yu Qiuli (1914)	Deputy Secretary General and Director, PLA General Political Dept
Zhang Aiping (1908)	Deputy Secretary General and Defence Minister

State Council

Zhao Ziyang	Prime Minister
Li Peng	Deputy Prime Minister
Tian Jiyun	Deputy Prime Minister and Secretary General
Wan Li	Deputy Prime Minister
Yao Yilin	Deputy Prime Minister

State President

Li Xiannian   President

Ulanhu   Deputy President

(f) female

12   Regime and Citizen in the Soviet Union, Eastern Europe and China

STEPHEN WHITE

Generalisations, even across a limited group of nations, are always fraught with difficulty, and the states represented in this volume are no exception. Although all of these states may be described as communist, at least in the sense that they adhere officially to Marxism–Leninism, they vary enormously in their area and population, their culture and society, their level of economic development and their historical experience. The states represented within this volume, for instance, include an officially atheist state (Albania) as well as one in which organised religion plays a central role in social and political life (Poland); they include at least one state whose living standards are broadly at the same level as those of the developing world (China) as well as several (such as the GDR and Czechoslovakia) whose levels of prosperity compare with those of Western Europe; and their historical experience ranges from states in which communism was independently established (such as the Soviet Union, China and Yugoslavia) to those in which it was a foreign importation and still lacks the support of a basic popular consensus (most obviously Poland). Nevertheless, for all their differences, the communist states represented in this volume share a common ideological allegiance, they generally (though with local variations) have economies in which resources are allocated administratively rather than by a market mechanism, and political power is exercised in all of them by a hegemonic Communist or Workers' Party within which the central leadership is normally in a dominant position. Most of them, moreover, are members of Comecon and of the Warsaw Treaty Organisation, both of which come under the effective control of the

216

Soviet leadership and thereby serve as a means of bloc integration.

For all their differences, then, the communist states represented within this volume share a number of important similarities; and given those similarities and interconnections, it is perhaps not surprising that they have shown a tendency to manifest broadly similar achievements and difficulties at similar stages in their development. Among the achievements of the communist states, it would generally be accepted, are the establishment of comprehensive health, education and welfare programmes, a substantial degree of income equality, cheap or at least subsidised housing, transport, cultural facilities and so forth. Until recently it would also have been agreed that the communist states could also lay claim to a number of economic achievements, such as an absence of overt unemployment, low rates of inflation, and a rapid rate of economic expansion. The first two of these elements still held true, at least for most of the communist states, in the early 1980s. The third element, however, a rapidly expanding economy, became increasingly inapplicable as the 1970s progressed, and by the mid-1980s it became apparent that the communist states faced, if not a full-scale crisis, then at least the end of the growth dynamic which at one time had been thought to ensure their ability to overtake the capitalist countries in aggregate and even per capita economic terms. It is a recurrent theme in the chapters of this volume, as well as in the academic literature on communist politics, that this deterioration in their economic performance will have serious implications for the political legitimacy of the regimes in the Soviet Union, Eastern Europe and China, based as it is upon a 'social compact' between rulers and ruled under which the citizens exchange a degree of political liberty for an assurance of a modest but nonetheless stable and gradually improving standard of living (Pravda, 1979, pp. 215–16).

It is certainly clear that the rate of economic growth (however defined) has declined markedly in almost all of the countries represented in this volume since at least the 1950s. In the Soviet case, for instance, the average annual rate of economic growth (in the Soviet definition) declined from 11.4 per cent in 1951–5 to 9.1 per cent in 1956–60, 6.5 per cent in 1961–5, 7.1 per cent in 1966–70, 5.1 per cent in 1971–5, 3.9 per cent in 1976–80, 3.2 per cent in 1981 and only 2.6 per cent in 1982 (Drewnowski, 1982, p. 158; *Guardian*, 14 July 1983.) The following year saw some improvement, to 3.1 per cent, (*Pravda*, 29 January 1984), but the early 1980s generally have seen the lowest rates of economic growth in Soviet post-war history and on some accounts, taking population increases into account, there has been no real per capita growth at all (Ellman, 1982, pp. 131–42). The position in Eastern Europe is more varied, with Bulgaria generally performing well and Poland exceptionally badly, but the general trend is broadly similar. According to CIA data, the rate of growth for these countries taken together averaged 3.8 per cent in 1961–5 and 3.7 per cent in 1966–70; it improved somewhat to 4.7 per cent in 1971–5 but thereafter fell to 3.2 per cent, 2.8 per cent, 2.7 per cent, one per cent and then unprecedentedly –0.6 per cent and –0.9 per cent in the years 1976–81 respectively. Performance on a per capita basis was even worse (US CIA, 1982, pp. 42–3). Levels of economic growth in China and Yugoslavia varied more widely, according to the same source, but both are estimated to have achieved no more than a 1.5 per cent increase in national income per capita in 1981, the second worst or worst figures respectively that have been recorded since the 1960s (US CIA, 1982, pp. 42–3). These falling rates of economic growth may not yet amount to a systemic 'crisis', as some have argued (Goldman, 1983; Drewnowski, 1982; Hedlund, 1984; Burks, 1984); the CIA itself has cautioned against such exaggerated conclusions, and it remains true that the economic performance of the communist nations, taken as a group, still compares favourably with that of their major western counterparts (World Economic Survey, 1983, p. 86). It is none the less clear that the communist states have generally experienced a significant and still continuing slowdown in their rates of economic growth; that this in turn relates to deep-seated problems of innovation and efficiency with which the regimes have found it difficult if not impossible to cope; and that this has serious implications for the 'social compact' between regime and citizens to which attention has already been drawn.

The 'social compact', broadly speaking, embraced security of employment, stable prices, an easygoing industrial discipline, modest but acceptable and steadily rising living standards, comprehensive health, education and welfare services, and a substantial degree of occupational mobility. In return for this the populations concerned, brought up in political cultures which generally conceived of rights in collective and economic rather than individual and political terms, were expected at least to acquiesce in a situation in which their ability to influence the decisions of central government remained extremely limited if not entirely negligible. All of this is threatened by the economic slowdown. It has led, for instance, to a series of sharp price rises, particularly for energy and services but in some cases for foodstuffs. It has also led to attempts to stiffen industrial discipline on the shopfloor, to a reduced degree of social mobility and an increasingly hereditary class structure, and to a series of increasingly bitter and overt disputes about the allocation of resources between national, social and occupational groups (such as the military). Beyond this again, there is an abundance of evidence from various sources to suggest the existence of what might be called a moral crisis in the Soviet Union, Eastern Europe and China. There has been a loss of optimism with the failure to catch up with and overtake the West, an alienation from the party and the official ideology, an orientation towards private life and the 'second economy', and an apparent increase in overt religiosity, drug-taking, alcoholism, corruption, street crime and sexually-transmitted diseases. Serious social problems such as poverty and juvenile delinquency have also become more prominent, and in some cases – notably Solidarity in Poland and (to a much lesser extent) Charter 77 in Czechoslovakia – an active and influential opposition movement has developed.

All of this might suggest that the communist regimes, lacking the formal or procedural legitimacy conferred upon their western counterparts by competitive elections and other generally-accepted mechanisms for the formation of a government, may be placed in an increasingly difficult position by the apparent erosion of their ability to provide a satisfactory alternative in terms of their socio-economic performance. Indeed a number of commentators, most notably Richard Löwenthal, were arguing even before the present economic difficulties in the communist world that in the long run there could in fact be no satisfactory basis for legitimacy other than the electoral mechanism. Löwenthal, basing himself particularly upon the experience of the Soviet Union, China and Yugoslavia, has pointed out that, although communist systems have some major achievements to their credit in socio-economic terms, no regime can in practice guarantee a continuously successful performance in these respects. If the system is regarded as legitimate, an improvement in performance will be sought by a change in government personnel rather than by a change in the system as such. In communist regimes, however, there are no established procedures which are generally believed to provide an opportunity for bringing more competent or at any rate more popular leaders into power and to provide some assurance that better-considered decisions will be made in the future on major matters of public policy. Communist regimes, in other words, can at best be temporarily and precariously legitimated by their socio-economic performance; in the long run 'there is no alternative to legitimacy based on institutional procedures' (Löwenthal, 1976, pp. 81–118, at 107).

This 'legitimacy crisis' theory may be challenged in a number of ways. In terms of their socio-economic performance, for instance, it is certainly true that the communist states have experienced a decline in rates of growth in recent years; but they have generally maintained full employment, low and stable prices for basic foodstuffs, housing and transport, and comprehensive welfare services. The more modest economic gains of recent years, moreover, have generally been allocated disproportionately to blue-collar workers rather than to other sections of the population, thereby strengthening support among the social group upon which the regimes most crucially depend for their stability. It is also possible to argue that comparisons with the West, with its massive unemployment, low economic growth and industrial disorders, are not nowadays in all respects to the disadvantage of the communist systems and by extension their political leaderships. In this chapter, however, attention will be focused on the political rather than the economic side of the legitimacy 'equation' and more generally to reassert the 'primacy of politics' in place of mechanical and determinist approaches that see the communist regimes as largely helpless in the face of their deteriorating economic performances (Paige, 1978, pp. 361–71). It will be suggested that to talk of a 'crisis' in these countries is generally at least premature; that economic difficulties exist, but that these can be mediated by political action; and that although competitive elections are undoubtedly absent, there are several 'mechanisms of adaptation' available to the ruling élites through which they can absorb and process popular demands, expand the consultative capacities of their regimes, give people a 'stake in the system' and thereby strengthen its legitimacy (White 1975: 297–304). Legitimacy in western countries, it should be noted, is based not simply upon the existence of competitive elections but upon other factors as well, such as an apparent willingness to take account of public opinion at other times and indeed socio-economic performance (Denitch, 1978). There is often no obvious party or ideological stake in issues such as housing, education, youth and women's issues with which communist publics appear to be particularly concerned, and the governing authorities have accordingly little to lose, and much to gain, by at least appearing to take popular preferences into account in the making of their decisions on such matters. As the economic bases of legitimacy apparently decline, the political bases of legitimacy may at least potentially be strengthened by recourse to such means. Among a variety of possible 'mechanisms of adaptation' four are singled out for particular attention.

The first of these is *electoral linkage*, or in other words the increasing use by communist regimes generally of the electoral mechanism (and indeed of elected bodies themselves) to provide, if not a genuine choice, then at least a degree of apparent choice from a range of officially-sponsored candidates. Twenty years ago even a restricted degree of choice was an isolated phenomenon in the communist world. By the mid-1980s, however, it was characteristic of about half of the world's communist-ruled systems, and was still gaining ground (White, Gardner and Schöpflin, 1982, p. 76; Pravda, 1982, pp. 169–95). Poland was one of the first of the communist regimes, in 1957, to establish a practice of putting forward more candidates than seats available in the legislature, albeit on a 'list' system with a heavy bias towards officially-approved candidates (Staar, 1982, p. 157; Sakwa and Crouch, 1978, pp. 403–24). The extension of electoral choice was discussed in the USSR in the 1960s and also in the GDR, with reference to the local level only, but in the event was not instituted (Hill, 1980, pp. 4–30; Staar, 1982, p. 109); in Bulgaria a modification of the electoral law in 1973 provided for the possibility of multiple candidacies, but no such candidacy has as yet occurred (Brunner, 1982, p. 39). The electoral law introduced in Czechoslovakia in 1967 also provided for the nomination of more than one candidate in each constituency, although on a 'list' system with a strong bias towards officially-approved candidates; no elections, however, were held under this system, and the 1971 electoral law reintroduced the standard Stalinist system popularly known as 'choice Paradise-style' (God said to Adam: 'Here is Eve, the woman of your choice'). This system still obtained in the early 1980s (Ulč, 1982 p. 116).

Elsewhere, however, rather more use has been made of the electoral mechanism as a means of providing some degree of at least ostensible choice and thereby conveying at least the impression of popular influence upon the composition of law-making bodies. In Romania, for instance, the 1975 elections were the first to be held under conditions of electoral choice, with two candidates standing for 139 of the 349 seats in the Grand National Assembly. At the subsequent elections in 1980 the degree of electoral choice was widened somewhat: in 151 of the 369 constituencies there were two candidates, and in a further 39 there were three (Ulč, 1982, p. 87; *Scinteia*,

11 March 1980). In Hungary multiple candidacies were first permitted in 1967, when there were nine. In 1971 there were 49, including one triple candidacy; in 1975 there were 34 double candidacies, and in 1980 there were 15 (Radio Free Europe (RFE) Situation Report: Hungary, 1 August 1983). Despite this declining trend, it is intended to extend the scope of electoral choice further at the next national elections in 1985. Following a July 1983 meeting of the Central Committee of the Hungarian Socialist Workers' party, it was announced that double or treble selections for seats in the National Assembly were to be made mandatory, with a separate national list for elder statesmen who wished to hold themselves above the electoral mêlée. The same provisions were to apply to local council elections (RFE Background Report: Hungary, 26 September 1983). 'The world will not collapse if two, three or even four candidates are featured on the nomination lists', as Mihaly Korom, a Politburo member and Central Committee Secretary, explained in a radio interview in May 1983. 'Nor will it collapse if the person who is not the official candidate of the PPF (People's Patriotic Front) happens to come in first in the elections. Believe me, the socialist system of society will not collapse even if the number of affirmative votes does not amount to 98 per cent or 97 per cent or some similar percentage' (RFE Situation Report: Hungary, 1 August 1983). The principle of electoral choice was reported to have extended itself to party as well as state affairs with the election of a party secretary in Somogy country from between two competing candidates in September 1983, the first such elections in the history of the Hungarian Socialist Workers' Party; trade union elections are to be reformed along similar lines (RFE Background Report: Hungary, 26 September 1983).

In Yugoslavia, where the complex multi-level representative system provides for the nomination of more candidates than places available at the first stages only, there have been authoritative calls for the further extension of electoral choice and for an end to the meaningless practice of a 'race with a single horse', as a Yugoslav political theorist has called it (RFE Background Report, Yugoslavia, 30 December 1983). In China, an electoral law was adopted in 1979 which for the first time provided for the nomination of more candidates than vacancies, again at the preliminary stages only of elections to the National People's Congress and local councils. Up to twice as many candidates are to be nominated as seats available, and elections are to be direct not only at the basic level but also (for the first time)

at the county level. The practice of holding by-elections has also been
revived (Zihua, 1979, pp. 15–18; Goodman, 1984, pp. 282–3). In
Poland, notwithstanding its extremely serious political and economic
difficulties, the ruling authorities have similarly been inclined, not to
suspend electoral choice, but cautiously to widen it, as for instance in
a law adopted in February 1984 which provides for pre-election
meetings at which voters are to be consulted about the candidates to
be placed on the electoral lists. At the local elections which took
place in June 1984 220 834 candidates competed for 110 428 seats
(RFE Situation Report: Poland, 25 February 1984; *Trybuna Ludu*,
20 June 1984). No comparable developments appear to have taken
place in the remaining state represented in this volume, Albania;
none the less, taken in conjunction with the greater degree of activity
that has been manifested over the past decade or so by legislative
bodies (and particularly their committees) and with the greater
emphasis that has generally been placed upon the powers and autonomy of local councils, the electoral mechanism does appear to offer
at least one means by which communist regimes can extend their
political base, develop their links with the population, and increase
the willingness of their citizens to accept unpopular decisions because
of their apparently greater degree of influence upon the selection of
those who make them.

A second mechanism is *political incorporation through membership
of the ruling Party*, both on the part of the population generally and
more particularly of the industrial working class. The ruling Parties of
the Soviet Union, Eastern Europe and China, for instance, have all
become more representative of their respective populations since the
1950s, with an increase in the proportion of the total population
enrolled within them from (typically) about 3 or 4 per cent to about 7
or 8 per cent by the early 1980s, with the rate of increase rather more
marked in the 1950s and 1960s than in the 1970s and 1980s (Shoup,
1981, pp. 82–5). Perhaps more important, there has been a substantial and still-continuing increase in the proportion of Party members
who are of working class origin (and conversely of the proportion of
the working class enrolled within Party ranks). In the USSR, for
instance, Party members of working-class origin accounted for 32 per
cent of total membership in 1957 but for 44.1 per cent in 1983 and for
over 59 per cent of new candidate members, a figure which more
accurately reveals current recruitment priorities (*Partiinaya Zhizn*,
15/1983: 21, 18). There have been similar or greater increases in the
proportion of workers by current occupation (rather than social

origin) in the ruling Parties of Albania (from 11.5 per cent in 1952 to 38 per cent in 1981) (Staar, 1982, p. 5; Shoup, 1981, p. 85); Bulgaria (from 34.1 per cent in 1953 to 42.7 per cent in 1982) (Staar, 1982, p. 5; Shoup, 1981, p. 86); Czechoslovakia (from 34.9 per cent in 1958 to 45.3 per cent in 1982 and about 60 per cent of new members) (Shoup, 1981, p. 5; Yearbook, 1983, p. 261; Wightman, 1983, pp. 208–22); and the German Democratic Republic, where workers accounted for 33.8 per cent of Party membership in 1957 but for 57.7 per cent in June 1982 (Shoup, 1981, p. 89; Yearbook, 1983, p. 271).

In Hungary an increase in the proportion of workers enrolled within the Party has also occurred, from 34.6 per cent in 1962 to 42.9 per cent in December 1982, although problems are reported to have arisen in respect of the recruitment of new worker candidates (down from 58.2 per cent in 1975 to 49.2 per cent of all recruits in 1982; the proportion of members under 30 has also dropped from 12.4 to 10.7 per cent over the same period) (*Communist Affairs*, 2/1984, p. 213). The level of membership of the ruling Party in Poland, the Polish United Workers' Party, has fluctuated more widely over the same period, increasing only slightly from 39–40 per cent in the early 1960s to a reported 44.7 per cent in 1981 (Staar, 1982 p. 173). In Romania, however, there has been a sharp and sustained increase in the proportion of Party members of working-class origin: up from 39.6 per cent in 1965 to 55.4 per cent in 1982, and a massive 84 per cent of new candidates (Shoup 1981, p. 94; Yearbook 1983, p. 325). The Yugoslav level has varied between 28 and 33 per cent over the same period, standing at 29.6 per cent in 1982 (Yearbook 1983, p. 368). Comparable if generally smaller increases have also been recorded in the proportion of workers represented in Party bureaux and committees at all levels (For USSR see *Partiinaya Zhizn*, 15/1983, p. 30).

Working-class recruitment into the ruling Party, in short, presents a varied picture, but it remains important as a 'mechanism of adaptation' particularly because its control rests in the hands of the Party leaderships and offers them at least potentially a means of incorporating selected social groups within the Party and binding them to the regime and to its purposes – or at least to the framework within which those purposes are determined. In this way the authorities can at least attempt to avoid a chasm of alienation and incomprehension opening up between them and the social groups to whose support they lay particular claim, particularly industrial workers. The political instability in Poland in 1970–1, for instance, was officially attributed to the weak representation of the Party within the working class; by biasing recruitment towards such potentially disaffected groups the Party authorities can at least attempt to incorporate them politically and to ensure that their aspirations find expression within the Party structure rather than outside it, where it might threaten the authorities' control and even the stability of the system itself. 'Still closer – the links between Party and people' is a mechanism of political adaptation and not simply a slogan in the communist countries of the Soviet Union, Eastern Europe and China.

A third and related 'mechanism of adaptation' is through the *role of associational groups*, particularly trade unions (what Alex Pravda has called 'institutional intermediation'). Since about the 1960s, it would generally be agreed, the authorities in the Soviet Union, Eastern Europe and China have placed increasing emphasis upon the role and importance of trade unions and other associational bodies, strengthening their leaderships and increasing their powers and autonomy both at the workplace and on a national level. Their motive for doing so is evidently the fear that an ineffective and discredited trade union organisation might fail to engage even a minimum of support and sympathy on the part of the workforce and might risk the emergence of an independently organised movement, as so conspicuously occurred in Poland in 1980. It was, for instance, apparently to pre-empt Polish-style developments that the Soviet leadership, early in 1982, replaced the chairman of the All-Union Central Council of Trade Unions with a younger and more energetic figure (S. A. Shalaev) and then, in June 1983, adopted a law on labour collectives providing for twice-yearly workers' conferences and (at least on paper) for greatly increased rights on the part of the workforce to influence management decisions (*Pravda*, 6 February 1982 and 19 June 1983). In Poland itself, although Solidarity has been dissolved, there has been no attempt to restore the discredited trade union bodies that existed before 1980. Rather, new and more effective institutions are to be developed which will respect the leading role of the Party but nonetheless defend their members' interests, although these were being constituted rather slowly in the difficult political circumstances of the early 1980s (RFE Situation Report: Poland, 26 October 1982 and 25 May 1983). Perhaps the most interesting developments in this connection have occurred in Hungary, where Sandos Gaspar, head of the trade union movement from 1965 until December 1983, presided over a considerable increase in the powers and autonomy of the unions in which the unions, for instance, have the right to veto management decisions if these violate the collective contract between management and workforce. It is perhaps worthy of note that Gaspar has been advising the Polish authorities on the reconstitution of a trade union movement in that country subsequent to the suppression of Solidarity (White, Gardner and Schöpflin, 1982, pp. 149–50; RFE Situation Report: Hungary, 12 January 1984; see also 4 March 1982 and 21 December 1983).

Once again it seems possible to see the development of a degree of autonomy on the part of associational groups, such as trade unions, as providing at least potentially a means of insulating the regimes from the difficulties they increasingly face in these areas by allowing them to be dealt with at a sub-systemic level rather than by the central authorities themselves. Many of the disputes that arise between workforce and management concern issues such as working conditions, overtime and industrial safety in which the Party leadership itself has no obvious interest at stake, and it would seem to have little to lose and much to gain by allowing such issues to be regulated by a bargaining process in which the management were not necessarily the victors in every case. The workforce is more likely to have confidence in a trade union organisation which can demonstrate its ability to negotiate effectively over such matters; and in turn it is less likely to give support to movements which conceive of their objectives in terms of opposition to the system as such rather than in terms of opposition to a number of individual decisions by officials at the local level. There is in fact not a great deal of evidence that workers in communist countries habitually conceive of their objectives in an anti-systemic manner; the Party and state leadership, as a result, have some room for manoeuvre in attempting to absorb the very particular, bread-and-butter complaints of most workers within institutions to which a greater degree of autonomy and effectiveness can in most cases safely be delegated. In Yugoslavia the principle of workforce autonomy has in fact been extended to include strikes, 'thousands' of which have occurred since the institution of the present framework of self-management in 1958. The majority are reported to have been successful (RFE Background Report: Yugoslavia, 17 May 1983).

Elections take place infrequently, Party members represent a small proportion of the total population, and even trade union membership is limited to the employed workforce, leaving out younger people, pensioners and a few others. Of particular importance, therefore, applying as it does to the total population at all times, is a fourth mechanism of adaptation, *letters to Party and state bodies, and above all to the press*. In the Soviet case mechanisms of this kind have been in greater use since the 1960s, culminating in the establishment of a letters department in the CPSU Central Committee apparatus in 1978 (White, 1983, pp. 43–60, particularly pp. 47–8). The Central Committee itself receives about half a million letters every year, and the major national newspapers receive comparable numbers. Some information on current practices in these areas was provided by the head of the Central Committee letters department, Boris Yakovlev, in an article in *Pravda* early in 1984. In the previous three years (1980–3), Yakovlev reported, the Central Committee had received over two million letters, and over 70 000 citizens had visited the Central Committee offices in person. Over the same period local Party organs had dealt with over 10 million written and oral communications from citizens; and in 1983 alone more than 60 dossiers had been prepared for the Party leadership and other bodies by the letters department, based upon the correspondence it had itself received (*Pravda*, 3 February 1984). Another example of the extension of 'epistolatory democracy' has occurred in China, particularly since the present leadership came to power in 1978. More letters are published in, for instance, *People's Daily* than ever before, more letters have been received (about 3000 a day in the case of *People's Daily*), and the letters are reportedly more direct, more critical and more interrelated. One recent study of such matters has concluded that the letters department of the *People's Daily* had 'come close to becoming a forum for public discussion' by the early 1980s (Chu and Chu, 1983, pp. 175–224, at 176–7, 214).

In Romania, similarly, the development of such mechanisms of consultation has proceeded at a swift pace, particularly since the Jiu valley miners' strike of 1977. General directives regarding communications with the population were issued by the Central Committee of the Romanian Communist Party a year later, and these were extended further at a Central Committee meeting in March 1982 which approved a report on the manner in which Party and state bodies were required to handle the suggestions, proposals, complaints and observations put forward by the mass of the citizenry (RFE Situation Report: Romania, 2 June 1982). The weekly paper *Flacara* has opened a regular complaints column (RFE Situation Report: Romania, 7 March 1983), and the number of workers' complaints in letters to Party and state bodies more generally is reported to have almost doubled, from 1 million in 1965 to 1.8 million in 1981, or one for every five or six members of the working population. Of these some

1.4 million were individual complaints, of which over 40 per cent were considered justified; 'collective memoranda' have also been received. The complaints raised in letters generally related to matters such as poor housing and working conditions, inadequate food supplies, shortcomings in public transport and so forth; substantial numbers also criticised the behaviour of individual officials. Preliminary evidence suggested that the total number of complaints received in 1982 would in turn be almost double the total received in 1981. The Romanian Communist Party has officially praised this work as representing a 'broad dialogue and direct broad contact with the working people' (RFE Situation Report: Romania, 1 June 1982).

In Romania, as elsewhere, letters to the press can serve a sort of 'ombudsman' role in this connection, exposing at least lower-level state and other officials to legitimate public criticism, correcting abuses and cases of maladministration and alerting the Party leadership to major issues of public concern which, if entirely neglected, might lead to demonstrations of public indignation of an extra- or even anti-systemic character. In turn they may help to strengthen regime legitimacy by providing at least the impression that popular complaints and grievances reach the relevant levels of the Party and state leadership and that they are taken into account at least to some extent, in the making of decisions on major matters of public policy. The evidence that is available, from Romania, the Soviet Union and elsewhere, suggests that such complaints generally concern housing, transport, working conditions and other matters rather than abstract issues such as the justification for Party dominance or the validity of Marxism–Leninism; here, as elsewhere, the Party leaderships have no obvious interest at stake and have little to lose and much to gain by responding so far as they can to such expressions of popular sentiment. Soviet evidence at least suggests that letters to the press and other bodies may in fact be seen as the most effective – or least ineffective – means of influencing the authorities in their decisions on such matters (White, 1983, pp. 56–7).

In conclusion, then, this chapter has tried to argue that the Soviet Union, Eastern Europe and China face serious economic difficulties, if not perhaps a full-scale crisis (at least outside Poland). The political leaderships, however, are not simply the playthings of inexorable forces, economic or otherwise, but can modify, anticipate and even forestall the seemingly inevitable. By means such as those indicated in this chapter, it has been suggested, they may be able at least to some extent to pre-empt popular grievances by expanding the consultative capacities of their systems and incorporating potentially disaffected groups, and thereby strengthen the political bases of their legitimacy to compensate for whatever loss of legitimacy they may have suffered in terms of their socio-economic performance. These remain, of course, authoritarian regimes, in which a range of civil liberties taken for granted in liberal democracies are largely or entirely absent. Naked force, however, has rarely proved a satisfactory ruling formula for long periods of time, and scholarly consensus in recent years has generally conceded that these are 'authoritarian but consultative' regimes, permitting at least a degree of popular influence upon the making of public policy provided overall Party dominance remains unchallenged. As the communist regimes enter a period of perhaps prolonged economic difficulties, it seems reasonable to expect that their leaderships will increasingly make use of the mechanisms of consultation at their disposal in order to compensate for the socio-economic performance they will find it more and more difficult to deliver.

References

Adelman, Jonathan R. (ed.) (1982) *Communist Armies in Politics*, (Boulder, CO., Westview Press).

Alexiev, A. (1979) 'Party–Military Relations in Eastern Europe: The Case of Romania', ACIS Working Paper No 15, University of California, Los Angeles, Center for International and Strategic Affairs.

Alexiev, A. (1981) 'Romania and the Warsaw Pact: The Defense Policy of a Reluctant Ally', *Strategic Studies*, no 1, March.

Artisien, P. F. R. (1984) 'A note on Kosovo and the future of Yugoslav–Albanian relations: a Balkan perspective', *Soviet Studies*, vol. XXXVI, no 2, April.

Artisien, P. F. R. (1985) 'Albania in the post-Hoxha era', *The World Today*, vol. 41, no. 6, June.

Artisien, P. F. R. and R. A. Howells, (1981) 'Yugoslavia, Albania and the Kosovo riots', *The World Today*, vol. 37, no 11, November.

Anon. (1981) *A Magyar Forradalom és Szabadságharo a hazai rádióadások tükrében, október 23–November 9* (San Francisco, L. Faþó).

Bacon, W. M. (1978) 'The Military and the Party in Romania', in Dale R. Herspring and I. Volgyes (eds) *Civil–Military Relations in Communist Systems* (Boulder, CO., Westview Press).

Bacon, W. M. (1981) 'Romanian Military Policy in the 1980's', in D. N. Nelson (ed.) *Romania in the 1980's* (Boulder, CO., Westview Press).

Bacon W. M. (1983) 'Romania', in R. Wesson (ed.) *Yearbook on International Communist Affairs* (Stanford, CA., Hoover Institution Press, Stanford University).

Bartke, W. (1981) *Who's Who in the People's Republic of China* (Brighton, Harvester Press).

Barton, Paul (1954) *Prague à l' Heure de Moscou. Analyse d'une démocratie populaire* (Paris).

Bauman, Z. (1976) *Socialism: The Active Utopia* (London, George Allen & Unwin).

Bauman, Z. (1979) 'Comment on Eastern Europe', *Studies in Comparative Communism*, Summer–Autumn.

Beck, C. *et al.* (1973) *Comparative Communist Political Leadership* (New York, Mackay).

Berindei, M. and A. Colas (1984) 'L'abolition du salariat', *L' Alternative*, no 25, January–February.

Bethell, N. (1969) *Gomuɫka: His Poland and His Communism* (London, Longman).

Bialer, Seweryn (1980) *Stalin's Successors: Leadership, Stability and Change in the Soviet Union* (Cambridge University Press).

Bialer, Seweryn (1983) 'The Political System', in R. F. Byrnes (ed.) *After Brezhnev: Sources of Soviet Conduct in the 1980s* (Bloomington, Indiana University Press).

Bieńkowski, W. (1969) *Motory i Hamulce Socjalizmu* (Paris, Institut Literacki).

Braun, Avrel (1978) *Romanian Foreign Policy since 1965: The Political and Military Limits of Autonomy* (New York, Praeger).

Braun, Avrel (1983) *Small State Security in the Balkans* (London, Macmillan).

Breslauer, George W. (1982) *Khrushchev and Brezhnev as Leaders: Building Authority in the Soviet Union* (London, George Allen & Unwin).

Bromke, A. and J. Strong (eds) (1973) *Gierek's Poland* (New York, Praeger).

Brown, Archie (1966) 'Plurastic Trends in Czechoslovakia', *Soviet Studies,* vol. XVII, April.

Brown, Archie (1980) 'The Power of the General Secretary of the CPSU', in T. H. Rigby, Archie Brown and Peter Reddaway (eds) *Authority, Power and Policy in the USSR* (London, Macmillan).

Brown, Archie (1984) 'Political Power and the Soviet State', in Neil Harding (ed.) *The State in Socialist Society* (London, Macmillan).

Brown, J. F. (1965) 'The Bulgarian Plot', *The World Today*, June.

Brown, J. F. (1966) *The New Eastern Europe The Khrushchev Era and After* (New York, Praeger).

Brown, J. F. (1970) *Bulgaria under Communist Rule* (New York, Praeger).

Brunner, George (1982) 'Legitimacy doctrines and legitimation procedures in East European systems', in T. H. Rigby and Ferenc Feher (eds) *Political Legitimation in Communist States* (London, Macmillan).

Bunce, Valerie (1981) *Do New Leaders Make a Difference? Executive Succession and Public Policy under Capitalism and Socialism* (Princeton, N.J., Princeton University Press).

Burg, Steven L. (1983) *Conflict and Cohesion in Socialist Yugoslavia* (Princeton, N.J., Princeton University Press).

Burks, R. V. (1984) 'The Coming Crisis in the Soviet Union', *East European Quarterly*, vol 18, no 1.

Carter, April (1982) *Democratic Reform in Yugoslavia The Changing Role of the Party* (London, Frances Pinter).

Ceauşescu, Nicolae (1968–9) *România pe drumul desăvirşirii constructiei socialiste*, 3 vols (Bucharest, Editura politică).

Ceauşescu, Nicolae (1970–83) *România pe drumul construirii societății socialiste multilateral dezvoltate*, 20 vols (Bucharest, Editura politică).

Chang P. H. (1978) 'The Rise of Wang Tung-hsing: Head of China's Security Apparatus', *China Quarterly*, 73, March.

Chang, P. H. (1983) 'Interview with Hu Yaobang', *Problems of Communism,* no 6 November–December.

Chernenko, Konstantin (1984) *Selected Speeches and Writings* (London, Pergamon Press).

Childs, David (1983) *The GDR: Moscow's German Ally* (London, George Allen & Unwin).

Chu, Goodwin and Leonard L. Chu (1983) 'Mass Media and Conflict Resolution: an Analysis of Letters to the Editor', in Goodwin C. C. Chu and Francis L. K. Hsu (eds) *China's New Social Fabric* (London, Routledge & Kegan Paul).

Cohen, Leonard J. (1977) 'Conflict Management and Political Institutionalization in Yugoslavia: A Case Study of the Parliamentary System', in Albert F. Eldridge, (ed.) *Legislatures in Plural Societies* (Durham N.C., Duke University Press).

Colas, A. (1982) 'Une situation explosive', *L'Alternative*, no 14, January–February.

Congresul al IX-lea al Partidului Comunist Român (1966) (Bucharest, Editura politică).

Congresul al X-lea al Partidului Comunist Român (1969) (Bucharest, Editura politică).

Daniels, Robert V. (1971) 'Soviet Politics since Khrushchev', in John W. Strong (ed.) *The Soviet Union under Brezhnev and Kosygin* (New York, D. Van Nostrand).

Dean, Robert W. (1976) 'Civil–Military Relations in Yugoslavia, 1971–1975', *Armed Forces and Society*, vol 3, no 1, November.

Deng Xiaoping (1983) *Deng Xiaoping Wen Xuan* (Beijing).

Denitch, Bogdan Denis (1976) *The Legitimation of a Revolution The Yugoslav Case* (New Haven and London, Yale University Press).

Denitch, Bogdan Denis (1978) 'Succession and Stability in Yugoslavia', *Journal of International Affairs*, vol 32, no 2, Winter.

Dittmer, L. (1983) 'The Twelfth Congress of the Communist Party of China', *China Quarterly*, 93, March.

Dobrogeanu-Gherea, C. (1977) *Opere complete*, vol 3 (Bucharest, Editura politică).

Domes, Jürgen (1980) *Politische Soziologie der Volksrepublik China* (Wiesbaden, Akademische Verlagsgesellschaft).

Drewnowski, Jan (ed.) (1982) *Crisis in the East European Economy* (London, Croom Helm).

Dziewanowski, M. K. (1976) *The Communist Party of Poland* (Cambridge, MA., Harvard University Press).

Ellman, Michael (1982) 'Did Soviet Economic Growth end in 1978?', in Jan Drewnowski (ed.) *Crisis in the East European Economy* (London, Croom Helm).

Farrell, R. B. (ed.) (1970) *Political Leadership in Eastern Europe and the Soviet Union* (London, Butterworth).

Fischer, M. E. (1980) 'Political Leadership and Personnel Policy in Romania: Continuity and Change 1965–76', in S. Rosefielde (ed.) *World Communism at the Crossroads* (Boston, M. Nijhoff).

Fischer, M. E. (1981) 'Idol or Leader? The Origins and Future of the Ceauşescu Cult' in D. N. Nelson (ed.) *Romania in the 1980's* (Boulder, CO., Westview Press).

Fischer, M. E. (1982) 'Nicolae Ceauşescu and the Romanian Political Leadership: Nationalism and Personalization of Power', Skidmore College, The Edwin M. Mosley Faculty Research Lecture.

Fischer-Galati, S. (1981) 'Romania's Development as a Communist State', in D. N. Nelson (ed.) *Romania in the 1980's* (Boulder, CO., Westview Press).

Fontana, D. G. (1982) 'Background to the Fall of Hua Guofeng', *Asian Survey*, XXII.

Foster, G. M. (1967) 'Peasant Society and the Image of the Limited Good' in J. M. Potter, M. N. Diaz and G. M. Foster (eds) *Peasant Society: A Reader* (Boston, Little, Brown and Co.).

Frank, Peter (1980) 'Leadership in Soviet-type Political Systems', *Government and Opposition*.

Frank, Peter (1984) *Political Succession in the Soviet Union*, Colchester, Essex University, mimeograph.

Gardner, John (1982) *Chinese Politics and the Succession to Mao* (London, Macmillan).

Goldman, Marshall (1983) *The USSR in Crisis: The Failure of an Economic System* (New York, Norton).

Goodman, David S. G. (1984) 'State Reforms in the People's Republic of China since 1976', in Neil Harding (ed.) *The State in Socialist Society* (London, Macmillan).

Góra, W. (1976) *Polska Rzeczpospolita Ludowa 1944–1974* (Warsaw, KiW).

Griffith, W. E. (1963) *Albania and the Sino-Soviet Rift* (Cambridge, MA., MIT Press).

Gyurkó, László (1982) *Arcképvázlat történelmi háttérrel* (Budapest).

Hammer, D. P. (1971) 'The Dilemma of Party Growth', *Problems of Communism*, no 4, July–August.

Hedlund, Stefan (1984) *Crisis in Soviet Agriculture* (London, Croom Helm).

Herspring, Dale and Volgyes, I. (eds) (1978) *Civil–Military Relations in Communist Systems* (Boulder, CO., Westview Press).

He Shiyuan (1981) 'Jiakuai minzu diqu jingjide fazhan', in *Lun caizheng zhidu gaige, di si ci quan guo caizheng lilun taolun hui wenxuan* (Beijing).

Hill, Ronald J. (1980) *Soviet Politics Political Science and Reform* (Oxford, Martin Robertson).

Hodnett, G. (1975) 'Succession Contingencies in the Soviet Union', *Problems of Communism*, no 2, March–April.

Hodnett, G. (1981) 'The Pattern of Leadership Politics', in S. Bialer (ed.) *The Domestic Context of Soviet Foreign Policy* (Boulder, CO., Westview Press).

Hough, J. F. (1980) *Soviet Leadership in Transition* (Washington, D.C., Brookings Institution).

Hoxha, Enver (1982) *The Titoites* (Tirana, The 8 Nëntori Publishing House).

Hu Qiaomu (1984) 'Guanyu rendao zhuyi he yihua wenti', *Hongqi*, no 2.

Hudson, Cam (1982) 'Bulgarian Economic Reforms: Between the Devil and the Deep Black Sea', RAD Background Report, no 142, Radio Free Europe Research, 2 July.

Janos, A (ed.) (1976) *Authoritarian Politics in Eastern Europe* (Berkeley, CA., University of California Press).

Joffe, E. (1983) 'Party and Military in China: Professionalism in Command?', *Problems of Communism*, no 5, September–October.

Johnson, A. Ross (1971) *The Yugoslav Doctrine of Total National Defense* (Santa Monica, CA., The Rand Corporation).

Johnson, A. Ross (1978) *The Role of the Military in Communist Yugoslavia: An Historical Sketch* (Santa Monica, CA., The Rand Paper Series).

Johnson, A. Ross (1980) *Yugoslavia: The Non-Leninist Succession* (Santa Monica, CA., The Rand Paper Series).

Jones, C. D. (1981) *Soviet Influence in Eastern Europe: Political Autonomy and the Warsaw Pact* (New York, Praeger).

Jowitt, Kenneth (1971) *Revolutionary Breakthroughs and National Development : The Case of Romania, 1944–1965* (Berkeley and Los Angeles, CA., University of California Press).

Jowitt, Kenneth (1978) *The Leninist Response to National Dependency* (Berkeley, CA., Institute of International Studies, University of California).

Jowitt, Kenneth (1983) 'Soviet Neotraditionalism: The Political Corruption of a Leninist Regime', *Soviet Studies*, vol. XXXV no 3, July.

Kardelj, Edvard (1966) 'The Principal Dilemma: Self-Mananagement or Statism?', *Socialist Thought and Practice* Belgrade, October–December.

Kaser, Michael (1979) 'Albania's self-chosen predicament', *The World Today*, vol. 35, no 6, June.

Kaser, Michael (1983) 'Albania's muscular socialism', *Contemporary Review*, vol. 243, no 1411, August.

Kautsky, John H. (1973) 'Comparative Communism versus Comparative Politics', *Studies in Comparative Communism*, VI.

Kemp-Welch, A. (1983) *The Birth of Solidarity* (London, Macmillan).

Kerov, Yordan (1980) 'Lyudmila Zhikova – Fragments of a Portrait', RAD Background Report, 253, RFE Research, 27 October.

Király, Béla (1982) 'The Aborted Soviet Military Plans against Tito's Yugoslavia', in Wayne S. Wucinich, (ed.) *At the Brink of War and Peace*,

Király, Béla and P. Jonas (1978) *The Hungarian Revolution of 1956 in Retrospect* (Boulder, CO., East European Quarterly).

Kolankiewicz, George and R. Taras (1977) 'Socialism for Everyman', in Archie Brown and Jack Gray (eds) *Political Culture and Cultural Change in Communist States* (London, Macmillan).

Kołomejczyk, N. and B. Szyzdek (1971) *Polska w latach 1944–1949*, (Warsaw, PZPS).

Korbonski, A. (1976) 'Leadership Succession and Political Change in Eastern Europe', *Studies in Comparative Communism*, Spring–Summer.

Korbonski, A. (1981) 'Eastern Europe as an Internal Determinant of Soviet Foreign Policy', in S. Bialer (ed.) *The Domestic Context of Soviet Foreign Policy* (Boulder, CO., Westview Press).

Korbonski, A. (1982) 'The Polish Army', in J. Adelman (ed.) *Communist Armies in Politics* (Boulder, CO., Westview Press).

Kovrig, Bennett (1979) *Communism in Hungary from Kun to Kádár* (Stanford, CA., Hoover Institution Press).

Kozik, Z. (1982) *PZPR w latach 1954–1957* (Warsaw, PWN).

Kusin, Vladimir (1978) *From Dubček to Charter 77 A Study of 'Normalization' in Czechoslovakia, 1968–1978* (Edinburgh).

Kusin, Vladimir (1982) 'Husak's Czechoslovakia and Economic Stagnation', *Problems of Communism*, no 3, May–June.

Lane, D. and G. Kolankiewicz (eds) (1973) *Social Groups in Polish Society* (London, Macmillan).

Lendvai, Paul (1969) *Eagles in Cobwebs Nationalism and Communism in the Balkans* (New York, Doubleday).

Lieberthal, K. (1983) 'China in 1982: A Middling Course for the Middle Kingdom', *Asian Survey*, 23.

Linden, R. H. (1981) 'Romanian Foreign Policy in the 1980's', in D. N. Nelson (ed.), *Romania in the 1980's* (Boulder, CO., Westview Press).

Löwenthal, Richard (1970) 'Development vs. Utopia in Communist Policy', in Chalmers Johnson (ed.) *Change in Communist Systems* (Stanford, CA., Stanford University Press).

Löwenthal, Richard (1976) 'The ruling party in a mature society', in Mark G. Field (ed.) *Social Consequences of Modernization in Communist Societies* (Baltimore and London, Johns Hopkins University Press).

Lowit, Thomas (1979) 'Y a-t-il des Etats en l'Europe de l'Est?', *Revue française de sociologie*, XX.

McAuley, Mary (1977) *Politics and the Soviet Union* (Harmondsworth, Penguin Books.).

McCauley, Martin (1979) *Marxism–Leninism in the German Democratic Republic The Socialist Unity Party (SED)* (London, Macmillan).

McCauley, Martin (1983a) *The German Democratic Republic since 1945* (London, Macmillan).

McCauley, Martin (1983b) 'Leadership and the Succession Struggle', in Martin McCauley (ed.) *The Soviet Union after Brezhnev* (London, Heinemann).

Meyer, A. G. (1970) 'Historical Development of the Communist Theory of Leadership', in R. B. Farrell (ed.) *Political Leadership in Eastern Europe and the Soviet Union* (London, Butterworth).

Meyer, A. G. (1983) 'Communism and Leadership', *Studies in Comparative Communism*, Autumn.

Mills, W. deB. (1983) 'Generational Change in China', *Problems of Communism*, no 6, November–December.

Mlynář, Zdeněk (1978) *Mráz přichází z Kremlu*, (Cologne). (An English translation was published in London in 1980 under the title, *Night Frost in Prague*.)

Mlynář, Zdeněk (1982) 'Normalization in Czechoslovakia after 1968', in W. Brus, P. Kende and Z. Mlynar, *'Normalization' Processes in Soviet-dominated Central Europe*.

Mołdawa, T. (1971) *Skład osobowy naczelnych organów państwowych Polski Ludowej*, Warsaw, Warsaw University mimeograph.

Moore, P. (1983) 'Romania in 1983', RAD Background Report, 294, RFE Research, 30 December.

Myant, M. (1982) *Poland: A Crisis for Socialism* (London, Lawrence & Wishart).

Nethercutt, R. D. (1983) 'China's Leadership', *Problems of Communism*, no 2, March–April.

Nethercutt, R. D. (1984) 'Deng and the Gun: Party–Military Relations in the People's Republic of China', *Asian Survey*, XXII.

Oksenberg, M. and S. C. Yeung (1977) 'Hua Guo-feng's Pre-Cultural Revolution Hunan Years, 1949–66: The Making of a Political Generalist', *China Quarterly*, 69, March.

Oksenberg, M. and R. Bush (1982) 'China's Political Evolution: 1972–82', *Problems of Communism*, no 5, September–October.

Omagiu tovarăşului Ceauşescu (1973) (Bucharest, Editura politică).

Oren, Nissan (1971) *Bulgarian Communism: The Road to Power 1934–1944* (New York, Columbia University Press).

Oren, Nissan (1973) *Revolution Administered: Communism and Agrarianism in Bulgaria* (Baltimore MD, Johns Hopkins University Press).

Paige, G. D. (1978) 'The Primacy of Politics', in Paul G. Lewis *et al.* (eds) *The Practice of Comparative Politics*, 2nd edn (London, Longman).

Paltiel, J. T. (1983) 'The Cult of Personality: Some Comparative Reflections on Political Culture in Leninist Regimes', *Studies in Comparative Communism*, Spring–Summer.

Pano, N. (1977) 'Albania in the Era of Brezhnev and Kosygin', in G. W. Simmonds (ed.) *Nationalism in the USSR and Eastern Europe in the Era of Brezhnev and Kosygin* (Detroit, MI., University of Detroit Press).

Pirages, D. (1972) *Modernization and Political Tension Management* (New York, Praeger).

Plenara Comitetului Central al Partidului Comunist Român din 22–25 aprilie 1968 (1968) (Bucharest, Editura politică).

Polonsky, A. and B. Drukier (1980) *The Beginnings of Communist Rule in Poland* (London, Routledge & Kegan Paul).

Polska (1974) *Zarys Encyklopedyczny* (Warsaw, PWN).

Pravda, Alex (1979) 'Industrial Workers: Patterns of Dissent, Opposition and Accommodation', in Rudolf F. Tökés (ed.) *Opposition in Eastern Europe* (London, Macmillan).

Pravda, Alex (1982) 'Elections in Communist Party States', in Guy Hermet, Richard Rose and Alain Rouquié (eds) *Elections Without Choice* (London, Macmillan).

Prifti, P. R. (1977) 'The Dismissal of Beqir Balluku, Albania's Minister of Defense: an Analysis', in G. W. Simmonds (ed.) *Nationalism in the USSR and Eastern Europe in the Era of Brezhnev and Kosygin* (Detroit, MI., University of Detroit Press).

Prifti, P. R. (1978) *Socialist Albania since 1944* (Cambridge, MA., MIT Press).

Rakowski, M. F. (1981) *Przesilenie grudniowe* (Warsaw, PiW).

Ramet, Pedro (1984) 'Political Struggle and Institutional Reorganization in Yugoslavia', *Political Science Quarterly*, Summer.

R. N. (1977) 'Bulgaria's Agro-Industrial Complexes after Seven Years', RAD Background Report, 34, RFE Research, 14 February.

Roberts, Adam (1976) *Nations in Arms* (London, Chatto & Windus).

RPiG (1957–83) *Rocznik Polityczny i Gospodarczy* (Warsaw, PWE).

Rotschild, Joseph (1959) *The Communist Party of Bulgaria: Origins and Development 1883–1936* (New York, Columbia University Press).

Rush, Myron (1974) *How Communist States Change Their Rulers* (Ithaca, Cornell University Press).

Rush, Myron (1976) 'Comment', *Studies in Comparative Communism*, Spring–Summer.

Rusinow, Dennison (1977) *The Yugoslav Experiment* (London, C. Hurst).

Rusinow, Dennison (1980a) 'After Tito', *American Universities Staff Reports*, 34.

Rusinow, Dennison (1980b) 'The Other Albania: Kosovo 1979', *American Universities Staff Reports*, 5 and 6.
Rusinow, Dennison (1982a) 'Yugoslavia's Muslim Nation', *UFSI Reports*, 8.
Rusinow, Dennison (1982b) 'Yugoslavia's First Post-Tito Party Congress', *UFSI Reports*, 39, 40.
Rusinow, Dennison (1983) 'Yugoslavia 1983: "Continuity" and "Crisis" ', *UFSI Reports*, 3.
Sakwa, George and Martin Crouch (1978) 'Sejm Elections in Communist Poland: an Overview and a Reappraisal', *British Journal of Political Science*, vol. 8, no 4.
Sanford, George (1980) 'Polish People's Republic', in B. Szajkowski (ed.) *Marxist Governments: A World Survey*, vol. 3 (London, Macmillan).
Sanford, George (1981) 'The Executive in a Communist Political System: the Polish Case', ECPR Joint Sessions, University of Lancaster.
Sanford, George (1982) 'Poland', in G. Walker (ed.) *Official Publications of the Soviet Union and Eastern Europe 1945–1980, An Annotated Bibliography* (London, Mansell).
Sanford, George (1983) *Polish Communism in Crisis* (London, Croom Helm).
Sanford, George (1984) 'The Polish Communist Leadership and the Onset of the State of War', *Soviet Studies,* vol. XXXVI, no 4.
Schapiro, L. B. (1972) *Totalitarianism* (London, Macmillan).
Schöpflin, George (1983) 'No Model for Reform', *Soviet Analyst*, vol. 12, no. 23.
Shafir, Michael (1981) 'The Socialist Republic of Romania', in B. Szajkowski (ed.) *Marxist Governments: A World Survey*, vol. 3 (London, Macmillan).
Shafir, Michael (1983) 'Political Culture, Intellectual Dissent and Intellectual Consent: The Case of Romania', *Orbis*, Summer.
Shafir, Michael (1985) *Romania: Politics, Economics and Society* (London, Frances Pinter).
Shoup, Paul (1968) *Communism and the Yugoslav National Question* (New York, Columbia University Press).
Shoup, Paul (1981) *The East European and Soviet Data Handbook* (New York, Columbia University Press).
Šik, Ota (1968) 'Jak zrálo střetnutí', *Kulturní noviny*, 29 March.
Simon, M. and R. Kanet (eds) (1981) *Background to Crisis Policy and Politics in Gierek's Poland* (Boulder, CO., Westview Press).
Skilling, H. G. (1966) *Governments of Eastern Europe* (New York, Crowell).
Skilling, H. G. (1976) *Czechoslovakia's Interrupted Revolution* (Princeton, N.J., Princeton University Press).
Solomon, Susan Gross (ed.) (1983) *Pluralism in the Soviet Union* (London, Macmillan).
Staar, Richard F. (1962) *Poland The Sovietisation of a Captive People* (Baton Rouge, LO., Louisiana University Press).
Staar, Richard F. (1982) *Communist Regimes in Eastern Europe*, 4th edn (Stanford, CA., Stanford University Press).
Stehle, H. S. (1965) *The Independent Satellite* (New York, Praeger).
Syrop, K. (1957) *Spring in October: The Polish Revolution 1956* (London, Weidenfeld & Nicolson).

Szczepański, J. (1973) *Odmiany Czasu Teraźnieszego* (Warsaw, KiW).

Taborsky, Edward (1961) *Communism in Czechoslovakia, 1948–1960*, (Princeton, N.J., Princeton University Press).

Teiwes, F. C. (1984) *Leadership, Legitimacy and Conflict in China* (London, Macmillan).

Tönnes, B. (1983) 'Grundlagen der albanischen Isolationspolitik', in R. Schönfeld (ed.) *Südosteuropa in Weltpolitik und Weltwirtschaft der achtziger Jahre* (Munich, Oldenbourg).

Ulbricht, Walter (1967) *Die Bedeutung des Werkes Das Kapital von Karl Marx für die Schaffung des entwickelten gesellschaftlichen Systems des Sozialismus in der DDR* (Berlin, DDR).

Ulč, Otto (1983) 'Legislative Politics in Czechoslovakia', in D. N. Nelson and S. White (eds) *Communist Legislatures in Comparative Perspective* (London, Macmillan).

UN *World Economic Survey* (1983) (New York, United Nations).

US CIA (1982) *Handbook of Economic Statistics* (Washington, D.C., US Government Printing Office).

Volgyes, I. (1982) *The Political Reliability of the Warsaw Pact Armies: The Southern Tier* (Durham, N.C., Duke University Press).

Wang, S. S. (1982) 'Hu Yaobang: New Chairman of the Chinese Communist Party', *Asian Survey*, XXII.

Weber, E. (1966) 'Romania', in H. Rogger, E. Weber (eds) *The European Right: A Historical Profile* (Berkeley and Los Angeles, CA., University of California Press).

Weydenthal, J. de (1978) *The Communists in Poland* (Stanford, CA., Hoover Institution Press).

White, Stephen (1975) 'Political Adaptivity', *Political Studies*, vol. 23 nos 2, 3.

White, Stephen (1983) 'Political communication in the USSR: letters to party, state and press', *Political Studies*, vol. 31, no 1.

White, Stephen, John Gardner and George Schöpflin (1982) *Communist Political Systems An Introduction* (London, Macmillan).

Wiatr, J. and K. Ostrowski (1967) 'Political Leadership: What Kind of Professionalism?', in J. Wiatr (ed.) *Studies in Polish Political System* (Wroclaw, Ossolineum).

Wightman, Gordon (1981) 'The Changing Role of Central Party Institutions in Czechoslovakia, 1962–67', *Soviet Studies*, vol. XXXIII, no 2.

Wightman, Gordon (1983) 'Membership of the Communist Party of Czechoslovakia in the 1970s: Continuing Divergences from the Soviet Model', *Soviet Studies*, vol. XXXV, no 2.

Woodall, Jean (ed.) (1982) *Policy and Politics in Contemporary Poland* (London, Frances Pinter).

Yearbook on International Communist Affairs (1983) (Stanford, CA., Hoover Institution Press).

Young, G. (1984) 'Control and Style: Discipline Inspection Commissions since the Eleventh Congress', *China Quarterly*, 97.

Zanga, L. (1984) 'The Latest Phase in the Hoxha Personality Cult', RAD Background Report, RFE Research, 3, 13, January.

Zaninovich, George (1981) 'Leadership and Change in Yugoslavia', *Current History*, April.

Zhonggongdang lishi zhuyao shijian jianjie (1982) (Chengdu).

Zhongguo gongchandang lishi jiangyi (1981) ii (Shanghai).

Zihua, Cheng (1979) 'On China's Electoral Law', *Beijing Review*, vol. 22, no 37.

Zinoviev, Alexander (1984) *The Reality of Communism* (London, Victor Gollancz).

Index